# Alice on Stage

Charles Bowland, Phoebe Carlo, and William Cheesman in the 1886
production of Henry Savile Clarke's *Alice in Wonderland* dream-play.

# Alice On Stage

**A History of the Early Theatrical Productions
of *Alice in Wonderland***

*Together with*

A Checklist of Dramatic Adaptations of
Charles Dodgson's Works

*by*

**Charles C. Lovett**

Meckler
Westport • London

Selections from *The Letters of Lewis Carroll,* edited by Morton N. Cohen with the assistance of Roger Lancelyn Green. The Letters of C.L. Dodgson © The Executors of the C.L. Dodgson Estate 1978. The selection, preface and notes © Morton N. Cohen and Roger Lancelyn Green 1978. Reprinted by Permission of Oxford University Press. Additional material published by permission of A.P. Watt and the C.L. Dodgson Estate.

**Library of Congress Cataloging-in-Publication Data**

Lovett, Charles C.
  Alice on stage: a history of the early theatrical productions of Alice in wonderland, together with a checklist of dramatic adaptations of Charles Dodgson's works/by Charles C. Lovett.
    p. cm.
  Bibliography: p.
  Includes index.
  ISBN 0-88736-390-3: $
  1. Carroll, Lewis, 1832–1898. Alice's Adventures in Wonderland.
  2. Carroll, Lewis, 1832–1898—Stage history.  3. Carroll, Lewis, 1832–1898—Adaptations.  I. Title.
  PR4611.A73L68  1990
  792.9'5—dc20                                89-9248
                                              CIP

**British Library Cataloguing in Publication Data**

Lovett, Charles C.
  Alice on stage: a history of the early theatrical productions of Alice in Wonderland.
  1. Fiction in English. Carroll, Lewis, 1832–1898.
  Dramatisations. Productions, 1850–1988
  I. Title
  792.9'5

  ISBN 0-88736-390-3

Meckler Corporation, 11 Ferry Lane West, Westport, CT 06880.
Meckler Ltd., Grosvenor Gardens House, Grosvenor Gardens,
  London SW1W 0BS, U.K.

Printed on acid free paper.
Printed in the United States of America.

# Contents

# Acknowledgments

Gracious thanks are due to Mr. Philip Jaques of the Estate of Charles Dodgson and to the Alfred C. Berol collection of New York University for permission to quote from Dodgson's letters to Henry Savile Clarke.

Thanks also to Mr. Frank Walker and the staff of the Berol collection, Mr. Alexander Wainwright and the staff of the Parrish Collection at Princeton University, the Pierpont Morgan Library, and the staff of the Wake Forest University Library for their invaluable assistance.

I owe a special debt of gratitude to Mr. Joseph Brabant, Dr. Selwyn Goodacre, and Dr. Sandor Burstein, who spent hours sorting through their collections of theatrical ephemera in order to assist in compiling the checklist. Thanks also to Mr. Ed Wakeling for his help with the checklist and to Mr. Stan Marx, whose collection of theatrical items was most helpful.

Gracious thanks to Janet Jurist and Pam Krisulewicz for their assistance with various research projects, and to Frances Gregory for her assistance in the final preparation of the book.

Thanks also go to all those people who answered my inquiries about theatrical productions of Dodgson's works: Bettye Chambers, Greta Cooper, Jaz Dorsey, Robyn Flatt, Robert Fleming, Joanne Forman, J.L. Fuller, Teddy Giles, Margaret Hodges, Nigel J. Luhman, Sally McGill, Margaret Meachem, Katherine Minehart, Christopher Morgan, Horst Muggenburg, J. Murphy, Tessa Panter, Mark Richards, M. Mackenzie Robinson, and others who never gave me their names.

Finally, to my wife, Stephanie, whose assistance, encouragement, and advice at every step of the way made this book possible.

For Doug

The Theatre is certainly not what it was.

## WHERE IS WONDERLAND

"Alice" *was* a book
That every fancy took,
   And oh my ! how it did sell !
It was illustra-
ted in wondrous way
   By our Mister TENNIEL.

Thus immortalised,
It was dramatised
   By a Savile-Clarkely hand;
And the Globe Theay
ter *en matinée*
   Is the present Wonderland.

–*Punch*, 19 Jan. 1889

# Charles Dodgson & The Theatre

I CHARLES LUTWIDGE DODGSON, more widely known as Lewis Carroll, was born in the small Cheshire village of Daresbury on January 27, 1832. Charles was the eldest boy in a family of seven sons and three daughters, and much of his childhood was occupied by entertaining his siblings. From these early days of performing for the family date not only Charles Dodgson's talent as a storyteller, but also his interest in the theatre.

When Charles was eleven years old, the family moved to the village of Croft-on-Tees in North Yorkshire, where his father, the Rev. Charles Dodgson, had been appointed rector. It was here that, as his nephew Stuart Dodgson Collingwood records, young Charles would perform conjuring tricks for his brothers and sisters, "arrayed in a brown wig and a long white robe."[1]

Charles was educated at Richmond School from 1844-1845, and beginning in 1846 at Rugby School. He matriculated at Christ Church, Oxford, in 1851, and took his Bachelor of Arts degree in 1854. In 1855 he was appointed to a Mathematical Lectureship at Christ Church. Throughout his school years, Charles continued to entertain his siblings in various ways. In 1845, he began producing a series of domestic magazines which contained pieces by himself and other members of the family. He also, according to Collingwood, "made a troupe of marionettes and a small theatre for them to act in."[2]

Though there is some question as to when this theatre was constructed (an extant theatre supposedly built by Dodgson has been dated at around 1880), Dodgson was certainly entertaining his family with marionette performances as early as 1855, and possibly much earlier. While home for Easter vacation in 1855, he recorded in his diary that

> we got up an entertainment for the assembled party with the Marionette Theatre. I chose 'The Tragedy of King John,' which went off very successfully . . . A Christmas book for children that would sell well:—Practical hints for constructing Marionettes and a theatre (we have managed to get up the whole thing with about twenty figures, for a very few shillings). This might be followed by several plays for representation by marionettes or by children. All existing plays for such objects seem to me to have one of two faults—either (1) they are meant for real theatres, and are therefore not fitted for children, or (2) they are overpoweringly dull—no idea of fun in them. The three already written for our theatre have at least the advantage of being tested by experience and found to be popular (*D*, 46).[3]

This entry, made when Dodgson was 23, illustrates not only his increasing interest in the theatre, but also the fact that that interest was linked to his love for children, a connection which would remain for the rest of his life. Of the three plays Dodgson mentions as having been performed in his marionette theatre, only one remains today. This is a "Ballad Opera," titled *La Guida di Bragia*,* which was intended to be a parody of *Bradshaw's Railway Guide*. Dodgson had always been fascinated by the railway; he had even constructed a toy railroad, with elaborate rules for its use, in the garden at Croft, so this was a logical choice of subject matter.

*Bradshaw's Railway Guide*, first published as *Bradshaw's Railway Timetable* in 1839 and renamed in 1841, was a most familiar work by 1850, about which time Dodgson wrote his play. Denis Crutch describes the play as

> a ballad opera which tells of two friends Mooney and Spooney,—one foolish and the other stupid!—who are expelled from court to take up positions as officers on the railway. After

---

* Manuscript now in the Berol collection at New York University.

a series of ineptitudes involving various intending passengers including a Kaffir, a lady much given to malapropisms called Mrs. Muddle, a young husband called Orlando, and a Mr. Lost, they discover that one of the terms of their employment was that they should sing at their work. As they have failed to do this, the ogre Bradshaw, who rules the railway, punishes them by making the trains run at the wrong times and to the wrong destinations, thereby causing great confusion. It has a Preface spoken by Mr. Ben Webster, a noted character actor of the day and an Epilogue by Mr. Flexmore, the pantomime clown. The play is full of witty nonsense and good-humour, and contains many amusing parodies of songs well-known in the mid-Victorian drawing room.[4]

Though certainly not on a level with Dodgson's later fantasies, this early work contains elements which would surface in his more famous books, specifically his parodies of popular songs. Dodgson's interest in marionette theatre continued, and on July 10, 1855, he recorded that he had "a new idea for a drama for the Marionette Theatre—*Alfred the Great*, but [had] not yet begun to write it. His adventures in disguise in the neatherd's hut, and in the Danish Camp will furnish two very effective scenes" (*D*, 55). There is no evidence that Dodgson ever wrote this play.

In January of 1856, Dodgson conceived the idea of having "slides of a magic lantern painted to represent characters in some play, which might be read aloud—a sort of Marionette performance" (*D*, 75). To this end, he arranged to purchase a magic lantern during his Christmas vacation that year. Dodgson recounted in his diary the performance which he gave using the new device:

> *Dec. 31.* First exhibition of the Magic Lantern: the largest audience I ever had, about eighty children, and a large miscellaneous party besides of friends, servants, etc.
>
> I expected the whole thing to last about an hour and a half, so as to be over soon after 3; as it turned out it did not begin until after 2, instead of 1:30, and lasted till nearly half past four. I divided it into two parts, of twenty-four and twenty-three pictures, with a rest of about half an hour between. I introduced

thirteen songs in the course of the performance, six for myself
and seven for the children.

As a whole I think it proved successful, though the first part
was rather too long, several of the views may safely be omitted
in the next performance (*D*, 99).

Dodgson records another magic lantern performance much later, in
1893 when he presented three stories ("The Epiphany," "Children lost in the
Bush," and "Bruno's Picnic") at the annual Christmas party for children of
College servants. Though large audiences were unusual for Dodgson, the
pattern of performing for children would remain with him all of his life, as
he entertained them individually or in small groups with his stories, games,
puzzles, and drawings. Children would also play a major role in Dodgson's
theatregoing, often accompanying him to plays and pantomimes in London
and elsewhere.

Throughout his life, the roles of playwright and performer would
occasionally return to Dodgson, usually in the context of the amateur or
family theatricals which were so popular in Victorian England. On two
occasions he wrote prologues for such performances given at the home of
his friend Dr. Edwin Hatch, whose daughters Beatrice and Evelyn were
special friends of Dodgson. The first of these he wrote for a performance
of *Loan of a Lover* by J. R. Planche and *Whitebait from Greenwich* by J. M.
Morton given on November 1–2, 1871. This prologue consists of a long
rhymed speech about the acting and the plays, interrupted by a short but
amusing scene between Miss Crabb and Miss Verjuice, who discuss how
dreadful theatricals are*.

The second of these prologues was written on February 14, 1873, for
a performance of *Checkmate*, a two-act drama by Andrew Halliday. This
prologue is a good deal shorter and consists of a dialogue between Beatrice
and Wilfred, her brother, about the "fuss and clatter" which have accompanied the family preparations for the play.

Dodgson also occasionally wrote songs for his friends' performances,
though unfortunately none of these has survived. In 1865, while visiting in

---

*All of Dodgson's writings relating to the theatre which are mentioned in the text appear
in Appendix C.

Whitburn, he wrote some songs for a pantomime of *Bluebeard* and *Whitting-ton and his Cat*. On January 13, 1876, he recorded: "The children went to help in acting *Puss in Boots* at Mrs. Head's, for which I wrote them a song, and got fifty copies printed to distribute among the audience" (*D*, 349), and again on January 9, 1879, "the Fendalls ... had some very third rate private theatricals in the evening: some tableaux, and [J. M. Morton's] *Poor Pillicoddy*, for which I wrote them a song to the tune of 'So Early in the Morning'" (*D*, 377).

One song which does survive is "Miss Jones," a medley song based on many popular tunes of the day. Dodgson composed this piece with the assistance of his sisters at Croft in 1862. He felt that the song might fit into a popular entertainment and sent it to his friend Edmund Yates for that purpose in October of 1862. Yates liked the song and said he would use it in his entertainment *Invitations* that Christmas, but in the end it was not included. Dodgson also sent the song to entertainer John Parry and to manager/entertainer Thomas Coe; both liked the song, but neither ever used it on stage.

It was not only as an author of songs and prologues that Dodgson assisted with family theatricals. On many occasions he assisted with rehearsals and helped in other ways. In December of 1891, he helped in the production of the printed programme for a set of four plays enacted at the Royal Cowper Theatre by Isa Bowman and her family. Isa was one of Dodgson's closest child friends, and had acted as Alice in the 1888 version of Henry Savile Clarke's operetta.

On rare occasions, more often in his younger years, Dodgson would take part in the entertainment, reading aloud from a play or even acting in one. On August 28, 1855, while on long vacation, he "read parts of *Henry VIII*, feeling angry with [himself] almost the whole time for the miserable way in which [he] fell short of even [his] own conception of that glorious play" (*D*, 62). A few days later he "read aloud the farce of *Away with Melancholy*, a decidedly more successful performance" (*D*, 63). The following day, September 4, Dodgson took part in the acting of a charade which he described in his diary:

We had a thoroughly theatrical evening: commencing with the Charade 'Den-mark', in which William, Freddy, Edward, Katie,

Georgie, Caroline, Louisa and I appeared: I took an old man part, with something of Mr. Trimmer's voice. The chief fault of the performance was its too great length (*D*, 63).

During Easter vacation in 1856, Dodgson again gave a reading of *Away with Melancholy*, this time to a party in Ripon. Dodgson's excursions into the world of performing were to become rarer and eventually cease altogether as his life grew more distant from the carefree days of performing for his family at Croft. His persistent stammer may also have been a contributing factor in this trend.

One cannot say that Dodgson ceased all sorts of performing, though, for throughout his life he engaged in the occasional preaching of sermons, and in his later years, he frequently addressed groups of school children, mixing educational material with his stories and puzzles. His greatest performances, however, were reserved for his child friends, who, in ones and twos, heard him weave his tales.

Dodgson's talent as a dramatist was not reserved strictly for marionette plays and amateur theatricals. Not only do his children's books contain some of the most charming and witty dialogue in the English language, but two of Dodgson's adult works were written in dramatic form. The first of these was one of his Oxford satires, *The Vision of the Three T's*, written in 1873. This pamphlet criticizes Christ Church's new Belfry (shaped like a "Tea chest"), a Trench at the south-east corner of Tom Quad, and the double arched Tunnel entrance to Christ Church Cathedral. It's three "chapters," are written as dramatic dialogue and even include directions on entrances and exits.

Dodgson's major work on the various Victorian theories on Euclidian geometry *Euclid and his Modern Rivals*, is also written in dramatic form. Published in 1879, this book uses the structure of a four-act drama to prove Euclid's superiority to his modern successors. It contains over 250 pages of dramatic dialogue and is a marvelous example of Dodgson's ability to write witty, logical conversations.

With the exception of his musings about an *Alice* drama, Dodgson only once seriously considered the possibility of writing a play intended for professional production. On January 17, 1866, Dodgson went with some young friends to the pantomime of *Little King Pippin*, by E. L. Blanchard, at the Drury Lane Theatre. He noted that "Percy Roselle's acting was quite the gem of the whole thing: Miss Terry tells me he is eighteen or nineteen,—he looks about eight" (*D*, 239).

Dodgson was impressed enough with Roselle's performance that, a few days later, he began work on a play intended as a vehicle for the young actor. After discussing his ideas for the play with his close friend and associate Robert Faussett, another Christ Church mathematics don, Dodgson "spent two or three hours in writing out, to send to Tom Taylor" (*D*, 239), an outline of the play.

Taylor, later the editor of *Punch*, was a well-known playwright whose works Dodgson had seen performed on many occasions. Dodgson had met Taylor for the first time on October 1, 1863, and the two had since become good friends. Dodgson sent Taylor a detailed description of the action of the play, together with an outline of scenes on January 25. His diary contains a briefer description of the play:

> The main plot is [Roselle's] being stolen away at the instigation of his father's younger brother—his mother (a widow) to be played by Miss Terry. I drew out two incidental scenes: one a street in a winter night, and the boy wandering by the house where (unknown to him) his mother is, and singing—the scene changing to the interior where they hear the singing and open the window, but too late; the other to be the concluding scene, after the lost child is recovered, and the villain has died in misery— a group of the widow, her old father, and her two children, seen by firelight: the children sing their grandfather to sleep, and the curtain falls in silence on the peaceful group (*D*, 239).

Taylor responded to Dodgson's letter immediately, saying that he took a "favourable view" (*D*, 239) of the drama, and offering to show it to Miss Terry and to enquire as to the availability of Percy Roselle. On February 3, Dodgson again discussed the play (by this time titled *Morning Clouds*) with Faussett, and spent another three hours working on it.

This promising beginning for Dodgson's drama was cut short,

however, when he met with Tom Taylor on April 5. Taylor had shown Dodgson's outline to Miss Terry, but

> their opinion seem[ed] to be that it [was] unpracticeable—even [his] favourite ending. The public taste demands more sensa-tion. [Taylor] mentioned as a minor flaw the bringing in the husband (who ought to have a leading part) so late in the piece. Besides all this, there is the fatal obstacle that Percy Roselle is not to be had (*D*, 240-41).

There is one more mention of Dodgson's play in his diaries, on May 11, 1867, when he visited Thomas Coe, a theatrical manager whom he had befriended. Dodgson wrote that Mr. Coe had "read and approves of, the sketch of *Morning Clouds* and wants me to try and do a bit of dialogue" (*D*, 259). The project went no further, however, and Dodgson never again undertook to write an original drama. Perhaps if drama had been a more literary art at the time, he would have persisted, but playwrighting was the least memorable part of Victorian theatre, and Dodgson rightly chose to leave his mark elsewhere.

In spite of his talents as an entertainer and playwright, it was as a member of the audience that Dodgson was most actively involved in the theatre. He first records attending a performance on February 19, 1855:

> Went to the Town Hall [Oxford] to hear Mrs. Fanny Kemble read *Henry V*. I can hardly criticise her performance, as I have never heard anything of the kind before, nor any Shakespeare on the stage, but she seemed to give the conversations with great spirit: long speeches and soliloquies sunk at times into recitation—it must be almost impossible to avoid this, labouring under such disadvantages as the want of dresses and scenery (*D*, 41).

Dodgson first recorded attending the theatre in London during his summer vacation of 1855. On June 20, he attended the opera at the Drury Lane, where he saw Bellini's *Norma*, of which he wrote "music delicious—scenery, dresses, and specially performers, poor." Of the grand ballet which followed, he recorded that he "was completely disappointed . . . Talk of the poetry of motion! The instinctive grace of cottage children dancing is something far more beautiful; I never wish to see another ballet" (*D*, 52).

After another night at the opera (he saw Rossini's *Il Barbiere di Seviglia* at the Covent Garden) Dodgson went to the Princess's Theatre on the twenty-second to see *Henry VIII* with Charles Kean in the role of Cardinal Wolsey. Dodgson described this as "the greatest theatrical treat I ever had or ever expect to have" (*D*, 53). He was especially impressed by an effect of angels descending from the skies. Dodgson believed quite strongly that the theatre should be a place of purity and reverence, and such a vision conformed precisely to his ideas about the perfect theatre.

This strong desire for purity in the theatre no doubt offset some of the guilt which Dodgson must have felt, at least in his younger years, about attending the theatre. His father was staunchly opposed to the theatre, and, had Dodgson taken priest's orders rather than stopping his religious training at the level of deacon, he would have been forbidden from attending.

The years in which Dodgson first attended the theatre were years of transformation for the British stage, and the theatre which Dodgson attended bore little resemblance to the theatre to which his father so violently objected. In the early part of the nineteenth century, theatre in London had degenerated from its standing as a Court entertainment during the Restoration period into a largely lower class entertainment. Theatres were frequently the sites of fights and even riots, and the performances were often crude and sexually suggestive. Those members of the upper class who wished to see a stage performance limited themselves to the opera.

By the mid-1800's, however, legitimate theatre had begun to return to the London stages. Shakespeare was performed at Drury Lane and Covent Garden, and when the monopoly of these two Patent Theatres on the production of plays was abolished in 1843, many of the minor theatres were taken over by managers who brought them out of the gutter and into the realm of respectable entertainment.

Though the Victorian era was not one which produced great plays, it was a time when the English stage was graced with some of its greatest actors, and, in his years as a playgoer, Dodgson would see not only Charles Kean and Fanny Kemble, but also Henry Irving, Ellen Terry, the Bancrofts, and many others.

From his first recorded visit to the London theatre in 1855 until the end of his life, Dodgson continued his pattern of theatregoing, especially during vacations, when he could freely travel to London for several days at a time. Such was his enthusiasm as an audience member that he occasionally even went to court to watch cases be tried, and once he went to a hospital to observe an operation. His diary records nearly 300 plays which he saw during his life, and there were almost certainly many others. On November 20, 1897, less than two months before his death, he attended the theatre for the last time, seeing J. M. Barrie's *The Little Minister*. He wrote that it was a play he "should like to see again and again" (*D*, 542).

Dodgson often took his child friends to the theatre, and he took special delight in introducing a young girl to the stage for the first time. He was especially careful in chosing plays for his young companions, for he did not wish them to be exposed to anything which he considered vulgar, coarse, or irreverent. He would occasionally note in his diary that a particular play was unsuitable for children, and at times went so far as to write to the manager of the theatre pleading that the offending matter be removed.

One by-product of Dodgson's constant quest for plays appropriate for children was his attempt to create an edition of Shakespeare's plays suitable for young girls. In 1882, Dodgson wrote both a circular and a letter to the editor of the *Monthly Packet* asking readers to suggest about fifteen plays which would be suitable for such an edition. On February 15, 1884, he met with Miss Cooper, mistress of the Edgbaston High School who had "offered to help [him] with [his] *Schoolroom Shakespeare*" (*D*, 424). When Dodgson compiled his list of literary projects in March of 1885, *Girls' Own Shakespeare* was listed as number twelve (of fifteen) with the notation "I have begun on *The Tempest*" (*D*, 434); however, the project was never completed.

Another result of Dodgson's theatregoing, and one in which he took great pleasure, was his friendship with so many members of the London theatrical community. He befriended scores of actors and actresses, both children and adults, as well as playwrights and managers. Many of his child friends were young actresses, and of those few adult women with whom he was able to engage in friendships, several, such as Isa Bowman and Ellen Terry, were stage personalities. Dodgson contributed to the careers of several child actresses by introducing them to established stage figures or managers, and he frequently took pleasure in the delight he could add to an evening at the theatre by introducing his young companion to the "star" of the play.

He befriended the entire Terry family, always reserving a special affection for Ellen. Even young boys, whom Dodgson avoided as a rule, were open to his affection if they were involved in the theatre. Throughout his life, Dodgson indulged in a certain degree of lionizing, ironic because of his own strong resistance to being sought after, and doubtless his desire to meet theatrical personalities was increased by this factor. There can be no doubt, however, that the majority of these friendships were completely sincere, especially that with the Terry family.

Dodgson was quick to compliment a good performance, but he also did not hesitate to criticize his friends' acting when he felt necessary. His letters to Ellen Terry reveal a thoughtful critique of her acting and of the productions in general, and he would occasionally suggest that some phrase or action which he found offensive be removed or altered.

Dodgson's involvement with the legitimate theatre did not end with his role as an enthusiastic audience member who befriended those on the other side of the footlights. He entered the lists, as "Lewis Carroll," on two stage-related topics: stage children and stage reverence.

On July 16, 1887, the *St. James Gazette* printed "an account of a large ladies' meeting 'to prevent children under 10 acting in theatres'" (*D*, 452). The ladies felt that the physical strain placed on a child by the rigors of theatrical life was not only unhealthy, but could even be fatal. As Dodgson had a special love of seeing youngsters on stage, this was an issue on which he felt strongly. He knew that children could be taken advantage of and abused by theatrical managers; in 1874 he spoke with the mother of Lizzie Wells, a young actress then engaged at the Sadlers' Wells, and learned that "they [were] killing the poor child with overwork, and she [was] suffering from some malady in the throat from so much singing. She [lay] in bed all day, and almost [lived] on port-wine and oysters" (*D*, 325).

In 1887, however, Dodgson's immediate experience with children in the theatre was the successful engagement of numerous children in Henry Savile Clarke's *Alice* operetta. On July 14, Dodgson had journeyed from his summer lodgings in Eastbourne to Brighton to see a performance of *Alice*, which was then in its provincial run. The following day, again in Brighton, he spent the afternoon with Phoebe Carlo, who played Alice;

Dorothy d'Alcourt, who played the Dormouse; and Lizzie Carlo, who had a minor role in the production.

When Dodgson read the next day that a group of ladies wished to ban children under ten from theatres, he responded with a letter signed "Lewis Carroll" describing the previous day and explaining that he had spent five hours with these "exceedingly happy and healthy little girls." He wrote:

> I think that anyone who could have seen the *vigour of life* in those three children—the intensity with which they enjoyed every-thing, great or small, which came their way—who could have watched the younger two running races on the Pier, or could have heard the fervent exclamation of the eldest at the end of the afternoon, 'We *have* enjoyed ourselves!'—would have agreed with me that here at least was no excessive 'physical strain,' nor any *imminent* danger of 'fatal results.'[5]

Dodgson went on to explain that these youngsters had been engaged in *Alice in Wonderland*, "with only a month's interval, ever since Christmas," and that they had acted every night that week, and "*twice* on the day before [he] met them, the second performance lasting until after half past ten at night."[6]

In spite of Dodgson's protest, the views of the ladies were widely held, and in 1889, an amendment to the Prevention of Cruelty to Children Bill was proposed in Parliament which would ban children under ten from the stage. During the debate over this amendment, Dodgson, as Carroll, wrote a letter which appeared first in *The Sunday Times* and later in *The Theatre*. In this letter he proposed that child actors should be more closely regulated rather than prohibited from performing.

Dodgson's scheme included an annually renewable license for actors under the age of sixteen, renewable only if the child passed the appropriate school examination; a limit on the number of weeks per year and hours per day a child could be employed; a minimum number of hours per day during which the actor must attend school; and a provision for a sufficient escort for young ladies.

Many other theatrical figures expressed similar opinions, and by the time Dodgson's letter was published in the September 2 edition of *The*

*Theatre*, the bill had been reworded to allow children from seven to ten to be employed in theatres under certain conditions.

Dodgson's second public stand on theatrical matters was also printed in *The Theatre*, and also under the name Lewis Carroll. On February 18, 1887, Dodgson wrote that Clement Scott, editor of *The Theatre*, had agreed to receive a paper from him on the stage version of *Alice*. The paper was titled "Alice on the Stage" and published in April of that year. Dodgson envisioned this as the first in a series of papers on the theatre, but he wrote only one more, titled "The Stage and the Spirit of Reverence," which was published in June 1888.

Dodgson begins this article by stating that "reverence" does not necessarily connote a religious belief or faith, but can simply mean reverence towards what is inherently good and, likewise, repulsion from that which is evil. Dodgson argues that audiences' reactions to evil on stage (a low hiss) and to good (a ripple of applause) illustrate their natural inclination towards reverence.

The article then turns to a discussion of reverence in the more specific context of religion. Dodgson gives many examples of irreverence in society, literature, and even in the pulpit—occasions on which a Bible phrase, a blasphemous profanity, or an "evil spirit" is treated as a jest, rather than with the serious reverence which these ideas, good and evil, deserve. He draws a distinction between the light and jesting use of oaths on the stage, which he finds profane, and the more grave employment of them, which may be acceptable in the proper context.

Dodgson also enumerates those things which he feels should be treated with reverence on the stage, giving examples of their irreverent treatment: the act of prayer, places of worship, and ministers of religion, except, in the case of the latter, "when they deserve it." Also the subjects of evil spirits, hell, and future punishment should be treated, if not with reverence, with a serious tone. In Dodgson's mind, these are not topics to be taken lightly or with a jest, as in the case of a production of *H.M.S. Pinafore* which he saw acted entirely by children. Dodgson wrote of this play that

> one passage in it was to me sad beyond words. It occurs when
> the captain utters the oath 'Damn me!' and forthwith a bevy of

sweet innocent-looking little girls sing, with bright happy looks, the chorus, 'He said "Damn me!" He said "Damn me!"' I cannot find the words to convey to the reader the pain I felt in seeing those dear children taught to utter such words to amuse ears grown callous to their ghastly meaning. Put the two ideas side by side—Hell . . . and those pure young lips thus sporting with its horrors—and then find what *fun* in it you can! How Mr. Gilbert could have stooped to write, or Sir Arthur Sullivan could have prostituted his noble art to set to music, such vile trash, it passes all my skill to understand.[7]

Dodgson contrasts this with a scene in *David Copperfield* in which Steerforth is referred to as a "damned villain." In this case, he feels that the oath is perfectly well placed, and should not be objected to. The article concludes with a note on the dramatic tone of the Bible, and how the story of the Prodigal Son would make a fine drama.

Dodgson's feelings may seem a bit extreme, especially in the case of a play like *Pinafore*, where the oath is used as a comic device, but it was precisely this comic use of a phrase which, though we may have forgotten it, has a deadly serious meaning, to which Dodgson objected. The article was very much in keeping with Dodgson's constant screenings of plays to ascertain if they were suitable for his young lady companions.

In September of 1886, Henry Savile Clarke, then working on the *Alice in Wonderland* operetta, wrote to ask Dodgson's opinion on the idea of creating a special theatre for children. Clarke had discussed this idea with a Mr. Barber, and felt that Dodgson, as a lover of both children and theatre, was in a position to contribute his thoughts. Dodgson's response touches on many of the points which defined his relationship with the theatre—the fact that the theatre was still considered a vulgar mode of entertainment by much of society, his ideas about reverence in the theatre, thoughts on children as actors, and thoughts on appropriate material for the entertainment of children. Although this project was never undertaken, Dodgson outlined his utopian children's theatre in a letter dated September 17:

It could do no good, I think, for you to discuss with Mr. Barber the bare idea of "a theatre devoted to plays intended for children." But I shall be happy to put my theory before you (I have never put it down on paper), & shall be glad to have your opinion, & his, as to its feasibility.

And I must begin with the rather Irish remark that one principal item in my theory is that it should not be a "theatre" at all. The audiences, to be hoped for, would be largely composed of those excellent people who regard all theatres as irredeemably bad, & would not go inside one on a consideration whatever. These people at present have no satisfaction for their natural craving for dramatic amusement except the "German Reed" entertainment: & I attribute its success, with its entirely third-rate acting (always excepting Conney Grain), largely to the circumstance that it is the only theatre in London to which such people can go with an easy conscience, owing to Mr. Reed's having had the happy thought of avoiding the terrible *name* "theatre"—I would therefore have the *building*, needed for my scheme, called by some such innocent name as "St. Nicholas Hall." (St. Nicholas is the patron saint of children, for which reason the chief American Magazine for children bears his name)—

The second essential part of my theory is that the "censorship of the stage" should here be of the most rigid kind. Love-stories, of course, would be admissible, but (to put it in plain words) sexual vice, of all kinds, should be absolutely ignored. It ought to be such an entertainment that any lady could take her Daughters to without the slightest fear that anything would be introduced that she could possibly object to their seeing or hearing.

Thirdly, as to the sources from which the necessary plays could be drawn. These have scarcely been used at all as yet, & they are practically inexhaustible. The plays should be of 3 kinds:—

(1) Serious drama—not exactly 'tragedies,' but melodramas with a pathetic element, relieved by comic scenes. For these I would suggest the dramatising of serious tales, such as those written by Miss Yonge, Mrs. Molesworth, Miss Montgomery, &c &c. I could easily get from my lady-friends a list of at least 50 such books, well-tested favourites with children, who would

*delight* to see on the stage books they almost know by heart.
Those I have named are all *girls'* books: but of course *boys*
should have their tastes consulted as well. There are plenty of
good books for boys, (such as Kington's) which would drama-
tise admirably. "Masterman Ready" on the stage would be a
tremendous success.

(2) Operettas—For this you have the whole range of Nursery
Tales. I would lay down *rigidly* the rule that only one Tale
should be used in each. And it would be worth while to get the
best musical composers—write a really good version of "Cinderella" (her history, *previous* to the ball, would bear almost
indefinite expansion), & give Sullivan £500 or £1000 to set it to
music, & you may run it for a year.

As to *writers*. There must be scores of them in the market: men
who have been for years writing plays that managers won't
accept, & would gladly give their labour & long experience of
stage requirements, in writing, for a fixed remuneration the
dramas required.

As to *actors*. These should largely consist of children: but I
would certainly use adults as well—specially in the serious
plays.

As to the *building*, I would suggest that it should be *small*. In
the days of Albert Smith's 'Mont Blanc,' it was often said that
one of the causes of his great success was that the room was so
small that the seats were all bespoken for a week on. Once let
people think they can go to a thing *any* day they like, & they put
it off *ad libitum*, & perhaps never go at all.

As to *hours*, I would make it *afternoons* only, not evening:
thus it would not come into competition with evening theatres—
Afternoon performances seem to be growing in popularity.

As to *seasons*, if it were found that it did not fill all the year
round, it would be easy enough to close it now & then, as so many
theatres do. But, so long as London can furnish audiences for
"Mikado" (which goes on all, or nearly all, the year), it would
also furnish audiences for "St. Nicholas Hall."

Now you have a fairly complete account of my theory—I wish

I were a moneyed man, & could add "Here are £10,000—keep the thing going till that is spent, at any rate—" But alas, I can only offer suggestions.

The thing has never quite been tried—It would be a complete novelty, &, I fully believe, a great success . . . [8]

It is a pity that Dodgson was not financially able to back such a venture, but he would help in the effort to bring two of those "well-tested favourites with children" to the stage—his own *Alice's Adventures in Wonderland* and *Through the Looking-Glass, and What Alice Found There*.

# Staging Alice:
# Early Attempts

**II** GIVEN DODGSON'S LOVE of all things theatrical, it is not surprising that, when he realized that his book *Alice's Adventures in Wonderland* was gaining an unexpected measure of popularity, his mind turned to thoughts of bringing his dream-child to the stage. Dodgson negotiated with authors, composers, and actors for nearly twenty years before realizing his vision of a theatrical *Alice*, and those negotiations were marked by Dodgson's own conflicting feelings regarding the project.

The road to *Alice*'s staging illustrates a dichotomy in Dodgson's character between perfectionism and modesty. On the one hand, Dodgson longed to have control over the process of bringing *Alice* to the boards; however, at the same time, he felt himself inadequate to perform the task of dramatizing the book. Dodgson's modesty led him to seek out several potential collaborators, but for years he failed to commit himself wholeheartedly to the project, always bowing out because of his own inadequacies, or indefinitely delaying collaborations.

Dodgson first mentions his interest in staging *Alice* in a letter to his brother Edwin on March 11, 1867, less than two years after the book's initial publication. Dodgson had been the guest of Mr. Thomas Coe, then associated with the Haymarket Theatre, for an afternoon, having accepted Mr. Coe's invitation for a behind-the-scenes look at his *Living Miniatures*, which Dodgson had seen performed some time earlier. Dodgson gives his brother a detailed account of his experience backstage, adding:

> After I got back here, an idea occurred to me, and I sent off to
> Mr. Coe that medley-song of "Miss Jones" [see above p. 7]

... He writes to say he thinks it very funny, and if one of his boys can manage it he will introduce it into the performance. I have also presented him, as an appropriate return for his entertainment, with a copy of *my* 'juvenile entertainment' *Alice*. I have vague hopes (though I haven't suggested the idea to him) that it may occur to him to turn it into a pantomime. I fancy it would work well in that form. (*L*, 102).[1]

Already the seed had been planted, and though Dodgson was proud enough to hope that a theatrical manager might see promise in his work, he was too modest to suggest the possibility of a dramatization himself. While his initial vision of *Alice* was as a pantomime, this was no doubt due to the fact that the pantomime was the standard format for the staging of children's stories at the time. Two months later, Dodgson called on Coe, who "[thought] *Alice's Adventures* would work into an extravaganza, but that it is too good for a pantomime" (*D*, 259). Many years later, he would tell Henry Savile Clarke that the "piece ought to be an Operetta . . . and not a Pantomime" (*L*, 637).

In spite of Mr. Coe's encouraging remarks, Dodgson seems to have neglected the idea of a staged *Alice* in favor of other pursuits until the fall of 1872. On September 28 of that year, he saw an entertainment featuring a young girl of eight years named Lydia Howard, and noted that "she would do well to act 'Alice' if it should ever be dramatised" (*D*, 314). With this thought perhaps lingering in the back of his mind, he read *The Principles of Comedy and Dramatic Effect,* by drama critic and theatre historian Percy Fitzgerald. This work, which much impressed Dodgson "with the reality of [its] dramatic criticism and the deep study . . . given to the principles of success in writing and acting" (*L*, 180), turned Dodgson's mind firmly towards the possibility of seeing *Alice* on the boards, and for the next several months he explored that possibility in some depth.

On October 18, 1872, he wrote to Mr. Fitzgerald:

I have published two books for children . . . and the idea has been suggested to me of making one or the other into a drama (or extravaganza) for children. I know no one more competent than yourself to give an opinion as to the possibility of doing this and

therefore I venture to ask the favour of your looking at the books
with that idea. Unless you happen to possess them already, may
I send you copies?

Of course, if the thing were done, much would depend on the
writer chosen, the actors, and the "properties." But the first
question to settle is whether either book has sufficient dramatic
element to warrant the attempt to exhibit it.

The *books* have been so wonderfully popular among children
that I am encouraged to hope they would also be popular as an
'entertainment' (*L*, 180).


Fitzgerald replied to Dodgson that he did think the *Alice* books suitable
for the stage, but advised against a proposal which Dodgson had put forth—
that they be acted by children (*D*, 315).* With his feelings that the *Alice*
stories could be dramatized confirmed by one whom he viewed as an expert
on the subject, Dodgson was encouraged to pursue dramatization more
actively.

On November 26, he wrote to his publisher Macmillan "Will you
kindly . . . have *all* the speeches in *Alice* and *Looking-Glass* written out, with
the names of the speakers, and such directions as 'Enter the White Rabbit'
. . . and *get them registered as two dramas*" (*LM*, 99). Dodgson was under
the impression that this action would make it illegal for anyone to dramatize
*Alice* without his approval. Macmillan had the dialogue copied out, noting
to Dodgson that "Wilkie Collins protects himself in this way, and effectu-
ally" (*LM*, 100n). The precaution was, in fact, to prove ineffectual some five
years later, but at the time it seemed a logical step to take before further
pursuing the project of dramatization, so the works were summarily registered at Stationer's Hall as dramas during December of 1872.

On January 13, 1873, Dodgson dined with Percy Fitzgerald, whom he
had met for the first time the previous week. Joining the party was Augustus
Dubourg, a minor dramatist. Dodgson mentioned the idea of staging *Alice*
to Dubourg, with whom he dined again on January 20.

---

*Dodgson eventually adopted Fitzgerald's advice on this matter, and when Henry Savile
Clarke suggested that the play be acted entirely by children, Dodgson argued that adult
actors should be used as well (see below p. 38).

The following day, Dodgson took three of his child friends to see *Happy Arcadia*, an opera by W. S. Gilbert and Frederick Clay, performed by the German Reeds. Thomas German Reed and his wife Priscilla had for some years been presenting "Mr. & Mrs. German Reed's 'Entertainments'," a series of "dramatic performances with music, rather than full scale theatrical pieces, usually given in concert halls and designed to provide respectable entertainment for audiences who would not normally attend the theatre" (*L*, 92 n). Dodgson had frequently attended the Reeds' productions, and had become acquainted with the Reeds personally. On that particular night, he dined with Mr. Reed following the opera.

Seeing their performance so shortly after his conversation with Dubourg, Dodgson realized that the German Reeds' Entertainments would be an ideal forum for a dramatized version of *Alice*. He had already discussed with Dubourg the possibility of approaching Arthur Cecil Blunt, a well-known actor who frequently appeared with the German Reeds, with the idea of staging *Alice*, and on January 26, Dodgson wrote to Mr. German Reed "suggesting the idea of producing a drama founded on *Alice* or the *Looking-Glass*" (*D*, 319).

Dodgson wrote to Augustus Dubourg on February 1, not to "trouble [himself] to broach the subject of a dramatised *Alice* to Mr. Blunt, as I have myself done so with Mr. German Reed—with what effect, remains to be seen" (*L*, 183).

Mr. Reed at first seemed enthusiastic about the project, replying to Dodgson on February 2 that he was interested, and imagined a production "with endless fairy visions of surpassing prettiness" (*L*, 183 n). However, Reed ignored Dodgson's next two letters, finally replying on June 5 that

> a combination of circumstances have interfered with my [desire] . . . to further the subject we are both interested in . . . I must now with much regret, resign the pleasure I had anticipated in being associated with charming little Alice in her dramatic introduction to the public . . . I am still faithful to my first belief that if properly placed on stage, with an appropriate representative, she cannot fail to enlist the sympathies of the intelligent classes (*L*, 183 n).

Despite Reed's kind remarks, Dodgson's first attempt at having *Alice* staged had failed, and he showed no more interest in the project for some time.

In fact, just a few months later, when Mrs. H. L. Bateman, a member of another prominent theatrical family, inquired through Mr. Dubourg about the possibility of dramatizing *Alice*, Dodgson responded, in a letter dated November 23, 1873, "I hope that, while dissuading you from entertaining the idea at present, [Mr. Dubourg] expressed to you, as fully as I did to him, my sense of compliment paid me by your having thought of it" (*L*, 199).

On December 7, 1874, Dodgson attended what was almost certainly the first *Alice*-related stage production. The performance was a private family theatrical of the "Mad Tea-Party," produced at the home of Thomas Arnold of University College. Dodgson had made the acquaintance of Mr. Arnold and his daughters in April of 1871, and young Ethel Arnold would be one of the few of his child friends with whom he continued his friendship into adulthood. The only record of this performance is a brief entry in Dodgson's diary:

> Went to the Arnolds in the evening, to see a performance of the 'Mad Tea-Party', which was very creditably done by Julia, (The hatter), Ethel (March hare), Beatrice Fearon (Alice) and Maud (Dormouse) (*D*, 335).

Beatrice Fearon would also become one of Dodgson's child friends, and he later took her to the theatre on several occasions.

Attending this modest performance may well have put ideas of a properly staged *Alice* into Dodgson's head, for in January of 1875, he again discussed the idea of an *Alice* production with the German Reeds, and his diary on the twenty-ninth of that month records that he "heard from Mrs. German Reed, on the subject we talked about on the 13th, the dramatising of *Alice*. They have no definite idea as yet of undertaking it" (*D*, 337). In fact, the Reeds never did stage *Alice*, and thoughts of a dramatization were set aside until February of 1876.

During that month, Dodgson was contacted by William Boyd, who had previously set to music several of the songs from *Alice* and *Looking-Glass* with Dodgson's permission. Boyd was seeking Dodgson's "leave to use the pictures [from the *Alice* books] in 'a lecture for children' on [the] books at the Polytechnic," and he inquired "what terms he should ask for vesting the "right of representation in [himself]" (*LM*, 122).

The Royal Polytechnic Institute had been established in London in the 1820's, and this institution combined scholarly instruction with the entertainment of the general public. Visitors to the Polytechnic could view exhibits dealing with science, exploration, and other topics. In addition, the Polytechnic offered entertainments which were both amusing and educational—combining, for instance, an enactment of a favorite fairy tale with a presentation on scientific discoveries.

Dodgson granted Boyd permission to use the pictures at the Polytechnic, but pointed out that he could "not vest such a right in any one person, as [he] had already given leave for them to be published as magic lantern slides, which of course involve[s] the right to *exhibit* the slides" (*LM*, 122).

Meanwhile George Macmillan had received a letter from the Polytechnic which not only asked for Dodgson's permission to stage an *Alice* entertainment but also implied that Dodgson should pay them for producing it. Macmillan wrote to Dodgson,

> I enclose a letter which we think must be meant for a joke! The idea is too delicious, that you should pay them something for doing what they have no earthly right to do without your permission. If the copyright were ours, we should be inclined to ask them to pay something like £500 for the right to present *Alice* on the stage. It would be just reward for their insolence (*LM*, 123 n).

Dodgson replied to Macmillan, in a letter dated March 1, that he was

> writing to Mr. Boyd to ask what sort of entertainment is proposed, as, if it is dramatic, or involves the recitation of the book, I can not give leave without knowing more about it . . . It certainly does not look like a case in which payment should be expected from *my* side (*LM*, 122).

Dodgson did eventually give his permission for the entertainment which opened on April 17, 1876. It was billed as a "new fanciful, spectacular, and musical entertainment, entitled Alice's Adventures; or The

Queen of Hearts and the Missing Tarts."[2]  The adaptation was done by Mr.
George Buckland, a musical entertainer who also served as narrator.  Also
on the bill with *Alice* was a lecture titled "A Sunbeam, and how to weigh it,"
and a pictorial lecture titled "From England to Philadelphia."

    Although Mr. Buckland's adaptation was far from being true to the
original text, it must be regarded as significant, not only as the first public
stage appearance of *Alice*, but also as the longest-running *Alice* drama
presented in London in Dodgson's lifetime.  The entertainment was something between a dramatic reading and a true dramatization, and was
accompanied by both music and dissolving views.  The *Times* reviewer
described the performance as

> pleasing alike to old and young, and, though played for a first
> time, went through without a hitch, the only fault which could
> possibly be found with it being that Mr. Buckland had endeav-
> ored to give a little too much.  The onlookers were taken through
> some pleasant scenes of country life, and many little touches at
> passing events were given.  Alice attended a spelling bee, and
> one word propounded was 'Empress.'  This was, amid the
> applause of a large audience, spelt 'Queen.'[3]

Dodgson saw the performance on its second day, April 18, and recorded in
his diary that

>     it lasted about one and a quarter hours.  A good deal of it was
> done by dissolving views, extracts from the story being read, or
> sung to Mr. Boyd's music; but the latter part had a real scene and
> five performers (Alice, Queen, Knave, Hatter, Rabbit) who
> acted in dumb show*, the speeches being read by Mr. Buckland.
> The 'Alice' was a rather pretty child of about 10 (Martha
> Wooldridge) who acted simply and gracefully.
>     An interpolated song for the Cat, about a footman and house-
> maid, was so out of place, that I wrote afterwards to ask Mr.
> Buckland to omit it (*D*, 352).

---

*Dodgson later suggested to Henry Savile Clarke that a dumb show be used to act out "The
Walrus and the Carpenter" (see below p. 39).

Beginning May 29, the production was presented in a new, revised version, billing itself as "More wonders in Wonderland, a second edition of Alice's Adventures, with new views, songs, and illustrations by Mr. G. Buckland."[4] Dodgson saw this "second edition" on June 10, and recorded that it was "very much the same, except that for the 'footman' song is substituted one about a 'naughty little boy,' part of which I think I must protest against as too horrible to be comic" (D, 353). He saw the production for a third and final time on June 21.

Mr. Buckland's *Alice* entertainment, billed variously as *Alice in Wonderland* and *More Wonders in Wonderland* continued its run into the summer. In mid-July, the performance was seen by the Prince and Princess of Wales on their visit to the Polytechnic. The run finally ended on August 19, after over four months of performances. During most of this period, it was performed twice daily, with various other entertainments on the bill.

*Alice* had made her debut on the public boards, but, in spite of its lengthy run, the entertainment was far from a fully blown theatrical production, and it did not in any way satisfy Dodgson's desire to see a real dramatization of his story. So, some eight months later, in January of 1877, Dodgson renewed his efforts, this time beginning with the musical aspect of the project and with a letter to Arthur Sullivan.

That Dodgson chose to write Sullivan says a great deal about his attitude towards the project, for in the world of light theatrical music in mid-Victorian England there was no more respected or successful composer. Dodgson's second letter to Sullivan is full of modesty, but also makes quite clear his perfectionist attitude, apparent enough in the fact that he chose to write the quintessential composer of operettas.

Sullivan had responded to Dodgson's initial inquiry, not recognizing Dodgson's connection with *Alice*, with a somewhat perfunctory reply, stating that "I am very glad indeed to get good words for music. But I do not accept commissions to set words, preferring to buy the right to use them" (L, 273 n). Dodgson responded with a letter dated March 24, 1877:

> I thank you for your letter. I thought it needless to trouble you with any particulars till I knew if my proposal were at all possible. And now, though your answer gives little or no ground to hope, I think I may as well, before giving up all hope, tell you

what it is I want, as perhaps it might change your view of my
question.  I am the writer of a little book for children, *Alice's
Adventures in Wonderland*, which has proved so unexpectedly
popular that the idea of dramatising it has been several times
started.  If that is ever done, I shall want it done in the best
possible way, sparing no expense—and *one* feature I should
want would be good music.  So I thought (knowing your
charming compositions) it would be well to get 2 or 3 of the
songs in it set by you, to be kept for the occasion, if that should
arrive, of its being dramatised.  If that idea were finally abandoned, we might then arrange for publishing them with music (*L*,
273-74).

Sullivan responded with more enthusiasm this time, in a letter dated March
30:

I wrote hurriedly, overlooking the obvious fact that you were
*the* Lewis Carroll who has delighted and charmed old and young
alike. I have often thought that an *Alice* might be dramatized, but
to my thinking it would have to be done with much aid from
scenery and music. It would make a beautiful 'fairy piece.'  If
you should ever give practical effect to your notion, I shall be
very glad indeed to enter into it with you. I may now explain that
*Song writing* is the largest source of my income, and as I keep a
royalty on each, I could not afford to write a song, and part with
it outright except under conditions which would be thought
absurdly extravagant.  I will gladly give you any information in
my power to enable you to get a proper return for your words, if
they are set to music either by myself or others (*L*, 274 n).

Dodgson immediately replied to this encouraging response; however,
he shied away from Sullivan's offer of assistance with a dramatic production, concentrating rather on the possibility of setting songs to music for
some nebulous future dramatization.

Why Dodgson declined to enter into a collaboration with Sullivan is
not entirely clear.  Certainly he felt himself inadequate to write a libretto for

such a fine musician as Sullivan, but he had initiated the contact, and continued to negotiate for some musical settings. Perhaps Dodgson simply wanted to see his work set to music by Arthur Sullivan whether or not he eventually dramatized *Alice*.

In any case, his next letter to Sullivan, dated March 31, made it clear that, while he was very interested in obtaining musical settings for his songs, he had no immediate interest in working out an entire dramatization. He wrote:

> I have again to thank you for a letter which, like the last, is nearly final, but just leaves the gate of Hope ajar. Excuse my troubling you with more questions, but I should much like to know what the sum is, which you say you thought "absurdly extravagant" for the copyright for the musical setting of a song: and also what the terms would be, supposing you had a "royalty" for every time it was sung in public. For my own part, I think the "royalty" system the best of the two, usually: but the other has the advantage of finality.
>
> You speak of your readiness to enter on the matter, if I should ever carry out the idea of dramatising *Alice*—but that is just what I don't want to wait for. We might wait an indefinite time, and then, when the thing was settled, have to get our music prepared in a hurry—and, worse still, *you* might not then be able or willing to do it. That is my reason for wishing to get something ready beforehand: and what I know of your music is so delicious (they tell me I have not a musical ear—so my criticism is valueless, I fear) that I should like to secure something from *you*, now, while there is leisure time to do it in (*L*, 274).

Sullivan did not respond to this letter for six weeks, and then only after Dodgson sent him a reminder. It is likely that, as Dodgson had no apparent interest in staging *Alice* at the present, Sullivan considered the matter, at least temporarily, closed.

After Dodgson sent him a note on May 12, Sullivan tried once more to propose a dramatization. In a letter dated May 17, he wrote "I still think it would be better to treat the whole work dramatically than to set single

Songs . . . My idea would be to make it into a delicious little extravaganza, with a great deal of delicate music of various kinds, Solo and concerted. Carefully mounted, it would be a great success, artistically and financially" (*L*, 278 n).

It is unfortunate for us that Dodgson did not accept this offer of collaboration, for such was Sullivan's talent that he would likely have produced an *Alice* much more full of magic and imagination than that eventually created by Henry Savile Clarke and Walter Slaughter.

Nonetheless, Sullivan finally acquiesced to Dodgson's request for the cost of setting individual songs, and on May 23 wrote "as [to] the songs in *Alice* . . . I would set them to music for thirty guineas each, merely stipulating that if the sale of each reached 5000 I should then receive a royalty of 6*d.* a copy on all sold beyond that number" (*L*, 278 n).

The high cost quoted by Sullivan extinguished any possibility of Dodgson's obtaining settings for all the *Alice* songs from Sullivan. He did write once more, partly to express his belief that the price was too high, and partly to ask if Sullivan would undertake a commission for a single song, another indication that perhaps all along Dodgson wanted his words set to Sullivan's music more than he wanted songs to use in a staged production.

Dodgson's final letter to Sullivan, dated July 5, 1877, reads in part:

> Now the question occurs to me (looking at the matter commercially), supposing *Alice* were produced as a drama, and I were to pay 30 guineas each for the 8 songs in it, and (say) another 160 for additional songs and incidental music—i.e. 400 guineas in all. Now I do not know the amounts of author's royalties on plays, but I have an idea that 10s. a night would not be an unusual amount. This would require a "run" of nearly 2 years before the outlay on the music alone would be repaid. Is it at all reasonable to expect such a run?
>
> My own feeling is that such a plan would end in heavy loss, which I should hardly be justified in risking, and that I should be inclined to ask you, if such a drama were contemplated, whether we could not arrange that, I supplying the libretto and you the music, we should divide the profits, if any, equally between us, and that *I* should bear the loss, if any.

That, however, is all visionary.  As a practical conclusion to
my letter, if you do not mind undertaking so small a commission,
I should very much like you to try one song in *Alice*—any that
you prefer (except of course those that were written for existing
tunes, such as "Will you walk into my parlour? and "Beautiful
Star")—or in *Looking-Glass*.

The music would *not* be published (at any rate not at present)
but laid aside in hopes of the book being dramatised some day
(*L*, 278).

Although Dodgson had made a reasonable proposal for a financial
arrangement, that arrangement was based on his own composition of a
libretto, which he still described as "visionary," and so the relationship,
which might have proved so fruitful, was ended, as Sullivan did not accept
the single song commission.

Newman Flower, in a 1932 article in the *Radio Times,* said that
Sullivan "liked [*Alice*] greatly . . . He tried hard to set it.  He sat up all hours
of the night over it.  But the odd meter beat him out.  He said he couldn't get
attuned to it."[5] Judging from his correspondence with Dodgson, though, it
seems that it was Alice's creator that Sullivan was unable to "get attuned to."

Near the end of his correspondence with Sullivan, Dodgson received
another letter from the Polytechnic, this time from Mr. Owen, one of the
directors, asking for permission to stage *Alice* once again.  Carroll, in a letter
dated June 18,  declined to grant permission, saying that "(1) [he] objected
to interpolations, and meant any future dramatic version to be the book itself;
[and] (2) [he] meant to charge a royalty if it were ever to be done again" (*D*,
363).

Though this response no doubt seemed harsh to the group who had
staged *Alice* just a year before, it seems much more in keeping with
Dodgson's perfectionist attitude about his books.  Though he had so far been
unable to bring *Alice* to the stage himself, he had no desire to see his work
bastardized and misrepresented.  The previous Polytechnic production had
been only loosely based on Dodgson's text, and he had no reason to believe
that a future production would be any more faithful.

His reaction was similar in late 1877 when he learned that the Elliston
family  planned to present an "Alice" entertainment in Eastbourne.  This

time, however, Dodgson discovered that the precautions he had taken by
registering his stories as dramas had no legal strength.    In a letter to
Macmillan dated December 27, 1877, he reports:

> I have just got the legal opinion on dramatic copyright which
> I told you (in my letter of December 18) that I would ask for.  It
> is entirely against me, and is to the effect that any one may
> dramatise a book, and that if the author does so, and registers the
> drama, it only secures the drama from being copied, not the
> book.  So we cannot interfere with the Elliston family.  What did
> you say in your letter to them?  I should still like to see their
> drama, if a copy is to be had (*LM*, 142).

The entertainment, titled "Alice in Fairy-Land," was performed by
"The Elliston Family of Burlesque Entertainers" on September 27 and 28,
1878, at Diplock's Assembly Rooms in Eastbourne. Dodgson, who saw the
performance on September 28, reported that "it was a very third-rate
performance . . . none of them could articulate so as to be audible:  and the
singing was painfully out of tune" (*LM*, 143 n).

Nonetheless, Dodgson did not appear to hold a grudge against the
Ellistons because of the performance.  He had called on them just a few
weeks before it took place and met their daughter Clara, and in January of
1879 he called on them and recorded that "Clara seems prettier than ever"
(*D*, 376).  In June of that year, he visited with Clara again, and again
described her as "prettier than ever" (*D*, 380).

*Alice* had now appeared twice on the public stage, though still not in
a full-blown production, but a dramatic *Alice* had yet to appear in print. This
changed when a little book titled *Alice & Other Fairy Plays for Children* by
Kate Freiligrath-Kroeker was published by W. Swan Sonnenschein and
Allen of London.  The book was dated 1880, but Dodgson received a
complimentary copy in early November of 1879, writing Miss Kroeker on
the sixth to request an inscribed copy and stating "when I have time to read
and consider the *Alice* drama, I may perhaps write again" (*L*, 354).

According to Collingwood "Mr. Dodgson most gladly gave his
consent to the dramatisation of his story by so talented an authoress."[6]  Why
Dodgson gave permission which had so recently been denied others is only

a matter for conjecture. Perhaps he felt less threatened by a printed drama than by a staged one, or perhaps he really did feel that Miss Kroeker was a capable playwright. One must keep in mind, also, that Dodgson could not legally prevent her from adapting *Alice*, so he may have seen more nobility in granting her his kind permission.

Dodgson does not mention his reaction to the adaptation in his diaries, but when Mrs. W. Hunter wrote to him in November of 1888 requesting a copy of the Savile Clarke script, he mentioned in his reply that

> a dramatised version, specially meant for *children* to act, has been brought out by Mrs. Freiligrath-Kroeker, in a volume called *Alice and Other Fairy Plays for Children* . . . Whether it is well adapted for acting I do not know (*L*, 722).

Either Dodgson had never bothered to read the script, or, more likely, he felt himself unqualified to judge its dramatic quality. He did, however, see a production of Miss Kroeker's version on December 19, 1889, in Birmingham. His diary records only that it was "really capitally acted, the 'White Queen' being quite the best I have seen* (Miss B. Lloyd Owen)" (*D*, 476).

In 1882, Miss Kroeker issued a second collection of dramas titled *Alice Thro' the Looking-Glass and other Fairy Plays*, again with Dodgson's "kind permission."[7]

The American edition of Kroeker's *Alice*, published by Dick and Fitzgerald, consists of two acts, "Going to the Queen's Croquet Party" and "The Hatter's Tea-Party" and includes music for "Speak Roughly" and "Beautiful Soup." As is common with many later productions, characters from Looking-Glass Land are sprinkled liberally throughout the scenes, with the Walrus and the Carpenter and the Lion and the Unicorn making appearances at the tea-party.

Kroeker's *Looking-Glass* is limited to characters from Looking-Glass Land, and contains four scenes: Alice's meeting with the Red Queen; Tweedledee and Tweedledum; The White King, Hatta, and Humpty

---

*Previous White Queens Dodgson had seen were Kitty Abrahams (1886) whose bad acting he had singled out, and Irene Vanbrugh (1888).

Dumpty; and the final feast. The musical setting for "To the Looking-Glass World . . . " is also included.

Kroeker used the airs which Dodgson had parodied when he wrote the songs "Beautiful Soup" ("Beautiful Star" by J.M. Sayles) and "To the Looking-Glass World" (a Scottish melody used for Walter Scott's "Bonnie Dundee"). The tune for "Speak Roughly" is not credited.

In her introductory remarks to each play, Kroeker states that "masks and costumes should be copied as faithfully as possible from Mr. Tenniel's illustrations."[8]

It was over six years after his failed negotiations with Arthur Sullivan and three years after the appearance of Miss Kroeker's *Alice* drama that Dodgson again considered a potential collaborator for a musical version of *Alice*. This time he approached Sir Alexander Campbell Mackenzie, a composer of operas who had been recommended to him as a collaborator by James Taylor, organist of New College.

On August 6, 1883, Dodgson wrote to Mackenzie:

> I write to ask a business question, but must begin by introduc-
> ing myself. I shall sign my real name, but I have, as "Lewis
> Carroll," written 2 little books for children, called *Alice's
> Adventures in Wonderland* and *Through the Looking-Glass*. It
> has been suggested to me, as the books have turned out popular
> with children, to make, or get made, a drama embodying one or
> other of these books, and to have it set to music as an Operetta.
> I have enough friends in the stage-world to get it produced. Now
> of course the first question is as to the Composer, and not only
> have I been strongly recommended to apply to you, by a friend
> who is a first class professional musician, but I have heard
> enough of your work to feel sure for myself that you are a
> genuine and original musician, to whom I may with confidence
> commit the task, if you should ever be able and willing to
> undertake it.
>
> My one question, this time, is "Is there any chance, say within
> 2 or 3 years, that you would be willing to entertain such a
> proposal at all?" If you say "no," I need trouble you no further:
> if "yes," I will write in more detail (*L*, 502).

On August 14, Dodgson recorded in his diary that he had "heard from Mr. Mackenzie . . . that he will be glad to undertake the *Alice* operetta—at the end of '84 or beginning of '85. So I have a motive for trying to write it: but it is a formidable task" (*D*, 419).

During this interim, Alice made another brief appearance on stage, this time in the Christmas Pantomime at the Drury Lane in December of 1883. The production being presented was *Cinderella*, and the guests at the ball were represented by storybook characters, including Alice of Wonderland fame.

By early 1884 it seems that Dodgson had convinced himself that he was incapable of writing a libretto for *Alice*. Finally, after nearly a year without producing a script, Dodgson recorded in his diary on May 14, 1884:

> Wrote to Mr. Mackenzie, finally abandoning the idea of writing a libretto for an opera on Alice. I feel quite sure I have not the needful constructive talent. I leave it to him to try it himself, or get any writer he likes, adding that I want no remuneration, and will give him 'permission.' (He also abandoned the idea, not caring to try it without me) (*D*, 425).

Still, on March 29, 1885, when Dodgson made up his list of literary projects, he mentioned among "other shadowy ideas . . . a drama on *Alice* (for which Mr. Mackenzie would write music)" (*D*, 434). For the time being, though, Dodgson had failed in his dream of staging *Alice* because of his own inaction. It was clear that, if *Alice* were to tread the boards successfully, Dodgson would need to find not only a composer to set the songs, but a librettist to do the job Dodgson himself found impossible.

# Henry Savile Clarke

**III** IN 1886, DODGSON RECEIVED two requests for permission to stage *Alice*. The first came on April 1 from a Mr. Addison who wished to use the title *Alice in Wonderland* for a pantomime to be presented at the Soldiers' Recreation Room in Woolwich the following Christmas.* Dodgson gave his consent, on the condition that the piece contain no "coarseness or vulgarity."

On August 28, Dodgson received a request which marked the end of his long search for a professional stage writer to adapt *Alice*. Henry Savile Clarke applied to Dodgson "for leave to make a two act Operetta out of *Alice* and *Looking-Glass*" (*D*, 443). Savile Clarke was a minor dramatist and critic, born in 1841, whose works up to that time had included a three-act drama (*A Fight for Life*), a musical comedy (*The Duke's Doctor*), and a one-act comedy (*A Lyrical Lover*). Dodgson replied two days later in a lengthy, polite letter in which, for the first time, he revealed some of his specific ideas and wishes about staging *Alice*:

> There is one, and only one, condition which I should regard as absolutely *essential* before allowing my name to appear as "sanctioning" any dramatic version of *Alice in Wonderland* or *Through the Looking-Glass*. There are one or two *wishes* on the subject, which I will name for your consideration: but the only

---

*There is no record that this performance took place.

essential condition is that I should have your written guarantee that, neither in the libretto nor in any of the stage business, shall any coarseness, or anything suggestive of coarseness, be admitted . . .

I have two wishes as to what you propose.

One is, that it should not have a harlequinade tacked on to it. It is not that I have any objection to a *decent* harlequinade: but the two things seem to me to be entirely incongruous. This piece ought to be an Operetta . . . and not a Pantomime.

The other is, that only *one* of the two stories should be dramatised. I do not believe *any* genuine child enjoys mixtures. Their memory of stories (as you will know well if you have ever tried telling a story twice to the same child) is accurate down to the smallest detail, and any deviation from what they remember is unwelcome. In the London Pantomimes they constantly make the mistake of mixing two Nursery Tales together. I do not believe there is *one* child of the audience who would not be ready to say "Give us the one, or the other, but not *both* in one entertainment."

Of course, if you say, "There is not enough material in either book alone for an Operetta," I have no more to say: I am not learned in dramatic composition. Still, I believe that the *dialogues* alone, in either book, would take at least an hour to deliver\*, and I hope you will not think me very vain if I add that I believe any children, who know the books, would prefer to hear those dialogues reproduced *verbatim* to any *substituted* matter, however much better it might be as dramatic dialogue.

One thing more occurs to me to request. Several of the songs are parodies of old Nursery Songs, that have their old tunes, as old as the songs probably. I would much prefer, if you introduce any of these, that the *old* air should be used. The whole of the

---

\*Savile Clarke's play, which used both books, eventually contained approximately 570 lines of dialogue plus 22 songs, compared with about 500 lines of dialogue and 10 songs in *Alice's Adventures in Wonderland* alone. Dodgson later complained that the 1888 version of the play was too *short*, lasting over 2 hours with intermission.

poetry, in both books, has already been published, with music, many times: people are constantly applying for leave to do this: and they have simply spoiled such pieces as "Will you walk a little faster" by writing new airs. It would take a very good composer to write anything better than the sweet old air of "Will you walk into my parlour, said the Spider to the Fly" (*L*, 636-7).

Savile Clarke responded directly, affirming that he would comply with Dodgson's demands relating to coarseness. His vision, too, was of an operetta. Savile Clarke did, however, still wish to use both the *Alice* books for the subject of his entertainment, and to this request Dodgson acquiesced, asking only that the books not be mixed in any way, but each kept "to its own act."[2]

Savile Clarke had originally proposed that the play be acted entirely by children, but in a letter of September 2, Dodgson pointed out that,

by admitting grown up performers* you will certainly get a much higher sum total of skill, & probably much greater success— There is no reason why all the characters should be the same size as "Alice"—Many of them were much larger—at least, so far as my ideas went: Tenniel has rather reduced some more than I meant—the Kings and Queens ought sure to be grown up."[3]

This idea, prefaced by Dodgson's often used "One more suggestion I will venture to make," was the first of many submitted to Savile Clarke during the months of preparation for the production.

Fortunately, Savile Clarke seemed both willing and able to work with Dodgson over the next few months. Dodgson considered his own knowledge of dramatic structure to be limited, and so, though he was constantly making suggestions, he made it quite clear that they were just that— suggestions—and not demands, and he was not at all upset if they were not adopted. No doubt, Dodgson's own sense of inadequacy made this a much

---

*Percy Fitzgerald had advised against an all-child cast when he corresponded with Dodgson in 1872. The cast of the 1886 production included many adults, who played the parts of the Kings and Queens as well as the Hatter, Gryphon, Mock Turtle, and other roles.

more pleasant collaboration than that with John Tenniel, which was marred by Dodgson's overbearing perfectionism. Savile Clarke was responsible for penning the libretto, but Dodgson was no doubt happy to have someone who would listen patiently, and at length, to his suggestions, and would then, adopting some and discarding others, forge a dramatically coherent script out of the *Alice* stories. In the end, a few of Dodgson's ideas were used, but most were politely rejected.

In his same letter of September 2, Dodgson had also suggested acting out in a background dumb-show the action in recited verses, such as "The Walrus and the Carpenter." This idea was used in an adapted form for the "Father William" sequence, when magic lantern projections were used in the background to illustrate the action of the poem.

Throughout September and October, Dodgson continued to correspond with Savile Clarke frequently, asking about more details of the production. He was especially eager to know who was to be the composer, for, he wrote, "the fate of the piece depends *chiefly* on that . . . really good music will make up for many shortcomings in other ways."[4] Savile Clarke chose Walter Slaughter, a twenty-six-year-old composer, for this task.

Slaughter was born in London in 1860 and educated at the City of London School. By the time he was twenty, he had already studied music with composer and conductor Alfred Cellier, who conducted at the Opera Comique. He later studied with George Jacobi, the conductor at the Alhambra Theatre. Before working on the music for *Alice*, Slaughter had been employed as a cellist and pianist in various music halls. Though *Alice in Wonderland* was one of Slaughter's first musical theatre ventures, he would go one to write the music for several operettas, including *The Rose and the Ring*, another collaboration with Savile Clarke. He also conducted at most of the West End theatres, including three years at the Drury Lane, before his death in 1908.

On October 26, Dodgson suggested as a possible Alice "a dear little friend on the stage—Phoebe Carlo, now playing in 'The Governess.'"[5] Dodgson had first seen this young actress on January 1, 1883, in a production of *Whittington and his Cat* at the Avenue Theatre in London. She subsequently performed in *The Silver King* by Henry Arthur Jones, in which Dodgson saw her in March of 1883 and again in May of 1885. He called to make her acquaintance on May 15, 1885, and took her to see some paintings and to dinner. That evening he saw her performance and recorded that she did "*very* nicely" (*D*, 435). Phoebe visited Dodgson in Oxford twice that summer, one visit lasting four days. Dodgson suggested to Savile Clarke that she "might do you good service," imploring him at all costs not to "get an Alice that drops her H's."[6]

Whether Savile Clarke had already been considering Phoebe for the part of Alice is not known, but in any case, this was a matter upon which he and Dodgson concurred, for when Dodgson went to London on October 30 to meet with Savile Clarke, she had been engaged to play the part. Dodgson and Savile Clarke "had a long talk about the play of *Alice in Wonderland*" (*D*, 444), and the following day, Dodgson dispatched another lengthy letter, outlining several suggestions, some of which, no doubt, had first been discussed the day before.

Dodgson suggested a small change in the script at the Cook's entrance into the court, which would create the opportunity for a funny bit of business with pepper and sneezes. This bit of business was adopted together with three new lines which Dodgson put forth:

> King:  What's that soup made of ? [later changed to "What are those tarts made of ?"]
>
> Cook:  Pepper, mostly
>
> Dormouse:  Treacle!

He also recommended that the hatter "*drawl*, not *hesitate*, with long pauses between the words, as if half-asleep."[7]

Having begun his letter with two modest and reasonable proposals, Dodgson then overstepped his bounds. He suggested that the play be three acts rather than two, with *The Hunting of the Snark* serving as Act Two. His primary reason for this suggestion was to give Phoebe a longer rest between acts. Dodgson went on to request permission to have some singing and acting instruction given to Phoebe, and asked if he might be in charge of her costume. Dodgson states quite clearly that "a great deal of the success of the piece must necessarily depend on Phoebe" (*L*, 643-45) and many of his suggestions and much of his effort were directed at making her the best possible Alice.

Clearly, Savile Clarke rebuffed these later suggestions. He felt that acting lessons would merely be a distraction to Phoebe, he was not about to incorporate a third act into his libretto, and the idea of an Oxford don playing dresser to a young actress must have seemed ridiculous. Dodgson, however, accepted this rejection with grace, writing on the second:

> I will now execute that beautiful strategic movement known as 'giving way all along the line' & withdraw my suggestions 'en masse,' the 'dress' question included—Amateurs have no business to put in their oar: it only spoils things.[8]

One change which was eventually effected was the ending of "'Tis the Voice of the Lobster." Savile Clarke had requested that Dodgson pen some lines to finish the second stanza, which began:

> I passed by his garden, and marked, with one eye,
> How the Owl and the Oyster were sharing a pie—

but then broke off. Dodgson had included with his letter of October 31 a two-line ending which he had originally written for William Boyd's *The Songs From* Alice's Adventures in Wonderland in 1870:

> While the Duck and the Dodo, the Lizard and Cat,
> Were swimming in milk round the brim of a hat.[9]

Though no copy remains with Dodgson's letters to Savile Clarke, it seems likely that Dodgson also sent at this time, another ending written for the occasion. Collingwood records the alternate ending as:

> But the Panther obtained both the fork and the knife,
> So, when *he* lost his temper, the owl lost its life.[10]

In his letter of October 31, Dodgson says that he is enclosing verses which he has "shown . . . to no one" as they were written especially for Savile Clarke. Later that day, though, Dodgson wrote another ending which he felt was more satisfactory, and so wrote to Savile Clarke on November 2, asking that he please send him a copy of the verses which he has "totally forgotten," and mentions that he thinks the lines "contrary to the spirit of the story" since "one character . . . allude[s] to another character, of whose existence he is

not supposed to know."[11]   Here he is referring to the couplet written for
Boyd, but apparently he did not like the knife/life couplet either. Dodgson's
final version of the poem, dated October 31, reads:

> The Panther took pie-crust and gravy and meat,
> While the Owl got the dish as his share of the treat.
> When the plate was divided, the Owl, as a boon,
> Was kindly permitted to pocket the spoon;
> While the Panther received knife and fork with a growl,
> and concluded the banquet by eating the Owl.

In the manuscript, Dodgson has altered the third line to its final form:

> When the pie was all finished, the Owl, as a boon,[12]

On November 6, Dodgson, now quite pleased with the new verses,
wrote to ask Savile Clarke if he objected to using the enlarged "'Tis the
Voice . . ." in the new edition of *Alice*. Savile Clarke replied that he thought
the text should remain unchanged, but Dodgson responded that he liked the
new song better, and that he would break off the final line after "by," which
he suggests that Savile Clarke do also, as it would add to the humor of the
piece.

The new version of the poem was printed in the seventy-ninth
thousand of Alice, and Dodgson did, in fact, break off the final line before
its grisly conclusion. He also made one other minor change, substituting
"its" for "his" in the line "While the Owl got the dish as his share of the treat."
This new edition of *Alice* also included a preface explaining the origin of the
new lines. The new verses were also printed, with the final line intact, and
with "his" rather than "its," in the published version of Savile Clarke's
adaptation.

Throughout November, Dodgson continued to express concern about
the use of original airs upon which some of his poems had been based. On
November 7, he wrote Savile Clarke asking that he copy out the airs which
were to be used, for he had found that "in one instance at least, the old songs
have been published with different airs."[13]   Dodgson was anxious that the
airs he had in mind when writing the words should be the ones used, and

asked for the airs for five songs: 'Twinkle, Twinkle;' 'Will You Walk Into My Parlour;' 'Beautiful Star;' 'I Give Thee All, I Can No More;' and 'Bonnie Dundee;' these last two being the airs on which Dodgson based "The White Knight's Song," and "'To the Looking-Glass world it was Alice that said'."

On November 28, Dodgson sent airs for three of the songs, which he had prepared with the help of a fellow student knowledgeable in music, to Savile Clarke, together with his feelings about them:

> "I give thee all" is Moore's poetry, written to a "National Air," but of what Nation I know not. I like it, but am not so deeply attached to it as to care much whether your composer uses it or his own setting—specially as my verses are *not* a parody of the original. The *final* line is an imitation, but after that I went off on my own hook.
>
> "Twinkle, Twinkle" I *hope* will be used. It would be a *great* pity not to do so—specially as it fits so well to the endless repetition of the words, by the sleeping Dormouse. They are certainly the notes which the *writer* attaches to the words, if any weight may be given to that circumstance.
>
> "Will you Walk" is the only air that I am really anxious to have preserved. It is a favorite air with me, & the only one that realises to me the idea of the dance. I should be sorry if any other melody, however pretty in itself, were substituted for it.[14]

In the end, the original airs were used for "Beautiful Soup" ("Beautiful Star" by J.M. Sayles) and for "Will you walk . . ." ("Will you walk into my parlour?'" by Marry Howitts).*

In the same letter, Dodgson responds to Savile Clarke's inquiries about a title for the production by favoring the term "dream-play," agreeing that "'fairy' should not be made part of the name. It is *not* a fairy-tale."[15] The

---

* Presumably, the original air for "Twinkle, Twinkle" was also used, though no mention of it is made in Dodgson's letters or in the contemporary reviews. The book of Slaughter's music, published in 1906 (see Appendix B), did not include music for this song, though it did include the original airs for "Beautiful Soup" and "'Will you walk . . .'"

next day, responding to a less than enthusiastic reception by Savile Clarke of the term "dream-play," Dodgson wrote, "I hardly think that any of your audience, who have borne without wincing the books themselves, are likely to complain of such a title as too fanciful."[16]   Dodgson's title was in fact adopted, perhaps as much as anything because of what he had stated about the production—that "what you [Savile Clarke] are producing is not in any existing lines at all & cannot fairly be classified into any existing form of drama, & I would say 'for a new *thing* try a new *name*.'"[17]

About the same time, Savile Clarke had asked Dodgson to write some lines for the Cook to deliver as she brews her soup.  Dodgson, who claimed to be unable to write nonsense on the spot "tried to fancy [himself] watching the cook stirring the soup & listening to her 'wild whirling words'."  On November 30, he sent some lines to Savile Clarke:

> . . . Cook [*stirring soup & soliloquising*]  There's nothing like pepper, says I . . . Not half enough yet Nor a quarter enough [*recites like a witch's charm*]
>> Boil it so easily
>> Mix it so greasily
>> Stir it so sneezily
>> One!  two ! ! three ! ! !
> One for the Missus, two for the Cat & three for the baby [*hits baby's nose*].[18]

Though Dodgson wrote that he feared it wouldn't do ("this kind of writing isn't in my line; you'll have to use your own hand at it"), Savile Clarke adopted Dodgson's lines, and they appeared not only on the stage but also in the published version of the script.

In this same letter, Dodgson remarks on one of Tenniel's illustrations in an effort to prevent Savile Clarke from making the same error as the illustrator:

> Mr. Tenniel has introduced a false 'reading' in his picture of the quarrel of Tweedledum & Tweedledee.  I am certain that 'my nice new rattle' meant, in the old nursery-song, a *child's* rattle, not a *watchman's* rattle as he has drawn it.[19]

Early in December, Savile Clarke was involved not only in the preparation of the production, but also in have his "book of the words" published so that it could be sold in the theatre. On December 12, Dodgson wrote giving his permission for Savile Clarke to use some of Tenniel's illustrations for this book. The next day, Dodgson wrote:

It occurs to me to send you the enclosed cutting, as you *might* perhaps like to print them at the end of your 'book of the words.'

They are very complimentary to me, but I can't help that!

Putting aside that point, & knowing how dearly the British Public like to get plenty for their money, I feel pretty sure that the purchasers of the book would be well-pleased to find they had got "in," & over & above what they thought they were buying, so graceful a little poem as this, & one so appropriate to the book.[20]

The verses in question were by Miss M. E. Manners, and had been published under the title "Wonderland" in the Christmas 1885 number of *Sylvie's Home Journal*, where they were credited to "One who loves Alice." They read:

How sweet those happy days gone by,
  Those days of sunny weather,
When Alice fair, with golden hair,
  And we—were young together;—
When first with eager gaze we scann'd
The page which told of Wonderland.


On hearthrug in the winter-time
  We lay and read it over;
We read it in the summer's prime,
  Amidst the hay and clover.
The trees, by evening breezes fann'd,
Murmured sweet tales of Wonderland.

We climbed the mantelpiece, and broke
    The jars of Dresden china;
In Jabberwocky tongue we spoke,
    We called the kitten "Dinah!"
And, oh! how earnestly we planned
To go ourselves to Wonderland.

The path was fringed with flowers rare,
    With rainbow colours tinted;
The way was "up a winding stair,"
    Our elders wisely hinted.
We did not wish to understand
*Bed* was the road to Wonderland.

We thought we'd wait till we should grow
    Stronger as well as bolder,
But now, alas! full well we know
    We're only growing older.
The key held by a childish hand,
Fits best the door of Wonderland.

Yet still the Hatter drinks his tea,
    The Duchess finds a moral,
And Tweedledum and Tweedledee
    Forget in fright their quarrel.
The Walrus still weeps on the sand,
That strews the shores of Wonderland.

And other children feel the spell
    Which once we felt before them,
And while the well-known tale we tell,
    We watch it stealing o'er them:
Before their dazzled eyes expand
The glorious realms of Wonderland.

Yes "time is fleet," and we have gained
    Years more than twice eleven;
Alice, dear child, hast thou remained
    "Exactually" seven?
With "proper aid," "two" could command
Time to go back in Wonderland.

Or have the years (untouched by charms),
    With joy and sorrow laden,
Rolled by, and brought unto thy arms
    A dainty little maiden?
Another Alice, who shall stand
By thee to hear of Wonderland.

Carroll! accept the heartfelt thanks
    Of children of all ages,
Of those who long have left their ranks,
    Yet still must love the pages
Written by him whose magic wand
Called up the scenes of Wonderland.

Long mayst thou live, the sound to hear
    Which most thy heart rejoices
Of children's laughter ringing clear,
    And children's merry voices,
Until for thee an angel-hand
Draws back the veil of Wonderland.[21]

Savile Clarke decided not to use the verses, perhaps because of their length, but did write a pair of verses in praise of Carroll which appeared opposite the first page of text in the published script, as well as in the playbill (see below p. 51).

Much to his credit, Savile Clarke survived nearly four months of meticulous suggestions from Dodgson, and *Alice in Wonderland*, described in the playbill as "A Musical Dream Play, in Two Acts, for Children and others," was scheduled to open on December 23, 1886.

The play would be performed in the new Prince of Wales's Theatre in Coventry Street. The Prince of Wales's had opened as the Prince's Theatre on January 18, 1884, and was renamed the Prince of Wales's in October of 1886. The theatre was built by Edgar Bruce, who had at one time been manager of the old Prince of Wales's Theatre in Tottenham Court Road, home of the Bancrofts.

The architect for the new theatre was C.J. Phillips, who had already designed some 40 theatres. *The Times* proclaimed that "the site, size [capacity of 960], equipment, and dramatic aim of the new theatre place it at once in the first rank . . . a rare combination of comfort and prettiness in all parts of the house."[22]   The account of opening night goes on to describe the theatre:

> The theatre is situated in a new block of buildings facing Coventry-street and flanked by Oxendon and Whitcomb streets. The frontage, which is treated in the French *renaissance* style, is occupied by an hotel, but the greater portion of the block to the rear is devoted to the theatre, which has a distinctive exterior of red brick ornamented with Portland stone. At the corner of Coventry and Oxendon streets three imposing doorways open into a circular and vaulted vestibule, from which marble stairs and mosaic passages lead to the private boxes, stalls, and balcony. Foyers adjoin these parts of the house, and under the vestibule is a smoking room fitted up in the Moorish style, with grotto and feraery attached. Admirable as are these various adjuncts, they by no means exhaust the merit of the structural design, which is best realized in the interior of the theatre itself. There is not a bad seat in the house from floor to ceiling; the means of access and exit are ample;  there are no pillars anywhere but in the pit, and those very few in number; and brightness and refinement characterize the general scheme of the decoration, the upholstery being red orange plush, the walls Venetian red or Japanese bronze, the ceiling gold, contrasting with a dark-tinted lunette picture over the proscenium, and the whole being bathed in the soft light of electric lamps on the incandescent system. The interior of the house, in short, is a

model of snugness and elegance combined. It is not so much a temple as a boudoir of the drama.[23]

The theatre also had a seven-ton iron curtain, the second of its kind to be constructed and the first in London, which was lowered and raised between the house and the stage each night and which was intended to halt the spread of fire.

Edgar Bruce was joined by Horace Sedger in October of 1886 in producing *La Bernaise* at the Prince of Wales's, and the two men also cooperated in producing *Alice in Wonderland*. In November, Bruce, "wishing to retire from the cares of management, leased the theatre to Sedger for 21 years."[24] Sedger officially assumed the management on September 29, 1887.

Sedger was born in the United States, but had been educated at Cambridge and spent five years on the London Stock Exchange before entering the world of the theatre. His first venture was *Nita's First* which he produced at the old Novelty Theatre in 1884, and in which he also made his acting debut. Sedger remained manager of the Prince of Wales's until 1892.

When *Alice in Wonderland* was produced beginning in December of 1886, Sedger was both Lessee and manager of the Prince of Wales's, but Bruce, who still owned the theatre, continued to be involved with its operation, and was listed on the playbill as "sole proprietor."

The direction of the piece was left to Savile Clarke, who was assisted by Monsieur Claude Marius, the latter also serving as stage manager. Marius (C.M. Duplany) was a Frenchman who came to London in 1869, having been offered an engagement by a Mr. Mansell. Marius' experience in both acting and stage management was quite extensive when he joined the crew of *Alice in Wonderland* in 1886.

Also on the *Alice* staff were M. Lucien Besche, whose costume designs were inspired by Tenniel and executed by Monsieur and Madame Alias; Labhart, providing the properties; Mademoiselle Rosa, who arranged the dances; and Messrs. E. Banks and G. Prodger, who painted the scenery. The dissolving view effects for the "Father William" sequence in Act I were provided by John Bateman and Company.

In addition to Phoebe Carlo in the role of Alice, the cast included

Sydney Harcourt as the Hatter, and members of Mlle. Rosa's dance troupe in several roles, including Cook, Duchess, and White Queen. Mlle. Rosa herself played the Red Queen. The cast also contained several children, notably six-and-a-half-year-old Dorothy d'Alcourt as the Dormouse and the Pudding, Edgar Norton as the Hare, and Charles Adeson as the Cheshire Cat and the Lion.

The play was scheduled to open on December 23, 1886.

# The Curtain Goes Up

**IV** AT 2:30 IN THE AFTERNOON OF December 23, 1886, a crowd of
children and adults quieted as the electric lights of the Prince of
Wales's Theatre dimmed and the curtain went up on the first performance
of Savile Clarke's *Alice in Wonderland*. For many in the audience, it
"seemed too good to be true, to have the opportunity of beholding Alice and
the extraordinary and delightful 'creatures' which she met in her two famous
journeys"* In the playbill, they had read two gracious verses, penned by the
playwright and praising the author of the *Alice* books:

> A Nursery Magician took
>   All little children by the hand;
> And led them laughing through the book,
>   Where Alice walks in Wonderland,
>
> Ours is the task with Elfin dance
>   And song, to give to Childhood's gaze
> That Wonderland; and should it chance
>   To win a smile, be his the praise.

The playbill indicated that Act I would represent "Alice in Wonderland," and as the stage lights came up Alice was revealed sleeping peacefully

---

*Unless otherwise noted, all quotes in this chapter are from Pennell, E.R., "London
Christmas Pantomimes," St. Nicholas For Young Folks, XV (Jan. 1888), 180-89.

at the foot of a "large tree with wide-spreading branches" "in the middle of a forest."[1]   Alice wore a "simple white frock" and had "long hair hanging down her back."   Watching over her sleep was a group of fairies who were no older than Alice herself, and who, dancing around her, sang their song of enchantment which would send her to the dream-world of Wonderland:

> Sleep, maiden, sleep!  As we circle around thee,
> Lulled by the music of bird and bee,
> Safe in the forest since fairies have found thee
> Here where we come to keep tryst by the tree.
> Sleep, Alice, sleep !  These are magical numbers,
> Songs that we learnt from the mount and the stream.
> Ours be the task to keep watch o'er thy slumbers,
> Wake, Alice, wake to the Wonderland dream.*

As the fairies danced off either side of the stage, the scenery changed to reveal a garden in Wonderland.  On one side of the stage, the Caterpillar, as oblivious to Alice as she was to him, sat on a gigantic mushroom, quietly smoking his hookah.  Alice, waking into her dream, had hardly a moment to observe her new surroundings before the White Rabbit "'splendidly dressed' in a jaunty jacket . . . and in wooly rabbit-skin trousers, a high collar and bright red necktie" came dashing across the stage, looking at his watch and murmuring about the savageness of the Duchess.

If the costume of the rabbit seemed familiar to the audience, it was not surprising, for all the characters had been outfitted in costumes based on John Tenniel's illustrations to the stories.  The White Rabbit scurried away at the first word from Alice, leaving her to ponder her new environment.

Puzzled and confused, Alice tried reciting "How doth the little busy bee" only to find, as the audience had expected, that the bee had somehow turned into a crocodile.  Spying the Caterpillar on his mushroom, she crossed the stage to take up conversation with him.  The Caterpillar insisted that Alice recite "You Are Old Father William," and as Alice began, the foliage in the background parted revealing a surface upon which the audience was

----

*All songs in this chapter are from the 1886 first edition, under revision, of Savile Clarke's dream-play (see Appendix B).

treated to a magic lantern show of Father William and his insolent son.

When Alice had finished her recitation, the Caterpillar declared that it was "wrong from beginning to end," and both he and his mushroom were drawn off into the wing. Alice was not alone for an instant, however, as the White Rabbit entered and, mistaking Alice for his housemaid, instructed her to wait for the Duchess and the Cook.

"The Duchess, who was much better-looking than her picture, though ugly enough, came in with the baby; the cook, neat and pretty, her sleeves rolled up, a fresh white cap on her curly hair, followed with her pepper-pot and the Cheshire Cat, with his grin." "Alice [was] amazed at their actions, which [were] laughable in the extreme, the cook alternately peppering the the soup and the baby."[2] After the singing of "Speak Roughly" the Duchess sent the cook away, threw the baby offstage after her, and exited with the Rabbit and the Cat, announcing that she was "going to see the queen."

Soon, the Cheshire Cat reappeared on a tree limb and, after a brief conversation with Alice, showed himself to be an accomplished performer, as he danced with Alice, "grinning all the time" while they sang a duet:

> Al. Cheshire Puss, my thanks to thee,
> For the things you've told to me,
> You've such information rare,
> No cat with you can compare;
> How I wish my Dinah, too,
> Could converse as well as you,

> Both. For my [your] answers come so pat,
> I'm [you're] a Wondrous Cheshire Cat.

> Cat. Alice, you're extremely kind,
> Thus to praise my active mind;
> Let your Dinah to me come,
> At a reasonable sum;
> I will teach her all I know,
> Make her manners *comme il faut*:

Both.    Till folks marvel what I'm [he's] at
        I'm [he's] a wondrous Cheshire Cat.

With a final dance step, the two left the stage making way for the Hatter and the March Hare, who entered carrying their tea table, and quickly seated themselves as Alice returned.    Many of the children in the audience applauded as they saw that their favorite scene, "The Mad Tea-party," was about to be enacted.

"Among the cups and saucers and bread and butter was a soft grey something, curled up like a pussy-cat. The Mad Hatter picked it up, and put it on a chair between himself and the March Hare. It was the Dormouse—the tiniest, sweetest, sleepiest Dormouse you can imagine. Its little grey head was down on the table at once, and it was having its own dreams. The March Hare wore a staring red waistcoat, and around his left ear was a wreath of roses. He looked very mad. So did the Hatter, in blue and white plaid trousers and an enormous grey hat placarded with its price."

The conversation which ensued at the tea party was quite familiar to the audience, but nonetheless delightful.    One of the highlights of the afternoon came when the Dormouse, in "the prettiest little voice," related the story of the three sisters who lived in a well.    "But what a sleepy Dormouse!  Down went the little grey head after every few words, and the March Hare had to push and push it to keep it awake till the end of the story."

The tea party ended with another song which described the Hatter and the Hare:

Hare.    That poor hatter's very bad,
All.      So they say, so they say
Hare.    Most indubitably mad,
All.      So they say!
Hare.    Though why hatters mad should be, dear,
        Is a puzzle unto me, dear,
        But they *are* mad all agree, dear:
All.      So they say, so they say.

Hat.    Hares in March get very queer,
All.      So they say, so they say !

Hat.    Though the reason is not clear,
All.       So they say !
Hat.    They are sane through all the Autumn,
          But when Spring-tide winds have caught'em
          Very mad the world has thought'em;
All.       So they say, so they say.

Al.      He is very bad in March
All.       So they say, so they say !
Al.      And he lives on soap and starch,
All.       So they say !
Al.      He is mad and so's the hatter
          And I do not wish to flatter
          When I say it doesn't matter:
All.       So they say, so they say.

With the final "so they say" the ensemble danced off the stage, the Hatter and Hare taking the tea table with them.

Next came a parade of cards, led by the two, five, and seven of clubs (who lay face down at one side of the stage), and including the King, Queen, and Knave of Hearts. The queen surprised no one when she demanded that the prone cards be beheaded. After learning from the White Rabbit that the Duchess was under sentence of execution, Alice, on the King's hand, joined in the Grand Gavotte of Cards.

Following the gavotte, Alice noticed that the head of the Cheshire Cat had reappeared. The conversation which ensued between the Cat, Alice, and the King so infuriated the Queen that she summoned the Executioner to behead the cat at once. The Executioner, after explaining that a head cannot be beheaded without a body, was then described in a trio sung by the Royal couple and Alice:

He is the executioner and he thinks it very odd he
Is asked to cut a head off when it hasn't got a body.

Al.   He is the executioner and he thinks it very odd he
      Is asked to cut a head off when it hasn't got a body.

King.  Of old my executioner indubitably said he'd
       Be sure a thing that had a head could always be beheaded.

Al.   Of old his executioner indubitably said he'd
       Be sure a thing that had a head could always be beheaded.

Qu.   With all this idle argument my temper isn't suited.
       If something isn't done at once you'll all be executed;

Al.   With all this idle argument her temper isn't suited.
       If something isn't done at once we shall be executed.

As the song ended, the cards, no doubt in fear for their heads, left Alice and the Queen alone on the stage. Finding that Alice had not yet met the Mock Turtle, the Queen sent her off with the Gryphon, who had just entered, in search of this sad soul.

The Mock Turtle entered from offstage, and Alice begged to hear his story. As Alice stood "between the the tall green Gryphon, whose brilliant wings flapped with every movement, and the awkward Mock Turtle, whose long tail dragged on the floor," many were struck by how exactly the pose resembled Mr. Tenniel's depiction of that same scene.

The Mock Turtle entertained his listeners with a performance of "Beautiful Soup," sung to the familiar air "Beautiful Star," and later all three danced the Lobster Quadrille. After more talk about life in the sea, it was Alice's turn to sing, and she presented "'Tis the Voice of the Lobster," delighting the audience with several new lines written for the occasion.

When Alice's song was ended, the Gryphon declared that it was time for the trial to begin, and immediately the stage bustled with the court of cards, including the poor accused Knave of Hearts, chained and guarded. As the trial progressed, it became madder and madder, until Alice, arguing with the Queen from the witness stand, loudly declared her own verdict of "not guilty" and led the chorus in the first act finale:

Al.      Not guilty I declare,
         But let the Knave take care
            In future not to steal the tempting tarts,

King.   Not guilty, then I fear
            You cannot now, my dear,
                Behead for stealing that bad Knave of Hearts.
Qu.     Not guilty ! Oh, it's shocking,
            Miss Alice must be mocking,
                Don't tell me that the tarts themselves ran off,
                    and left the shelf.
Al.      Yes, that's the view I've taken;
            If your nerves, my dear, are shaken,
                I would venture to advise you just to execute yourself.
All.     It's very hard upon the Queen of Hearts,
            Who vowed the Knave stole tarts;
            To find that Knave by verdict of our friend,
            Not guilty in the end.
            Not guilty we declare,
            But let the knave take care,
                In future from the tarts to keep his hand;
            Not guilty ! now we know,
            Why these strange things are so,
                And why our Alice came to Wonderland.


With the end of this song, the curtain dropped on Act I, and children
and grown ups alike enjoyed tea or ginger ale in the Moorish Room during
the interval.

At the beginning of Act II, which was titled "Through the Looking
Glass," Alice was seen pondering what might be on the other side of the
mirror. She then climbed through the glass and disappeared. Quickly, the
scene changed to reveal the garden of live flowers in Looking-Glass Land.
The chessmen were on stage and they duly sang their chorus:

Here ranged in due order of battle we stand,
With red king and white king and queens on each hand;
The bishops move sideways to aid in the fight,
And see how erratic the course of the knight;
The pawns are our privates and both wings to guard,
The four sturdy castles keep due watch and ward.

There followed a dance by the chessmen, during which the White Queen, trying to help up a pawn who had fallen, managed to knock over both the White King and herself. Alice arrived to discover them on the floor and surprised them by lifting them up onto their feet. Alice's action caused a great confusion among the chessmen, and the scene ended with the White Knight's singing "Jabberwocky" followed by the exit of the chess pieces.

Alice was left alone in the garden where she discovered that the flowers could talk. While Alice was conversing with the flowers, the Red Queen entered, and Alice, who wanted to be a part of the chess game, was assigned the role of White Queen's Pawn. The Red Queen then led Alice off-stage to the next square.

Tweedledum and Tweedledee then entered and sang a duet comprising the verses of their namesake nursery rhyme. Dum and Dee were quite a sight—"fat overgrown boys with tiny caps on their heads," and when Alice entered a moment later, she recognized them at once. When introductions had been made, the trio joined hands for a lively game of "here we go round the mulberry bush," and as they sang they seemed to be having such great fun "that it made one feel like jumping up, joining hands, and going round the mulberry bush with them."

After such a game, it was time for a recitation, and Dum and Dee began to repeat "The Walrus and the Carpenter." The Walrus, the Carpenter, and even the little oysters entered and helped to recite and enact their story. After the demise of the oysters, Tweedledum discovered that his new rattle had been broken, and so Alice helped in the battle preparations as the Tweedles tied "blankets and bolsters around their waists, and [stuck] coal scuttles on their heads."

Before the battle could really begin in earnest, however, the lights on the stage began to dim and Alice spotted the crow in the distance. Frantically, the brothers rushed off-stage, and as the lights brightened, the White Queen's shawl came flying across the stage and was caught by Alice. The befuddled White Queen herself followed, and gave Alice a lesson in "living backwards." Before leaving, the Queen instructed Alice to "sing 'Humpty Dumpty' and you'll see what will happen."

As Alice sang the familiar verse, Humpty Dumpty himself appeared on a wall at the back of the stage. She tried her best to talk politely with him, but in the end, found him most unsatisfactory. Alice had just left the stage when suddenly, with a great crash, Humpty Dumpty fell off the wall. As promised, all the king's horses and all the king's men appeared on the stage, but they could only sing:

> Humpty Dumpty's fallen down,
> > Humpty Dumpty, Humpty Dumpty;
> Humpty Dumpty's cracked his crown,
> > Humpty Dumpty, Humpty Dumpty.
> > But the king keeps his promise
> > The king keeps his promise.
> The king keeps his promise though horses and men
> Can't put Humpty Dumpty together again;
> Though all the king's horses and king's men may race,
> 'Tis clear they can never restore to his place
> > Humpty Dumpty, Humpty Dumpty.

Alice then reappeared with the Red King, and the two watched the road for the King's Anglo-Saxon messenger, who eventually arrived in the person of Hare. Hare's entrance was followed shortly by that of the Lion and the Unicorn, who were in the midst of fighting for the crown. A loud chorus of "The Lion and the Unicorn" drummed everyone out of town and off the stage, leaving Alice alone once more.

She was not alone for long, however, for the White Knight soon entered to tell Alice that she was on the verge of becoming a queen. Alice followed him off stage, and returned with a crown on her head. At this point the Red and White Queens entered to give Alice her examination, which was followed by a blast of trumpets and a grand procession to the feast, where "To the Looking-Glass World" was sung.

"The Cook brought the Leg of Mutton on a big dish, and it jumped up and made a bow; the Plum Pudding walked in, and when Alice cut out a great slice, a little wee voice, very like that of the Dormouse [for it was the voice of the same young actress] cried from inside: 'I wonder how you would like it if I were to cut a slice out of you!'" Then the whole of the assembly drank a toast to Queen Alice's health, singing:

> Alice's health,
>   Long life and wealth;
> Never a monarch so mighty was seen.
>   Gaily fill up
>   Beaker and cup;
> Drink to our Alice, to Alice the Queen.

Then the stage went dark, and the voices of the fairies who had enchanted Alice's sleep were heard:

> Wake ! Alice ! wake ! now no longer a rover,
>   Fast fade the Wonderland visions away;
> Wake at the Elves' call—the dream-play is over
>   Wake ! Alice ! wake ! to the world of today.

Then the lights came up to reveal Alice, once more, asleep at the foot of the tree. With music in the background, she woke, and rubbing her eyes, delivered her well-known final line, "Oh, I've had such a curious dream!"

The audience was most appreciative, calling before the curtain not only Miss Phoebe Carlo, who played Alice, but "all the principal characters of the piece and those concerned with its production."[3] To many it seemed that this would prove to be the finest entertainment of the Christmas season.

To be sure, much of the enjoyment of the piece was rooted in the fact that the audience, especially the children, was already so familiar with Alice and her adventures. Savile Clarke was able to take great advantage of this familiarity, for his script, though it did not precisely follow the plots of the *Alice* books, contained very few speeches which were not taken directly from the books. With familiar words and familiar pictures, in the form of the costumes based on Tenniel's drawings, this "dream-play" truly brought the story of *Alice* to life, and this living version of a favorite tale delighted the audience.

The critics, too, were generally complimentary of the production. *The Daily News* commented, "A more sweet and wholesome combination of drollery and fancy, of humor and frolic, of picturesque beauty and brilliant pageantry, in brief, a more refined and charming entertainment has not been seen upon our stage for many a day."[4] *The Times'* critic wrote:

> Mr H. Savile Clarke . . . has, no doubt, had a somewhat difficult task in bringing the two stories together and working them into harmony, but he has evidently succeeded in no slight degree, and the manner in which the various parts were handled . . . gave an idea of completeness to the whole thing. Had Mr. Clarke confined himself to one of the stories, he might probably have secured a more pleasing effect, but this was found impossible, owing to the fact that these charming tales are too short to admit either of them being dealt with separately. Without doubt *Alice in Wonderland* must become a highly popular production. It is exceedingly pretty, and every scene is crammed with innocent jokes and witty sayings which cannot fail to amuse. It is, of course, eminently a children's play, but older folk will find in it much to charm them. The scenery and mounting are effective, but too much attention has not been given to spectacular display . . . Miss Phoebe Carlo played Alice excellently, and the other characters were in competent hands . . . Mr. Walter Slaughter's music is not the least attractive part of the play.[5]

Other critics characterized the production as "a delightful entertainment, and one earnestly to be pressed on the attention of the intelligent child who loves a comic story-book and a pretty tale, delightfully told"[6] (*Illustrated London News*); and "altogether one of the most charming as well as one of the most wholesome and innocent of the productions of the Christmas Season"[7] (*The Graphic*).

There was no argument on the fact that Alice's stage incarnation would appeal to children, especially those who were familiar with the books. There was, however, some question as to the extent to which adults would enjoy the performance. At the time, Carroll's books were still viewed as children's fantasies, not as monuments of nonsense suitable for all ages. The reviewer for *The Theatre* wrote that

> 'Alice in Wonderland' will not appeal to the children alone, it will be patronised, and largely too, by the older members of the

community, unless I am very much mistaken, who will go to join
their laughter with the youngsters, and appreciate once again the
simple, yet subtle, wit of Lewis Carroll's inimitable work.[8]

This opinion of the universal appeal of the play was not shared by all
who critiqued it, however. Especially revealing are two reviews of the play
published in *Punch* (where John Tenniel was still busily producing car-
toons). The first was a report from the youthful portion of the audience:

> Our Child-Critic says that the place to spend a really happy
> afternoon is at the Prince of Wales's Theatre, where *Alice in
> Wonderland* is being played. "They must know the book," she
> says, "and then they'll recognise all Mr. Tenniel's pictures
> walking about."[9]

Three weeks later, *Alice* was reviewed by a more mature critic:

> *Alice in Wonderland* will continue to delight children as long
> as there are any left in town to visit the Prince of Wales's, the
> home of the Bruce, which is crowded every afternoon. We
> suppose that all children over eight years of age must have read
> Lewis Carroll's book, so thoroughly conversant are they with its
> scenes and characters. It's a splendid re-advertisement for the
> book, and the Christmas Carroll ought to be grateful to Mr.
> Savile Clarke, the dramatiser of this work. But, mind you, it is
> not a work to please the elders. What delights the little ones will
> not suit their parents and guardians, who must be content with
> taking a back seat, and being enchanted to see a theatre filled
> with children thoroughly enjoying themselves.
> It is all very well for anyone, say over thirty, to take up the
> book, look at Mr. Tenniel's wonderfully fancy pictures, and to
> select here and there some nonsensical prose and funny verse.
> But to sit out nearly three hours of inconsequent dialogue and
> utterly idiotic songs, given with only one rest of ten minutes
> between two Acts, strikes us as uncommonly good preparation
> for being entered on the books of Colney Hatch. And then from

the experienced playgoer's point of view—for whom it was never written, and never intended, so he'd better not go and see it,—what effective chances have been lost! and, with the exception of the Gryphon, the Mock Turtle, the Hatter, the March Hare, and Tweedle-dum and Tweedle-dee, how unsatisfactory are the realisations of Mr. Tenniel's ideals! Why, the Chess Queens look like bottles of salad mixture, and the Pawns like overgrown fungi! Then the song of the Jabberwok [sic]—oh dear, oh dear—utterly lost. It ought to have been declaimed to music by a good reciter, and the fight with the Monster should have been shown by means of a magic lantern and electric light, or some such device.

However, it was written for the children, and not for their seniors, and the children could go and see it over and over again and never be tired. We recommend the Papas and Uncles who take them, to see a little bit of the beginning, then to retire to their Club, and, if they indulge in such a habit, smoke, or read the papers and return in time to see Tweedle-dum and Tweedle-dee in the Second Act. For which tip they'll thank us.[10]

The creators of the play could not be severely upset by such criticism, however, for, as the critic observed, the play was intended for children, and any enjoyment derived from it by adults was to be regarded as a pleasant by-product. Furthermore, the children for whom it was intended flocked to the theatre, and were delighted by what they saw. The reaction of the audiences, more than the comments of the critics, soon made it clear that *Alice in Wonderland* would be a great success.

# Revisions, London,
# & The Provinces

**V** ON DECEMBER 30, 1886, Dodgson went to London with Meta
Poole, whom he had first met some ten years earlier, and went with
her and Marie Van der Gucht, a twelve-year-old child to whom he would
later dedicate *The Nursery Alice*, to see Savile Clarke's *Alice in Wonderland*. He recorded his impressions of the play in his diary:

> The first act ('Wonderland') goes well, specially the mad tea
> party. Mr. Sydney Harcourt is a capital 'Hatter' and little
> Dorothy d'Alcourt (aet. 6 1/2) a delicious Dormouse. Phoebe
> Carlo is a splendid 'Alice.' Her song and dance with the
> Cheshire Cat (Master C. Adeson, who played the Pirate King in
> *Pirates of Penzance*) was a gem. The second act was flat. The
> two queens (two of the Rosa Troupe) were very bad (as they were
> also in the First Act as Queen and Cook): and the 'Walrus etc.'
> had no definite finale. But, as a whole, the play seems a success
> (*D*, 445).

Although he agreed with much of the positive assessment of the play,
Dodgson recognized that it left much room for improvement. He was
especially displeased with the members of the Rosa Dance Troupe, and
became increasingly critical of them—later saying that they had "largely
spoilt" (*D*, 462) the production.

Mlle. Rosa was ballerina turned choreographer and leader of a dance
troupe which had appeared before in such pantomimes as the spectacular

*Cinderella*, mounted at the Drury Lane in 1883. She had arranged the dances, and also played the roles of the Queen of Hearts and the Red Queen. Members of her troupe, including Kitty and Anna Abrahams, played several roles, including the Cook and the White Queen.

No doubt some of their failure was due to the fact that they were primarily dancers, not actors, and while their dancing was apparently satisfactory (one critic claimed "The celebrated Rosa troupe were to the fore in dancing"[1] ), their acting clearly left much to be desired. Doubtless the producers of the play saw no reason to hire additional adult actors for the roles of the Queens and the Cook when they already had women on the stage hired to be dancers. Dodgson's reaction to their performances, however, clearly shows his displeasure with this particular frugality.

On February 2, after seeing the play for a third time, Dodgson wrote to Savile Clarke:

> The second Act . . . is heavily handicapped by the bad acting of the two queens. They have no comic acting in them *whatever* (& the same may be said of the Queen of Hearts & the Cook), & it is a mystery to me how they ever got into the cast. The W. Queen seems to try her best to lay emphasis on the wrong word in every sentence you give her to say . . . I would not have thought that any one, with an atom of common sense, could have spoken so utterly without meaning.
>
> However Phoebe, Dorothy, & the hatter, make up for a good many short-comings.[2]

Clearly there was nothing that Dodgson could do to correct what he perceived as the problem of the Rosa Troupe, for they had already been engaged and integrated into the production. There were other aspects of the play, though, on which Dodgson felt he could offer suggestions for improvement, and on December 31, 1886 he wrote to Savile Clarke:

> I got a great deal of amusement and pleasure yesterday afternoon in seeing *Alice in Wonderland*. I think Phoebe *very good indeed*: and little Dorothy is a genius! I should like to have a long talk with you over the whole thing, and possibly might

make a useful suggestion or two: but I hope you *would* feel
perfectly free (and it won't wound my vanity a bit) to reject every
suggestion I may make.[3]

Clearly, the portion of the production in which Dodgson perceived the
immediate possibility for improvement was the finale (or lack thereof) to the
"Walrus and the Carpenter" section. So, he "conceived the happy thought
of making the ghosts of the victims jump on the sleeping forms of their
assassins, and give them bad dreams."[4]

On January 3, 1889, he recorded that he had written a "finale, which
[Savile Clarke] approved, for 'Walrus, etc.' bringing in three ghosts of
oysters" (*D*, 446):

> [WALRUS *and* CARPENTER *put remains of feast into
>          basket, yawning and half asleep.*

DUM.    The Carpenter he ceased to sob;
         The Walrus ceased to weep;
         They'd finished all the Oysters,
          And they laid them down to sleep—
DEE.    And of their craft and cruelty
          The punishment to reap

CAR.    Forty winks for me!          [*lies down and snores*
WAL.    Order another forty for me     [*lies down.*
                              [*ghost of first* OYSTER *appears.*
1*st.* OYS.    The Carpenter is sleeping, the butter's on his
                    face
               The Vinegar and pepper are all about the place!
               Let oysters rock your cradle and lull you into
                    rest;
               And, if that will not do it, we'll sit upon your
                    chest!                              [*seats herself*
               We'll sit upon your chest!     [CAR. *groans.*
               We'll sit upon your chest!
               The simplest way to do it is to sit upon your
                    chest!
                              [*Ghost of second* OYSTER *appears.*

2nd OYS.    O woeful, weeping Walrus, your tears were all a
                    sham!
            You're greedier for Oysters than children are for
                    jam.
            You like to have an Oyster to give the meal a
                    zest—
            Excuse me, wicked Walrus, for stamping on
                    your chest!                                    [*stamps*
            For stamping on your chest!      [*stamps*—WAL. *groans.*
                        For stamping on your chest!      [*stamps.*
            Excuse me, wicked Walrus, for stamping on
                    your chest!                                    [*stamps.*

[*Seats herself on* WALRUS.   *Ghost of third* OYSTER *appears. The
     Ghostly hornpipe, and ghosts go off*[5]

Roger Lancelyn Green has suggested that the final verse (that sung by
the second oyster) may not have been composed until 1888, for Empsie
Bowman, who played the Dormouse and ghost of the second oyster in the
revival of that year, told him that "Dodgson was so sorry that she had no lines
in her second part that he wrote the stanza specially for her—and she was
still able to sing it word-perfect sixty years later."[6]  Green, however, had not
had access to the second edition of the play (dated 1886, but published in
1887), which includes this final stanza, precluding the possibility that it was
written later.

If Dodgson had a particular young actress in mind when he wrote this
stanza, it would have been Dorothy d'Alcourt, of whose performance he
spoke so highly, for she was given the role of the second oyster. The other
oyster ghosts were played by two newcomers to the cast, Dot Hetherington,
who acted under the name Dot Alberti, and Isa Bowman, who would play
the role of Alice in the 1888 revival.

Dodgson saw the production again on January 7 and then on February
1, by which time his new verses had been added, and on which occasion he
wrote:

The oyster-ghosts are a great addition (Dorothy [d'Alcourt] is
No. 2; and No. 3 [Dot Hetherington] is a little sailor, and dances

the sailor's hornpipe!) and bring the Walrus etc. to an effective
end.  Also, the Christmas Waits [see below] made a funny
addition:  but the silent end to the play still seems to fall flat (*D*,
448).

Dodgson was quite pleased when "the spirit shown by the defunct
oysters in inflicting this (somewhat mild) retaliation drew applause from the
spectators."[7]

At about the same time that he added Dodgson's new ending to the
"Walrus & the Carpenter," Savile Clarke made another significant change
in the script. In the original staging, the White Knight had had only two lines
in his scene alone with Alice.  Savile Clarke revised this scene, expanding
the Knight's dialogue with Alice to include the discussion of bees, the box,
and the blotting paper pudding.  This new scene was capped by a song titled
"The Waits," which was sung by the White Knight:

> As custom was at Christmas time,
>     As ancient story states,
> We wander, singing doleful rhyme,
>     And call ourselves the waits,
>         The waits, the waits,
>     And call ourselves the waits.

> *Chorus*:  Folks jump out of bed, and put out each head
>         And straight begin to sneeze;
>         As waits we say, in the usual way,
>             "A trifle, if you please."

> And, as in all the olden days,
>     We sing in joyous tone,
> And wander in the midnight ways,
>     And play the gay trombone,
>         Trombone, trombone,
>     And play the gay trombone.

we sat next to a chatty old gentleman, who told me that the author of A*lice* had sent Phoebe Carlo a book, and that she had written to him, to say she would do her very best, and further that he is an 'Oxford man'—all of which I hope I received with a sufficient expression of pleased interest (*D*, 448).

Dodgson saw the play for a final time in London with Sissie Earle on February 15. The production had originally been scheduled to end its London run on February 20, but on the sixteenth, the following advertisement appeared in the *Times*:

> Owing to the extraordinary rush for places to see A*lice in Wonderland*, it has been arranged to give six extra matinées, namely Feb. 21st to Feb. 26th. These will be positively the last performances of this delightful play.[12]

By this time, some theatres had already been booked for a tour of the provinces, so it was impossible to indefinitely extend the London run. However, on February 26, when it was due to close, the play was advertised as being performed "every day up to March 2nd, inclusive," with a note added that "*Alice in Wonderland* cannot be played after Wednesday afternoon March 2nd."[13]

The reason for this deadline was the booking of *Alice* in the Theatre Royal, Brighton, for performances on Thursday, March 3 through Saturday the fifth. This Brighton run was to begin the provincial tour, but the demand for tickets in London was so great that Bruce managed to reschedule other provincial dates, and so was able to advertise on March 1:

> Mr. Edgar Bruce, by arrangement with Mr. Horace Sedger, and having succeeded in postponing some promised visits of his company to the provinces, has the honor to announce a few extra matinées of *Alice in Wonderland* at the Prince of Wales's Theatre commencing on Monday next, March 7th and continuing daily until further notice.[14]

So, after a successful three-day engagement in Brighton, the company returned to the familiar surroundings of the Prince of Wales's Theatre and continued playing to London audiences.

As the run of the play continued, Dodgson became increasingly disenchanted with both the adaptation and the management under which it had been produced. On March 7, he wrote to Savile Clarke:

> I am sorry the London 'run' of the piece continues & shall be very glad when this version is withdrawn from the public eye and you set about preparing a better thing altogether . . .[15]

And on March 13:

> I write another word about my hope to see the 'run' of Alice over for the present. Instead of saying 'this version' I should rather have said 'under this management.'
> Money is rolling in but not in the right direction, which would be into *your* pocket.[16]

On Tuesday, March 15, advertisements in the *Times* announced that the play would run "daily until Friday, next, inclusive,"[17] and the play finally finished its London engagement on Friday, March 18. Even then, it received attention, as "Mr. Punch" commented,

> If the manager and his Clarke are not above listening to a humble suggestion, I should say, Renovate, without removing it; and, with a few changes, you may run it, with *matinées*, right through the year. I venture to think it would be more crowded in spring and summer, when the children can walk to the theatre and back, than in winter.[18]

There would be only a brief rest for the cast before the provincial tour began in earnest. In a letter to Marion Miller dated April 11, Dodgson states that the cast is "going round to the provincial theatres now" (*L*, 673), so, at best, the performers had about three weeks rest before the tour began.

Dodgson commented publically on his impression of the London production in an article he wrote for *The Theatre* in February. The article, titled "Alice on the Stage," was published in the April 1, 1887 issue. In it, he describes the genesis of *Alice* and the *Snark*, and gives brief character sketches of several of his creations, calling the White Rabbit "Elderly, timid, and feeble;" the Queen of Hearts "a blind and aimless Fury;" the Red Queen "the concentrated essence of all governesses;" and the White Queen "stupid, fat and pale, and helpless as an infant."

He said of the adaptation,

> not that [it] is in any sense mine. The arrangement, in dramatic form, of a story written without the slightest idea that it would be so adapted, was a task that demanded powers denied to me, but possessed in an eminent degree, so far as I can judge, by Mr. Savile Clarke. I do not feel myself qualified to criticise his play, as a play.

Speaking of the performances, he said,

> None, I think, was better realized than the two undertaken by Mr. Sydney Harcourt, "the Hatter" and "Tweedledum." To see him enact the Hatter was a weird and uncanny thing, as though some grotesque monster seen last night in a dream, should walk into the room in broad daylight, and quietly say 'good morning!'
>
> . . . Of Miss Phoebe Carlo's performance it would be difficult to speak too highly. As a mere effort of memory, it was surely a marvellous feat for so young a child to learn no less than two hundred and fifteen speeches . . . But what I admired most, as realising most nearly my ideal heroine, was her perfect assumption of the high spirits, and readiness to enjoy *everything*, of a child out on holiday . . .
>
> And last (I may for once omit the time-honoured addition 'not least,' for surely no tinier maiden ever yet achieved so genuine a theatrical success?) comes our dainty Dormouse. 'Dainty' is the only epithet that seems to me exactly to suit her: with her beaming baby face, the delicious crispness of her speech, and the perfect realism with which she makes herself the embodied essence of Sleep, she is surely the daintiest Dormouse that ever

yet told us 'I sleep when I breathe!' With the first words of that
her opening speech, a sudden silence falls upon the house . . . and
the baby tones sound strangely clear in the stillness. And yet I
doubt if the charm is due only to the incisive clearness of her
articulation; to me there was an even greater charm in the utter
self-abandonment and conscientious thoroughness of her acting.[19]

In late March, Savile Clarke wrote to Dodgson asking if he thought the
play would do well in Oxford. Dodgson, who had already suggested the
possibility of an Oxford engagement on February 4, replied that he did feel
the piece would do well, but only if it played during Term. He added that
if Phoebe was not to play Alice he didn't "care 2d *where* it goes or doesn't
go: nor could I advise friends to go see it with such a wooden 'Alice' as
Mabel Love would make."[20]

Mabel Love was a thirteen-year-old actress who had been engaged to
play the role of the Rose. It was her first appearance on the London stage,
and she had been coached for the occasion by a Miss Carlotta Leclercq.
Apparently, she was Phoebe's understudy when the play closed in London.
The role of understudy for Alice was played for some time (though whether
in London or the provinces is not clear) by Isa Bowman, who played the title
role in the 1888 revival.

Collingwood records that the provincial tour "met with a fair amount
of success."[21] Dodgson saw the piece performed in Brighton on July 14, and
noted that it was "improved in 'cast'" (*D*, 452). On August 17, the play was
being performed in Eastbourne, but Dodgson, who had purchased tickets,
did not attend owing to the recent death of his cousin Margaret Wilcox. He
did, however, send his guest Irene Barnes, who would play in the revival of
1888, with his friend Mrs. Henry Gladwyn Jebb. Despite Dodgson's
positive recommendation, there is no record that the tour stopped in Oxford.

The provincial tour ended in late summer, and Dodgson recorded on
September 16 that he had "inscribed forty-one books to go to children who
had acted in *Alice*" (*D*, 455).

Despite Dodgson's disenchantment with the play in the later stages of
the run, *Alice in Wonderland* was a success in nearly every way. It had met
with critical approval, the demand for tickets by enthusiastic audiences had

caused repeated extensions of the London run, and it had been a financial success.

Before production of the play began, the sharing of profits or losses had been agreed upon as follows: if the play made a profit, 9/10 went to the producer Edgar Bruce, 1/24 to Henry Savile Clarke, 1/24 to Walter Slaughter, and 1/60 to Charles Dodgson; if the play lost money, Bruce would bear 9/10 of the loss, Savile Clarke 7/120, and Slaughter 1/24. Happily, the play produced a profit of over £7000, making Dodgson's share slightly over £118.

Though Dodgson was not particularly interested in the amount of his own share, his main desire simply being to see *Alice* on stage, he did feel that the split between producer and playwright was tilted too heavily in favor of Bruce. However, as Bruce bore the bulk of the expense of the production, and nearly all the risk of loss, it was not unreasonable that he receive nearly all the profit. In the end, Bruce pocketed a profit of about £6375, while Savile Clarke received roughly £295.

# Alice Revived

**VI** DODGSON HAD BEGUN giving thought to a revival of Savile Clarke's *Alice* drama even before the initial production was over. In his letter of March 7, 1887, he mentioned Savile Clarke's "preparing a better thing altogether," and on March 29 he "went to town and . . . had a long talk with Savile Clarke about the revised version of *Alice in Wonderland* I want him to do" (*D*, 460).

Dodgson himself was a great reviser of works—he continued to make minor alterations to *Alice* until just before his death—so it comes as no surprise that he wished to see the "dream-play" reworked. His eagerness to revise was especially evident in this case, for in the dramatic form, some things which appeared acceptable in print did not quite work when placed on the stage. Dodgson felt that any sections of the play that, when staged, had seemed weak or undramatic should be eliminated. Once this was done, new material could be added to create a new, and quite different, script.

The question of how to revise the play would become one of debate between Dodgson and Savile Clarke, for the playwright was of the opinion that, as the first production had been most successful, any revival should re-create that version, with only minor changes.

Despite this basic difference, the two continued to discuss the possibility of a revival over the next year. In mid-October of 1887 they made arrangements to meet and exchange ideas on the new version. Dodgson wrote to Savile Clarke on October 14:

> I am very glad you have given me an opportunity of saying my say, before committing yourself to . . . reviving "Alice." I have

a great deal to say, that may be worth your hearing.

I was very nearly calling the other day, & bringing Isa Bowman with me . . .

It is not clear if, at this time, Dodgson entertained any thoughts of suggesting Isa for the role of Alice, but the two were close friends, and it seems unlikely that the thought had not crossed his mind.

The following day, Dodgson wrote that he wished to discuss not "merely alterations . . . [but the] proposal as a whole . . . in which the question of sharing profits will come as a subordinate part."

On October 25, the two met in London, but there is no record of what transpired in this meeting. When the revival became a reality, Dodgson relinquished his claim to any share in the profits, though whether that was the "question of sharing profits" discussed at this meeting is not known. In any case, there was certainly no thought of reviving the play for the 1887 season, and nothing more is said of it in Dodgson's diaries or extant letters until June of the following year.

By that time, Savile Clarke seemed once again to be entertaining serious thoughts of a revival. Dodgson's correspondence with him during June and July was largely devoted to the question of who should play the role of Alice. Given Dodgson's interest in young girls, and particularly in young actresses, this was understandable.

On June 26, he wrote to Savile Clarke:

Are you still cherishing any idea of reviving "Alice in Wonderland?" And if so, have you considered, as possible representatives of "Alice," Minnie Terry and Vera Beringer? I have not seen Minnie on the stage, but, from all I hear, I feel certain she would make a charming "Alice." Vera I have seen, and I am absolutely certain in her case. She evidently has remarkable natural powers, but I attribute much of her success to the teaching she has had from Mrs. Kendall. The result has made me wish you had allowed me to carry out my idea of getting Mrs. Lewis [Kate Terry Lewis, Ellen Terry's sister] to give Phoebe Carlo a few hints as to her acting "Alice." You thought the only result would be to distract the poor child: but I now feel

convinced it would not only have done no harm, but would have
much improved her, and thus improved the whole piece, and
would have saved her from some rather bad mistakes in delivery,
which, when once she had acquired them, I found to be ineradi-
cable.[4]

Dodgson had first seen Vera Beringer on stage just a week before in
the title role of *Little Lord Fauntleroy*. He recorded in his diary that she acted
"with wonderful naturalness and spirit" and that she was "one of the
cleverest children [he had] seen on the stage" (*D*, 460).

Minnie Terry was the daughter of Ellen's brother Charles. On July 2,
Dodgson saw Minnie in *Bootle's Bottle*, and recorded that he was "a little
disappointed" with her. "She recites her speeches, not very clearly, without
looking at the person addressed" (*D*, 460). Following that performance,
Minnie ceased to be a candidate for the role of Alice as far as Dodgson was
concerned.

On June 20, Dodgson had seen Savile Clarke's tableaux on
Andersen's fairy-tales, and remarked that "Isa Bowman looked pretty as the
little match girl dying in the snow" (*D*, 460). It was perhaps this performance
that suggested to Dodgson the possibility of Isa as Alice.

On July 4, Dodgson "called on Mrs. Beringer, to make the acquaintance of her, Esme, and Vera." Later that day he visited Savile Clarke, again
discussing the possibility of a revival, and recorded in his diary "I hope he
will have either Vera or Isa as heroine" (*D*, 461). Despite the fact that Isa
was currently acting successfully in the Savile Clarke tableaux, the
playwright's attitude about the role of Alice was quite the same as his feeling
about the production in general. He did not wish to tamper with success, and
therefore suggested that Phoebe Carlo repeat her performance as Alice.

Though Dodgson had had nothing but praise for Phoebe at the time of
the original production, he became less enthusiastic about her performance
when reflecting upon it the next year. This was certainly partly due to the
fact that he had last seen her during the provincial tour when she had been
playing the role for several months, after which time any child's performance would likely become bland.

Following his meeting with Savile Clarke, Dodgson began a serious
campaign on behalf of Isa. Later that same day, he wrote:

One line in addition to what I said this morning about a successor to Phoebe—I very much *hope* you may find Isa good enough for it—So far as my own wishes are concerned I would far rather Isa should have it than any other child. Of course, I don't expect my wish to have any weight if another child were *distinctly* better—But 'ceteris pamibus' please take Isa! I've never heard her *speak* on the stage, & so have no idea whether she would make a good 'Alice' or not. I've only heard her sing, & I am no judge of musical matters.[5]

Dodgson's admission that he had "no idea whether [Isa] would make a good 'Alice'" indicates the personal nature of his recommendation.

On July 6, Dodgson again wrote to Savile Clarke. Apparently Savile Clarke was considering the possibility of seeing Vera's performance in *Little Lord Fauntleroy*, perhaps in order to evaluate her as a potential Alice, for Dodgson wrote "if you go to see Vera, I should be *much* interested to hear your opinion."[6] In the same letter, Dodgson asks if Isa might be able to have a few days off in order to come and visit him.

Isa did come to visit on July 11, staying until the sixteenth. On the first day, while still in London, Dodgson took her to see Vera's *Little Lord Fauntleroy* before returning with her to Oxford. Following his visit with Isa, Dodgson was even more eager to have her play the part of Alice. He visited with Savile Clarke on the sixteenth, after returning Isa, and by that time the candidates for Alice had been narrowed down to Phoebe and Isa. Dodgson wrote later that day:

After seeing you today, one or two things occurred to me in reference to the question "Phoebe or Isa?" which I would like to put before you—If possible, please don't think me needlessly officious & interfering.

Mainly, of course, it should be a question of "which is fittest?" As to this:—

(1) Phoebe seems to me too old and too tall for "Alice" now— In my book, "Alice" is supposed to be about 7.

(2) Friends, who saw the play in its latter days, thought that Phoebe was beginning to play *mechanically*, & with a want of

childlike freshness.  This seems a very likely result after repeat-
ing the part so often.

(3) Isa's "English" is better than Phoebe's.  In one special and
important point, the use of 'H' she is altogether better.

(4)  Isa *looks* more of a lady than Phoebe—

I do not know how much weight you would be disposed to
give to *other* considerations than mere *fitness*.  But I would like
to mention that

(5)  Isa seems to have, to some extent, a claim to be allowed to
take the first part, having been "under-study" so long, with a
constantly deferred hope of having a chance of playing it.

(6) Phoebe has had a very good "innings" already, & could not
fairly complain at some one else having a turn now.

*Both* children are nice, I think, & both are friends of mine: but,
on the whole, I, personally, would be glad to hear that you could
see your way to engaging *Isa* rather than Phoebe.[7]

In the end, Dodgson's view prevailed.  Though it is unlikely that Savile
Clarke engaged Isa solely because of Dodgson's desires in the matter, she
was engaged.  When Dodgson visited Savile Clarke on July 20, the two no
longer discussed the revival of *Alice* as a possibility, but as a reality.  Savile
Clarke had not only engaged Isa to play the role of Alice but her brother
Charlie was to play the White Rabbit and the Unicorn, her sister Emmie
would play the Dormouse, and sister Maggie would also have a minor role.

Only one of the Bowman children, Nellie, who was "still engaged in
*Joseph's Sweetheart* at the Vaudeville" (*D*, 462), would not be in the
production.  Also engaged for the revival was Clara D'Alcourt, whose sister
Dorothy had made such a charming Dormouse in the original version.  Clara
had played a small role in the provincial tour of the first production.  Also,
Sydney Harcourt would recreate his role as the Hatter.

Making her stage debut in the new *Alice* production would be a young
actress named Irene Barnes, who acted and later became famous as Irene
Vanbrugh.  Dodgson had first met Irene on March 4, 1887, and she had spent
several days with him at Eastbourne that summer.  At the time, Irene was
fourteen years old, somewhat past Dodgson's ideal age of seven, but he
seemed charmed with her nonetheless.

Dodgson had suggested Irene (and perhaps her sister Edith who was cast as "Cook" and "Rose") as a possibility for the White Queen (she also played the Knave of Hearts). Years later, she recorded:

> My first professional London engagement came to me through a college friend of my father's, the Rev. C. L. Dodgson—better known as Lewis Carroll . . .
>
> Lewis Carroll had written to Savile Clarke, who had adapted the play, suggesting me for the White Queen. Violet [Irene's sister] had just made a great success with Toole in *The Butler* by Herman Merivale, and some of her reflected glory shone on me. Alas! what were my feelings when Savile Clarke, meeting her one evening during rehearsals, told her I was hopeless and he thought he would have to get someone else for the part! I was heartbroken. However, Violet talked to me and went over the part with me and all was well, for I remained in the cast . . .[8]

There was a noticeable absence from the new cast, and Dodgson recorded in his diary on July 20, "It is good news that the Rosa Troupe, who largely spoilt the previous production, are no longer in it" (*D*, 462).

On August 5, Dodgson dispatched another lengthy letter to Savile Clarke, discussing some of the details of the new production:

> I hope your new "cast" will prove a success. You say that Dorothy's sister (Clara) is "new": but she was in it when they came to Eastbourne. She played in a scene of "all the King's horses & men," & I think was a fairy also.
>
> As to the 2 lyrics you ask for, it is well you mentioned the matter, as *I* have been waiting to hear from *you*. I thought it was understood that you & the composer were to settle what metres were wished for, & I suggested that he had better write the music *first*, & that you should give me a nonsense-verse to fit it, from which I could see what metre was wanted. Though I retain my opinion that he had better be content with the existing metres, & merely put new airs to them, I shall be very happy to alter them

into any other metres he prefers—*

Please bear in mind the two suggestions of mine, which you approved of—one, that *masks* (of heads of animals &c) should always partly show the human face: the other that *ladies should be warned that bonnets, or hats, are not allowed in the stalls & dress circle*. This last I consider a most important reform to make, for the sake of theatres *generally*: the other managers are almost sure to follow your lead, if once you have the courage to protest against the present senseless practice, by which numbers of the spectators have the pleasure entirely spoiled.

There are a few other matters I want to mention:

(1) In writing your new version of the play, would it not be well to begin by taking the existing one, & ruthlessly erasing all that experience has shown to be flat and ineffective?  Then you will see what room you have for new matter.

(2) If you keep the "King's horses & men," *don't* let them carry such absurdly small toy hobby horses that the wheels are completely off the ground!

(3)  I wish to withdraw, *absolutely*, my suggestion of letting boys act any female characters—You were quite right, & I was quite wrong.  It would *vulgarise* the whole thing.  The rule doesn't work both ways—I don't know why, but so it is.  Girls make charming boys (e.g. "Little Lord Fauntleroy") but boys should never be dressed as girls.

(4)  In giving out the parts to be learned, would it not be well to *underline* the words that ought to be made emphatic?  Very likely it wouldn't have saved the Red & White Queens from making nonsense of every sentence by leaning on the wrong word: but they were *exceptionally* idiotic: for people of ordinary common-sense it would be a great help in giving the dialogue its true meaning.[9]

In the same letter, Dodgson also suggested the possibility of selling copies of the People's Editions of the *Alice* books in the theatre.  The

---

*Apparently the idea of having Dodgson write new lyrics was dropped, for no new songs or verses by him were included in the revival.

People's Editions had been brought out in 1887 as a means to provide a less expensive alternative to the six shilling editions. The idea of marketing them in the theatre, with the producers of the play receiving that portion of the profits normally reserved for booksellers, was eventually adopted.

On August 19, Dodgson wrote to Savile Clarke much distressed:

A piece of news has reached me, part of which seems credible enough: the other part I entirely decline to believe, except on *your* assurance.

The first part is that Mr. Sedger (I forget what his connection is with the Prince of Wales's Theatre) has had a "misunderstanding" with Mr. Bruce (who I think you told me is the lessee)—

The other part is that, in consequence of this "Alice" is not to be played at Xmas ! It makes me indignant to think that it should be believed that you are so entirely dependent on these men that you cannot produce your own play without *their* assistance! From what you told me about Mr. Bruce, I shall be by no means sorry to hear that your arrangement with him is "off": & I trust you will now be able to do the thing "off your own bat," and, instead of getting only the narrow percentage you were going to get from him, that most of the profits will be in your hands, to divide with the composer & perhaps have "a trifle, if you please" for *me* as well.

I believe, if you could get the room at the Egyptian Hall, where Albert Smith used to give 'Mont Blanc', you would make a great success of it.

Poor Isa is much distressed, believing "Alice" to be smashed by the quarrel between these two workers: but I daren't say anything hopeful to comfort her, till I hear from *you*.[10]

The Prince of Wales's Theatre, in which *Alice* had been produced in 1886, had officially changed management since the original production of *Alice*. Edgar Bruce, the owner of the theatre, had leased it to his partner Horace Sedger beginning in November 1886, and both men had been involved in producing the original version of *Alice*. However, in September of 1887, Sedger had taken over sole management of the theatre, and apparently did not wish to cooperate in another *Alice* venture.

The temporary lack of a theatre did not deter Savile Clarke from his preparations, however, and on November 13 Dodgson was able to record that he had "heard from Mr. Savile Clarke that he has settled with Mr. [Richard] Mansfield . . . who has taken the 'Globe,' to produce *Alice* there in the afternoons, beginning on Dec: 26th" (*D*, 465-66). The Globe had been built in 1868 on the site of the old Lyons Inn in Newcastle Street, Strand. It was of similar size to the Prince of Wales's, with a capacity of about 1000.

Richard Mansfield was an American actor who had travelled to London in July of 1888 and presented his production of *Dr. Jekyll & Mr. Hyde* at the Lyceum. This he followed with *Prince Karl*, and when he was unable to continue the run of that production at the Lyceum, he took the lease on the Globe to begin December 21, and transferred there. As *Prince Karl* was giving only evening performances, Mansfield was happy to make arrangements with Savile Clarke and Edgar Bruce to produce *Alice* in the theatre during the afternoons.

Dodgson was present at some of the rehearsals, and Irene Vanbrugh recalled that Dodgson "made himself so entertaining to the children during rehearsal, with his stories and his fun, that more than once he was politely requested to leave the theatre by the worried stage manager."[11]

The new edition of the script, published in 1888 no doubt to be sold in the theatre, reflected several changes which were made from the 1886 version of the play. The majority of these were quite minor, and many involved changing a line or two so that the dialogue more closely resembled Dodgson's original. There were some alterations, however, which seem certain to have been suggestions of Dodgson.

The Tea-party was slightly revised to give several more lines to the Dormouse, whom, when played by Dorothy D'Alcourt in 1886, Dodgson had singled out for praise. The Pudding, played by the same actress, also received some additional dialogue in the final scene. The stage direction "*Appearance of the Jabberwock*" was inserted following the singing of "Jabberwocky," an addition which was noted by the *Times* reviewer.

The play's ending was the most extensively rewritten portion of the script. At the beginning of the final scene, Dodgson's "'To the Looking-glass world'" was replaced by a new song, titled "Sound the Festal Trumpets":

Sound the festal trumpets, set the bells a-ringing,
　　　Here are curried crumpets, crocodiles, and beans;
Raise on high the chalice in our honour singing,
　　　Welcome, welcome, Alice, with the noble Queens.

### CHORUS

Come, and fill up all the glasses just as quickly as you can,
Sprinkle everyone that passes with the buttons and the bran;
Put the cats into the coffee, and the mice into the tea
Mix the cotton-wool with toffee quite as nice as nice can be.[12]

Later in the scene, following Alice's encounter with the Pudding, the exchange between Alice and the Queens concerning poetry and fishes, taken verbatim from *Looking-Glass*, was added.

This conversation was followed by a singing of "'First the fish must be caught'," Dodgson's only song to be added to the new version. This song is then followed by the "Alice's Health" chorus and "Wake, Alice, Wake" which ended the earlier version. Though it is not surprising that this final scene was augmented in order to accommodate another song from the book, there is no apparent reason for the substitution of "Sound the Festal Trumpets" for "To the Looking-glass world." Certainly Dodgson would not have approved of such a change, though his opinions on the matter are not recorded in any extant source.

In addition to the textual changes, there was another difference in the 1888 version of the script, and this was almost certainly instituted at Dodgson's request. Throughout the script, words which should be emphasized were printed in italics. Though this was done to a certain degree in the 1886 versions of the script, it was much more extensive in the 1888 version. Dodgson's displeasure with the inability of the Rosa Troupe members to lay the emphasis on the proper word most likely lead to this alteration.

In Isa Bowman's copy of the script, Dodgson has underlined some twenty words in Alice's speeches which he felt Isa should lay emphasis upon. It is interesting that Isa's surviving copy of the script is of the 1888 edition, indicating that the script was probably printed before or during the rehearsal process, when Isa was learning her part.

Dodgson first saw the revival on January 3, 1889, on which occasion he recorded in his diary,

> Isa makes a delightful 'Alice,' and Emsie is wonderfully good as 'Dormouse' and second ghost, when she sings a verse and dances the Sailors' Hornpipe. Charlie [Bowman] is 'White Rabbit'; Dorothy d'Alcourt is speaking Oyster, first fairy, first ghost, and plum-pudding. As first ghost, she dances a mazurka with one of the Lockits. Edith Barnes is 'Cook' and 'Rose', and Irene is 'Knave of Hearts' and 'White Queen'. Both *speak* well, specially Irene . . . The chief addition to the play is the 'fish' song at the feast, sung by Miss Dewhurst (*D*, 467).

On February 28, in a letter to Winifred Holiday, Dodgson said he thought the revival "ever so much better than in 1886" and that his "little friend, Isa Bowman, was a more refined and intelligent Alice even than Phoebe Carlo, though *she* was a very good one" (*L*, 730).

Reviews of the new production were generally positive, the critic for *Era* writing that he

> could have hugged without hurting the dear sleepy little dormouse so cleverly played by Miss Emmie Bowman, who with her tiny voice made everybody understand clearly all that she had to say. Miss Isa Bowman made a pretty, engaging, and highly intelligent exponent of the part of Alice, and, although her singing voice was hardly strong enough to do justice to the songs, her dancing and her acting generally secured warm admiration.[13]

The *Theatre* critic praised the Bowman ensemble, saying "We have a charming *spirituelle* Alice in Miss Isa Bowman, who sings sweetly and dances gracefully, a quaint Dormouse in tiny Miss Emmie Bowman, and a funny little White Rabbit in Master Charles Bowman."[14]

*The Times* described Isa as "not only a wonderful actress for her years, but also a nimble dancer," and went on to say

> In its new surroundings the fantastic action of the story ... loses nothing of its original brightness and humour. Alice's adventures in Wonderland and through the looking-glass have the rare charm of freshness, both for children and their elders ... Even the dreaded Jabberwock pays an unconventional visit to the company by a descent from the "flies," and his appearance will not be readily forgotten.[15]

Despite his own and others' praise, however, Dodgson was not wholly satisfied with the production. Two incidents had greatly distressed him, and he wrote to Savile Clarke immediately after seeing the play on January 3:

> ... there are 2 points in the "Alice" I am so anxious you should attend to *at once*, that I must write tonight.
>
> First, let me say that I think the new version as a whole *very* successful, & that in *many* aspects it is quite superior to the old one: that Isa is in my opinion, *charming*: & Emmie simply *astonishing*! though I can't quite think her better than Dorothy, yet she is wonderfully good.
>
> But I have not time to go into details of praise.
>
> There are two matters I want earnestly to object to, under the clause of our agreement in which *you* undertook to eliminate all manner of impropriety, & *I* agreed to have myself named as giving my special sanction.
>
> (1) The White King, this afternoon, fell flat on his back, with his feet towards the audience who (at any rate in all the stalls) were thus presented with a view of him which—which I leave to your imagination.
>
> (2) The Red King, in order to dance (the regular abominable *ballet* dancing style) actually *drew up* the long series of rings which formed his skirt, nearly to his waist—I don't say he was not fully clad, in tights, beneath that skirt: and I don't say he *needed* the skirt: nor that there would have been any indecency

in appearing *without* the skirt; but I *do* say that, having the skirt on, it was *distinctly* indecent to pull it up—It is an inviolable rule in such matters that a dress should always *do all it is meant for*. A very short skirt may be perfectly decent, while a much longer one, a little pulled up, may be quite the reverse.

May I respectfully, but most seriously, beg for the immediate abolition of these two indecencies? I fear that you, however much you may *yourself* sympathise with my remonstrance, are to some extent not quite master of the situation—May I then arm you with a weapon for the occasion? If you find the acting managers decline to interfere in what I deliberately hold to be two pieces of real *indecency* you have my authority to tell them that in that case I exercise my right of demanding the immediate withdrawal of my name as sanctioning the piece—But I hope you may be able to manage the thing without taking this step, which I should be very sorry to take, as it would look so unfriendly towards yourself.

I am *specially* anxious for immediate steps to be taken, as I expect to be present again on *Monday* next, with a young lady friend, whom I would gladly spare the unpleasant spectacle I have described.

Forgive me if I seem *very* sensitive: & try to realize the feelings of an unfortunate writer who, having done his best to give English children a book of absolute *purity*, finds it brought into such foul associations.[16]

Savile Clarke was able to remedy the situation immediately, and on January 6, Dodgson wrote "Many thanks for your letter. I am most pleased by your action about the kings."[17]   After he saw the play again on January 7, he wrote to Clarke "the 'King' business is now all right & . . . I am much obliged to you for setting it right."[18]

To his long letter of protest, Dodgson added a post script with a few additional notes on the performance:

(1) Isa's dress, (as seen from the dress circle) looks a trifle too *long* for artistic effect (perhaps it may look alright from the

stalls)

(2) When Humpty-Dumpty fell off the wall, the crash came *much* too soon, while he was still visible!

(3) The "fish" song was perhaps over-accompanied: at any rate it was scarcely audible—and isn't the air a rather depressing one?

On the whole I congratulate you on the new piece & trust it will bring you in *heaps* of wealth![19]

This final comment proved somewhat ironic, for the economy of the production was soon to become a major issue. After seeing the play on January 7, Dodgson sent another list of notes to Savile Clarke:

(1) When, in the Tea Party, the Hatter says "lets all move *one* place on," I did *not* mean them to take their chairs with them! Surely it wouldn't be *much* extra trouble to bring in 5 chairs?

(2) Perhaps the above was only a piece of rigid economy, as I see they are now economical enough to omit the Magic Lantern for "Father William." If *economy* will bring in money for you, I hope you will get lots—I should think this omission will save *at least* a penny a day.

(3) I see you allow a wretched parody of "Father William"— an advertisement of something—to be printed on the cover of the play-book. So let it be, by all means, if you wish. But do you remember declining to print some really pretty verses, by Miss Manners, on 'Alice' that would have made a really pretty end to the book? [see above p. 45] You said "we would rather have nothing *but our own thunder*." If *this* poem is your "own thunder" then I apologise for calling it wretched.[20]

The poem, printed on the back cover of the 1888 edition of the play, was an advertisement for Dr. Ridge's Patent Cooked Food, and one can hardly take issue with Dodgson's calling it wretched. It was printed under the title "New Version of a Song" and reads:

"You are old, Father William," the young man said,
    "Yet seem young; you are healthy and slight,
You are active, at times wont to stand on your head,
    Do you think at your age it is right?"
"In my youth," Father William replied to his son,
    "I feared it might injure the brain;
But I took **Ridge's Food**, and it made it so strong,
    That I do it again and again.


"You are old," said the youth, "as I mentioned before,
    Yet seem young, a most curious vision;
Pray, what is the reason?" "Of course, **Ridge's Food**,
    You young fool," said his pa, with precision.
"For in my youth," said the sage as he shook his grey locks,
    "I kept all my limbs very supple
By using **R's Food**, price one shilling the tin,
    It's worth twenty guineas the couple."


"You are old," said the youth, "yet your jaws are so strong,
    You eat gristle, and easily chew it;
Why you ate that old steak, 'twas as tough as a nail,
    Pray how do you manage to do it?"
"In my youth," said his father, "I took **Ridge's Food**,
    And I owe to it peace throughout life;
For the muscular strength which it gave to my jaw,
    Killed my mother in-law and my wife."


"You are old," said the youth, "one would hardly suppose
    You like wine, and you never repent it;
It somehow has never disfigured your nose,
    Did you take **Ridge's Food** to prevent it?"
"I have answered three questions, and that is enough,"
    Said his father; "I'll kick you downstairs."
"If you do," said his son, "I shall  get **Ridge's Food**,
    For it executes neatly repairs."[21]

Not only did this bastardized version of Dodgson's poem appear on the rear cover, but the verses which Savile Clarke had written in praise of Dodgson were omitted from this edition. Following the complaint about the poem, Dodgson's January 7 letter continued:

> (4) I thought the *time* of the whole *very* short—it is over at 20 minutes to 5—10 or 15 minutes more wd. be no harm at all. Also I hear it is generally said there might be more songs with advantage. Also Edith Barnes has a very pretty voice. Now *do* think about it, & see if you can't find room for another song & allow me to write (or write yourself if you prefer it) a song for Edith to sing as "Rose"—I should like that pretty air I sent you, in that book, but if Mr. Slaughter liked to write another air, so let it be—Only, somehow, do let Edith sing![22]

Dodgson pursued this last matter in a letter dated January 20, in which he mentioned that he understood that "the conductor (Mr. German) ... thinks it a pity [Edith] should not sing."[23] Edith was eventually given the "Fish-Song" to sing. Dodgson, though happy that she was singing, felt that the song was "not an effective one; & if it were struck out, & the song, for her as "Rose" which [he had] devised, were put in . . . it would improve the play."[24]*

On January 11, Richard Mansfield closed *Prince Karl* as he had been ordered by his physician to take a break from the stage. The following day, he opened a production of *She Stoops to Conquer*, which starred Kate Vaughn, to play evenings in the Globe. By this time, it had become clear that there were serious problems with the management, whether related to Mansfield's illness is not known, and the early demise of the production is revealed in Dodgson's next several letters. On the eleventh, he wrote to Savile Clarke:

> I can't well express in words the indignation with which I heard Mr. Clarke's account of the treatment you and so many others

---

*Whether Dodgson had actually written a song for the Rose is not clear. In any case, no such song survives.

have had to put up with from one of the most arrogant managers
I ever heard of—and poor Isa! I could cry over the thought of that
dear, painstaking, conscientious child being so cruelly repri-
manded.

Mr. Clarke said something about what you would have done
or would do, if only you had the command of £1000—Why oh
why didn't you say it to me before you got entangled with this
man?  I would be glad to advance £1000 with the profits of the
play as my sole security for repayment, under certain conditions—I fear, however, it's no use talking about it, *now*, as the
conditions are not likely to be fulfilled.

If there were any chance of getting things put on a better
footing, I wd. gladly come and talk it over with you . . .[25]

The description of Mansfield (if Dodgson was in fact referring to
Mansfield and not Edgar Bruce) as arrogant was not without basis, for it is
said that he considered himself to be equal or superior to Henry Irving, who
at that time was at the height of his popularity.[26]   When his *Richard III*,
produced at the Globe later that year, failed to draw, he gave up the London
stage, disgusted with what he perceived to be the poor taste of the British.
Coincidentally, Isa Bowman,  mistreated during the run of *Alice*, was
featured as a young prince in *Richard III*.

On January 15, Dodgson received a letter from Savile Clarke concerning, among other things, the lack of sale of the People's Editions of the *Alice*
books in the theatre.  Again, Dodgson expressed his dissatisfaction with the
management, and his wish that some new material might be added to the
play:

I got your letter, and heartily sympathise with you in all the
worry you have undergone.

By all means, send me back all the unsold copies of the cheap
'Alice', since your manager (what a lot of managers you suffer
from!  Never was there a dish of broth with so many cooks!)
seems resolved that "there is no sale; there can be no sale; & there
*shall* be no sale!" I was there this afternoon, & saw no symptoms
of their being on sale at all. I feel no doubt that he is not allowing

the attendants any profit on the sale. The whole management seems smitten with a passion for "cheese-paring."

The thing ended about 4 30 today—I'm sure the audience wd. have liked another 15 or 20 minutes. And I'm sure that it adds to the popularity of a piece to have little 'extras' put in from time to time—and I'm sure the (rather flat) Rose & Lily scene would be much brightened up by a song—and I *think* the finale I wrote you for the Walrus and the Carpenter has been an addition of some value—But I don't want to tease you about it. If you are decidedly against any further addition I say no more—. . . [27]

By January 25, chances for a financially successful run seemed quite slim, and Dodgson outlined measures which he felt might save the production:

Here is one more matter that I hope you will find worth consideration.

It appears to me that the prospects of 'Alice' are in danger of suffering from want of *money*. Now I should be very glad to "put money into" the thing even though I get none *out*—I propose, then, to contribute £100, on condition that, so long as it lasts, the following conditions are observed:—

(1) Advertisement in papers to be a *single* one (instead of the two now appearing in a few papers)—to end with the words "Alice—Miss Isa Bowman"—to appear in the Times, Morning Post, Daily News, Standard, Daily Telegraph, Globe, St. James Gazette, Star, & Echo—

(2) That 6 posters, of the usual size, be placed at the following Metropolitan Stations—Charing Cross, (*west*-going platform), Praed Street (*east*-going platform), South Kensington (both platforms), Gloucester Road (one platform, it doesn't matter which), Victoria [ditto].

(3) That circular pictures, like those done on japanese paper last time, be *given* away to all *children* as they leave the stalls and dress circle.

(4) That 'Father William' be acted in dumb-show, while Alice sings the words, by two boys dressed after the pictures, the father being acrobat enough to "stand on his head" (& hands) at any rate. Instead of the "back-somersault" he might "turn a wheel" (In this case, the threatened "kick you downstairs" wd. of course be done by Father William, & Isa would be spared from doing what is certainly *not* a very graceful thing for a little girl to do).

If all this can be done for £10 a week I'll pay for it for 10 weeks—if £25 a week, I'll pay for it for 4 weeks, & similarly for intermediate amounts.[28]

Dodgson's proposition was not adopted, however, for within a few days, it was decided to terminate the run of the show. On this occasion there would be neither a provincial tour nor a profit. The advertisement for *Alice* in *The Times* on January 30 proclaimed "Last 10 Performances." On the twenty-ninth, Dodgson had written to Savile Clarke:

I am *very* sorry for your disappointment & loss & that the 2nd production of "Alice" has turned out so badly; but I can't say I am at all surprised—I believe that *most* of the people, ready to come & see it, are as yet entirely ignorant of the fact that it is going on *at all*. The advertising seems to me to have been wretchedly done—Take the "Globe" newspaper as an instance: very likely there are many people who, like myself, take in that paper, & no other: all such people wd. never have even *heard* of this new edition! And I conclude that the same niggardly economy has been observed as to many other papers—and the advertisements are so wretchedly short.

Look at the way Irving advertises
        "Macbeth—Mr. H. Irving
        Lady Macbeth—Miss Ellen Terry"
why shouldn't you have had
        "Alice—Miss Isa Bowman
        Dormouse—Miss Emmie Bowman
        Hatter—Mr. Sydney Harcourt"
and so on—

such an advertisement put into *all* the papers & posted at *all* the Metropolitan Stations, and liberally shown by "sandwich" men, would have cost another £100 a week, & have brought in another £300 a week.

Again: I was strongly of opinion, & the result confirms me in it, that the 2nd edition ought to have been *different* from the first—ineffective bits being cut out, & new songs, new dances, & new "business" being put in—I believe that would have added £100 or £200 a week to the receipts, because every body, who went *last* time, would go *again*, as soon as they heard "there's a lot *new* in it": but no doubt many people, when their friends told them "it's much the same as last time," didn't care to go & see only the old thing over again—I know *your* view was to keep it as much as possible the *same*: & I didn't expect my amateur notions to have any weight with you: but I certainly have seen other plays advertised on that very principle, & the fact, of there being many new features introduced, put forward as a special attraction.

It seems a great pity to cut the thing short when it has scarcely begun—If you were willing to consider any plan for carrying it on in some other theatre, or hall, or even room, I would come and talk it over with you—Of course, it must be now or never: in another week your company will have accepted other engagements. I would be happy to advance £1000 myself: but it would have to be on totally new conditions—& I will have nothing to do with any such arrangements as that we shd. bear *all* the risk & get 1/10 of the profits! It must be "all the risk, & all the profits"—I need not say it wd. be *essential* to advertise more liberally, & to alter the play enough to be able to announce "new effects, new songs, new dances, etc., etc."[29]

On February 5, the wording of the *Alice* advertisement in *The Times* was changed, giving the management's explanation for the impending closing. The new segment read, "In consequence of the action taken by the School Board of London these performances will cease after Saturday next."[30]

A complete understanding of the implications of this advertisement requires some background. In 1876, Lord Sandon's Education Act was passed. This act lay down that "no child might be employed at all below the age of ten, and no child might be employed between the ages of ten and fourteen without a certificate [indicating that he had passed certain standards of achievement and attendance]." The law also compelled parents to ensure that children between ages 5 and 14 "receive[d] efficient elementary instruction in reading, writing, and arithmetic."[31]

Power to enforce the laws of attendance was vested in local School Attendance Committees, or, in the case of London, the London School Board; however, the Board was not in the habit of enforcing the law against children who were employed in theatres. In 1886, a Royal Commission on Education was appointed and headed by Lord Cross. It issued a ten volume report in 1888. One of its recommendations was the enforcement of the law against those who employed children in theatres.*

This recommendation was taken up as the battle cry of the Moral Reform Union when they attended the meeting of the London School Board on November 8, 1888. *The Times* reported that a communication from that group

> expressed the hope that the recommendation of the Royal Commission . . . relating to the employment of children in theatres, pantomimes, and other places of public entertainment, might speedily be carried into effect . . . [The Union] asked the Board to exercise its powers to restrain the engagement of young children by theatrical managers and their agents . . . [urging] that the danger to health, education, and morals of children engaged in factory work was as nothing compared with that involved in the work at the pantomime . . . [The Union] asked the Board to bring into operation the provisions Section 5 of the Act of 1876 to prevent the employment at pantomimes and other public performances of young children under ten years of age.[32]

---

* According to the Act of 1876, employers of children under the age of ten were subject to fines of up to 40 shillings per offense.

The request of the Union was referred to the By-Laws Committee, which reported back to the Board on Dec. 13:

> Mr. Bayley asked the chairman of the late By-Laws Committee as to the steps which had been taken to protect children of school age employed at the theatres. The Rev. J. J. Coxhead replied that by the action of the committee notice had been given to the managers of the theatres where children were employed in pantomimes, that, for the protection of the children against their illegal employment, the Board would enforce the law against such managers in any case in which children of school age were employed.[33]

It was this "action" which was referred to in the February 5, 1889 advertisement regarding the closing of *Alice in Wonderland*. That the management failed to respond to an action taken before the play opened in December until it began to fail in February may indicate that this excuse was used to remove the blame for the production's failure from their own shoulders. Oddly enough, this explanation for the closing of the show was never offered to Dodgson, who took a keen interest in the debate over stage children, and became actively involved in that debate later in 1889 when an amendment to the Bill for the Prevention of Cruelty to Children specifically prohibiting the employment of children in theatres was proposed (see p. 14).

Despite Dodgson's disappointment with the failure of the second version of *Alice*, he felt that events had proven him correct in his original assessment that the play should have been completely revised. Savile Clarke, on the other hand, thought the failure due to the second production's following too closely on the heels of the first.

Whether the failure of the *Alice* revival was due to lack of new material and good advertising, as Dodgson claimed; the new production's following too closely on the original, as Savile Clarke claimed; the action of the London School Board, as the managers claimed; or some combination of the three can never be known for certain. In any case the curtain was brought down for good on February 9.

Dodgson did not want to close the door on future stage versions of *Alice*, and wrote to Savile Clarke on the day of the final performance:

... No need to discuss further whether failure of play was due to its being a repetition or want of fresh features, or insufficient advertising, or what not. It's too late to say anything more. And I fear *you* will never put "Alice" on the stage again—However you won't resent somebody else trying it, I daresay? Provided of course they make no use of *your* version . . .[34]

Three days later, on the twelfth, he wrote with another possible explanation for the failure:

> A strange idea has come into my head, with regard to what you tell me of the almost incredible, & unaccountable difference between the profits this time & those in 1886.
>
> I went 3 times myself; there was a good house every time— Friends, who went last Saturday tell me the house was "nearly full."
>
> I have a strong suspicion that the profits, this time, have been pretty nearly what they were in 1886, & that you have been egregiously cheated by *somebody*. It is a tolerably easy piece of swindling to *cook* the accounts, so as to make it appear that the payments have been only about 1/3 of what they really were.

In a postscript he continued to defend his opinion about the nature of revivals:

> P.S. A propos to a remark of yours, that you think the failure this time is due to its being "a revival"—I don't pretend for a moment that my story (though it has sold in undiminished amount for 22 years) has anything like the same elements of inexhaustible interest as (say) "Cinderella." Yet still ("to compare great things with small") just see how many "revivals such stories hear!" I shd. think *every* one of them is revived *every* year: but then they have (what to my mind is an essential part of a successful revival), new business, new songs, new dances, new *everything* except the story itself. If *I* were the author of an

"Alice" play, I shd. reproduce it, regularly, *every* Xmas—and people shd. ask each other "Well, what is the new 'Alice' like this time?"[35]

Dodgson was certainly not bitter with Savile Clarke because of their differing views on this matter; any real animosity he felt was directed towards the managers. On April 12, he wrote to Savile Clarke asking what the losses had been on the second version, and on June 16 he sent Savile Clarke a check for £118 4 (his profits from the first venture) to help defray Savile Clarke's portion of the losses.

The playwright was no doubt touched by this gesture, and Dodgson continued to correspond with both him and his daughter Kitty. In December of 1889 Dodgson sent Savile Clarke his own advance sheets for *Sylvie and Bruno*, which the playwright later reviewed.

Henry Savile Clarke died in 1893, and his *Alice* drama was not produced again in his, or Dodgson's, lifetime. It was revived at the Opera Comique for the 1898 Christmas season, under the management of Horace Sedger, who had helped produce the original version at the Prince of Wales's. Beginning with that production, the play began a long series of Christmastime productions (eighteen between 1898 and 1930) which confirmed Dodgson's own belief that his stories were popular enough to sustain frequent revivals on the stage.

# Other Productions
# In Dodgson's Lifetime

**VII** THOUGH *ALICE* WOULD not see another professional stage production in London until Savile Clarke's version was revived in December, 1898, after Dodgson's death, there were some more modest attempts made to stage her adventures during the last ten years of Dodgson's life. On December 31, 1888, some scenes from *Alice* were presented as part of the Christmas Entertainment at the Royal Free Hospital in London. A reviewer for *The Graphic* wrote:

> An entertainment of a miscellaneous character followed, consisting of vocal and instrumental music; the most interesting feature of which was scenes, in costume, from *Alice in Wonderland*, excellently performed by some of the lady medical students.[1]

Dodgson did not attend this performance (he was in Guildford at the time), and there is no indication that he even knew of it.

In November of 1891, Dodgson received an application through his cousin, Mrs. W. E. Wilcox, from one of her friends, for permission to dramatize *Alice*. By this time, Dodgson was quite familiar with the law governing adaptations, and responded, on November 26, in such a way as to wholly remove himself from the situation:

> Will you tell your friend the following facts as to her proposed dramatising, or acting. (1) If they are dramatising the book for

themselves, no permission is needed from anybody. (2) If they are using any published drama (such as Savile Clarke's, which was acted in London), they need the author's permission . . . (3) If they are going to charge for admission, they need a theatrical license (*L*, 874).

If this unidentified friend ever did dramatize Alice, there is no record of it.

Dodgson was probably aware by this time of another dramatic adaptation of *Alice* which had been published in New York in 1890. This version was titled *Alice in Wonderland. A Play for Children in three Acts*, and was dramatized by Mrs. Burton Harrison (Constance Cary Harrison). The drama was published by the de Wit Publishing House, and contained illustrations by Tenniel. In a letter to Mrs. C. H. O. Daniel of March 11, 1895, Dodgson wrote that he had "three dramatised versions of *Alice in Wonderland*, one by Mr. Savile Clarke, one by Mrs. Freiligrath-Kroeker, and one by Mrs. Burton Harrison" (*L*, 1056).

This same letter to Mrs. Daniel was in response to her application for permission to present a dramatized version of *Alice* in Oxford to raise money for St. Thomas Schools. Dodgson replied

> . . . As to your wish that I should give my approval of your performance of a dramatised *Alice* for the benefit of the St. Thomas Schools, well, you certainly put me rather into a 'fix' there, as the Americans would say . . . Long ago I made up my mind that I do *not* approve of that mode of getting money for charitable objects . . . and I have again and again declined to let it be said that 'it is done with the sanction of Mr. L. C.' . . . I don't in the least want to prevent your doing as you think right, in the way of giving this entertainment: *all* I ask is, that it shall not be announced as done with my approval (*L*, 1055).

This benefit production was eventually given four performances on June 13 and 15, 1895, in the garden of Worcester College, and Alan Mackinnon, no doubt attributing more approval and involvement by Dodgson than he actually showed, described the production as

an admirable little performance of Alice in Wonderland . . . was
personally superintended by the author . . . The scenes were
admirably arranged by Mrs. Dowson . . . During the rehearsals
in Worcester College gardens, Dodgson occasionally used to
look in, but being a shy man, he never allowed himself to come
forward; all we ever saw of him was a sly face peeping out from
behind a tree and smiling.[2]

Mrs. Dowson (Miss Rosina Filippi) not only "arranged the scenes,"
but was also "responsible for the excellence of the stage management."[3]
The role of Alice was played by Rachel Daniel (for whose first birthday
Dodgson had contributed a poem to *The Garland of Rachel*, published at her
father's private press in 1881).

In a biography of Rosslyn Bruce,  Verily Anderson describes the
production:

Rehearsals were reminiscent of Wonderland itself with actors
and little actresses resting on the grass beside Rosslyn's tame
white rabbit, brought to inspire the other . . . Permission had been
sought and was given by the author . . . the elderly . . . don . . .
Though he appeared to take no interest in the . . . production, he
was sometimes seen shuffling about the rhododendrons during
rehearsals.  Nigel Playfair produced the play, using only lines
from the original books . . . without any rewriting as in the
London production.  The costumes were taken from Tenniel's
illustrations.  Paul Rubens composed special music, and Emily
Daniel [Mrs. C. H. O. Daniel] printed the posters and program-
mes . . . The day before Alice was to be put on, the Vice-
Chancellor of the University announced that no money could be
taken for this kind of charity performance.  After some quick
thinking it was decided that the audience would be allowed to
come in for free, but would have to pay to get out [the four
performances produced a profit of £100].[4]

An anonymous review for *The Sketch* (Oxford) wrote that "the acting
was remarkably good," and that

The *ensemble* was excellent, the dance being especially spir-
ited.    There was, indeed, a quaint charm about the entire
performance which exactly suited the dainty fantasy of the story,
the author of which, "Lewis Carroll," is a well known Oxford
don.[5]

There is no evidence that Dodgson attended any of the performances,
and, as he had in the past recorded attendance at performances of *Alice* in his
diary, it seems unlikely that he witnessed this production.    Dodgson
recorded meeting Nigel Playfair for the first time several months later,
describing him as "an undergraduate . . . who . . . has a great deal to do with
the University amateur theatricals" (*D*, 522).    He makes no mention of
Playfair's involvement with the *Alice* drama, however.  Playfair would go
on to become the manager of the Lyric Theatre, Hammersmith.

This open-air production of *Alice* brought to a close Alice's British
stage incarnations for the duration of her creator's life.  Charles Dodgson
died on January 14, 1898, in Guildford, leaving behind him the legacy of
*Alice*.

# Epilogue

Despite Charles Dodgson's enthusiasm for Alice in Wonderland as a theatre piece, he cannot possibly have imagined the zealousness with which his dream-child would be brought to the stage in the twentieth century. Not only has *Alice* become a regular fixture among the London Christmas plays, but it has been adapted all over the world in virtually every form of stage presentation. Alice has tread the boards in the context of ballets, operas, experimental theatre, Broadway musicals, puppet plays, mime acts, and rock musicals. Characters and scenes from the Alice books have been used in all sorts of dramas for both children and adults. To a lesser extent, Dodgson's other works, especially The *Hunting of the Snark*, have been brought to life on stage, and Dodgson's own life has been the subject of several dramas.

With each year that passes new dramatic interpretations of *Alice* appear on stages across Britain and America and around the world. Without a doubt, *Alice's Adventures in Wonderland* has become one of the most dramatized works ever written, as the checklist which follows will attest. Though many of the theatrical interpretations of *Alice* would no doubt meet with the disapproval of her creator, Dodgson's prediction that something new could be done with his heroine each year has certainly come true.

The motivation of those who have provided us with this constant flow of Alician dramas is as irrepressible as the seemingly inexhaustible appeal of the books themselves. Just as the literary critics have been able to attach a limitless number of meanings to the *Alice* books, so have the dramatists each found their own way of translating *Alice* to the stage.

Each has had to face many of the same problems, but the largest of these is certainly the fact that Alice is not essentially a dramatic work. Dodgson's dialogue works marvelously in a theatrical context, and many individual scenes, such as the Mad Tea-party and the Mock Turtle's story, transfer quite well to the stage, but the work as a whole, which was not written with the intention of being staged, has no real dramatic unity.

The episodic nature of the book works quite well on the page, but drama requires a firm plot structure to hold it together. The audience must be curious as to what will happen next and what the consequences of the current action will be. In *Alice*, however, we have a series of loosely related episodes, each charming, which demonstrates no real dramatic coherency. This undramatic aspect of *Alice* is one of the chief elements which has attracted dramatists to the story, for here is a group of characters, well known and loved by youngsters and adults, upon whom the dramatist can hang his own ideas and interpretations, and playwrights seemed destined to re-interpret *Alice's Adventures* as long as those adventures continue to be read, or, in a word, forever.

# Appendix A
## A Checklist of Dramatic Adaptations of
## The Works of Charles Dodgson

This list includes dramatic adaptations, published and unpublished, of the works of Charles Dodgson. Also included here are dramas which use scenes or characters from Dodgson's works, and dramas which are in some way related to Dodgson's life and works. Not listed here are dramas written expressly for radio, television, and motion picture presentation.

Each entry includes information on the earliest production of the adaptation which has been located, as well as information on subsequent productions and publication. When possible, and especially in the case of major commercial productions, reviews have been cited, though no more than three are given for any one production. Publications described in the early editions of *The Lewis Carroll Handbook* are indicated by the citation "Williams & Madan" and the appropriate number.

Entries are arranged chronologically, according to the earliest known production, or, if no production is known, date of publication. Works in progress are described at the end of the list, as are undated scripts and productions for which no date is known. Productions for which the author is unknown have been given separate entries.

Every effort has been made to provide information which is as complete as possible; however, as so many of the adaptations here listed are unpublished and their production poorly documented, some information has proven unavailable. Doubtless there are collectors who will be able to amend and augment this list, and the author would welcome such changes to be included in future editions.

———

**1**      *The Mad Tea-Party*. Presented as a private theatrical at the home of Thomas Arnold in Oxford on 7 Dec. 1874. Cast included Ethel, Julia, and Maud Arnold and Beatrice Fearon as Alice.

**2**    Buckland, Mr. G. *Alice in Wonderland*. Music by William Boyd. Entertainment presented at the Royal Polytechnic, London, from 17 April to 19 Aug. 1876 (revised version beginning 29 May).

**3**    *Alice in Fairy-Land*. Presented by the Elliston Family at Diplock's Assembly Rooms, Eastbourne, from 27 to 28 Sept. 1878.

**4**    Freiligrath-Kroeker, Kate. *Alice and Other Fairy Plays for Children*. (London: W. Swan Sonnenchein and Allen, 1880). Published in America by Dick & Fitzgerald, New York (in both paper wrappers and illustrated boards).

The *Alice* portion of this book was presented at the High School, Birmingham, on 19 Dec. 1889.

**5**    Freiligrath-Kroeker, Kate. *Alice Thro' the Looking-Glass and other Fairy Plays for Children*. (London: W. Swan Sonnenschein & Co., [1882]). Williams & Madan 700. Binding variants in blue, olive, and rust cloth have been noted. Second edition published in 1896 (Williams & Madan 711).

Published in America in 1883 by Putnam, New York.

**6**    Clarke, H. Savile. *Alice in Wonderland, a Dream Play for Children, in two acts*. Music by Walter Slaughter. Presented at the Prince of Wales's Theatre, London, from 23 Dec. 1886 to 18 March 1887. A provincial tour followed. Phoebe Carlo played Alice.

See Appendix B for information on publication.

Subsequent London (and environs) productions, with opening dates (and Alices) were:

> 26 Dec. 1888- Globe Theatre (Isa Bowman)
> 22 Dec. 1898- Opera Comique (Rose Hersee)*
> 26 Dec. 1899- Brixton Theatre (Valli Valli)
> 19 Dec. 1900- Vaudeville Theatre (Ellaline Terriss)

---

*\*The Lewis Carroll Handbook* has listed Phyllis Beadon as playing Alice in this production and listed an 1899 production at the same theatre starring Rose Hearne. There was a Miss Beaden in the cast, in the roles of Rose and Oyster, and the play did run into early 1899; however there was only one Opera Comique production, and Rose Hersee, not Rose Hearne, played Alice.

20 Dec. 1906- Prince of Wales's Theatre (Marie Studholme)
23 Dec. 1907- Apollo Theatre (Maidie Andrews)
27 Dec. 1909- Royal Court Theatre (Ivy Sawyer)
26 Dec. 1910- Savoy Theatre (Ivy Sawyer)
23 Dec. 1913- Comedy Theatre (Cora Goffin)
26 Dec. 1914- Savoy Theatre (Ivy Sawyer)
24 Dec. 1915- Duke of York's Theatre (Ivy Sawyer)
26 Dec. 1916- Savoy Theatre (Vera Hamilton)
26 Dec. 1917- Savoy Theatre (Estelle Dudley)
27 Dec. 1920- Victoria Palace (Phyllis Griffiths)
26 Dec. 1921- Garrick Theatre (Phyllis Griffiths)
26 Dec. 1922- Royal Court Theatre (Evelyn Joyce)
20 Dec. 1926- Golders Green (Gwen Stella)
23 Dec. 1927- Savoy Theatre (Myrtle Peter)
22 Dec. 1930- Savoy Theatre (Joy Blackwood)

**7**      Scenes from *Alice in Wonderland* performed by the lady medical students of the Royal Free Hospital, Grays Inn Road, London, as part of the Hospital's Christmas Entertainment on 31 Dec. 1888. Rev: *The Graphic* 1/12/89.

**8**      Harrison, Mrs. Burton (Constance Cary Harrison). *Alice in Wonderland. A Play for Children in three acts.* (New York: The de Witt Publishing House, 1890). Williams & Madan 709.
       Also published by The Dramatic Publishing Co., N.Y. & Chicago.
       Also published in *Harper's Young People, an Illustrated Weekly* (1 April 1890).

**9**      Dowson, Mrs. (Miss Rosina Filippi), with Nigel Playfair. *Alice in Wonderland.* Presented in the gardens of Worcester College, Oxford, 13 & 15 June 1895. Rev: *The Sketch* 6/26/95. See Williams & Madan 710.
       Presented at the Royal Court Theatre, London, for a single performance on 24 May 1905. Rev: *Times* 5/31/05.

**10**     Griffiths, Miss H. Beatrice. *Sylvie and Bruno.* Mentioned by Dodgson in a letter of Sept. 1896, but apparently never printed or performed. Williams & Madan 712.

**11** Anon. *Alice in Wonderland*. [a dramatization]. (Boston: Barta Press, 1897). Williams & Madan 713.

**12** *Alice in Wonderland*. Music by Lewis S. Thompson. Directed by James Gilbert. Presented at Copley Hall, Boston, Mass., from 17 to 20 Feb. 1897 for the benefit of the Boston Art Students' Association. Possibly the same as number 11.

**13** Delafield, Emily Prime. *Alice in Wonderland a play compiled from Lewis Carroll's Stories* Alice in Wonderland *and* Through the Looking-Glass. "Originally presented, for the benefit of the Society of Decorative Art, at the Waldorf, New York, March thirteenth, 1897."
Published: New York: Dodd, Mead, 1898. Williams & Madan 714.

**14** B., S.S. *Charade from 'Alice in Wonderland' and 'Through the Looking-Glass.'* (London: Samuel French, Ltd.; New York: T. Henry French, [1898]). Williams & Madan 758. First published in thin pink wrappers; later reissued in heavier cardboard binding. There were several later printings, all undated.

**15** de Wagstaffe, W. *Alice in Wonderland*. Music composed and selected by Emil Huber and G. Scarano. Presented by Franklin Sargeant's Children's Theatre at the Carnegie Lyceum Auditorium, New York, beginning 10 April 1899. Rev: *NY Times* 4/11/99.
Presented at the Broad Street Theatre, Philadelphia, for approximately three weeks, beginning 8 May 1899.

**16** Knott, Y. *Alice through the Looking Glass*. Music by Walter Tilbury. Presented at the New Theatre, London, from 22 Dec. 1903 to 29 Jan. 1904. Rev: *Times* 12/23/03.
Published: under the title *Alice through the Looking Glass. Fairy Play, Founded on Lewis Carroll's Book*. (London: Hopwood & Crew, Ltd., [1904]). Williams & Madan 761.

**17** Hooper, Rebecca Lane. *Alice in Wonderland* . Music by Miss Mabel W. Daniels. Presented by the members of the Vincent Club, New

York, in April 1905.  An uncredited newspaper clipping gives the title as *Alice in Wonderland Continued*.

Published: Boston, Schirmer, ca. 1905.

**18**      MacDonough, Glen. *Wonderland*.  Music by Victor Herbert. Opened at the Majestic Theater, New York, on 24 Oct. 1905.  This musical was an amalgamation of the *Alice* books and Grimm's tale *The Twelve Dancing Princesses*.  It tried out in Buffalo under the title *Alice and the Eight Princesses*, and was revised while running in Chicago during October, with most of the *Alice* characters being dropped, and the title changing to *The Eight Princesses*.  When it opened in New York as *Wonderland*, only the King of Hearts was left from *Alice*.  Rev: *NY Times* 10/25/05.

**19**      Gillington, M. C. *Alice in Wonderland . . . An operetta for children*. Music by C. Hutchins Lewis.  (London:  J. Curwen & Sons: [1907?]). Williams & Madan 720.

**20**      *Alice thro' the Looking Glass*.  Presented at the Station Theatre, Cawnpore, India, from 9 to 11 Feb., 1907.

**21**      Justitia, Fiat. *The Porpoise and The Chancellor  A Skit on* "The Walrus and the Carpenter." (London: Women's Freedom League, [1908]).

**22**      Wheeler, Edith. *In Wonderland Fairy Operetta for children, in 2 Acts*.  Music by Florian Pascal.  (London: Joseph Williams; New York: G. Schirmer, [1908]).  Williams & Madan 723.

Also published (words only) in an edition printed by Geo. Barber, Furnival Press, London.  Williams & Madan 724.

**23**      Houseman, Laurence. *Alice in Ganderland*.  Presented at the Lyceum Theatre, London, on 27 Oct. 1911.  Play featuring the Mad Hatter, Hare, Dormouse, Bill the Lizard, Alice, and other Carrollian characters. Rev: *Times* 10/28/11.

**24**      [Abbott, Holker]. *Alice in Wonderland in eleven scenes*.  (Boston: Ellis, 1912).  Author uncredited.  Arranged for the Copley Society of Boston.  Williams & Madan 727.

**25**     Anon. *Alice's Adventures in Wonderland: fairy charade*. (New York: French, 1912). Williams & Madan 730.

**26**     Gaul, Harvey B. and Hariette A. *Alice in Wonderland. A musical play in three acts*. Music by Harvey Gaul. (Boston: White-Smith, 1912).

**27**     Lambdin, Augusta. *Alice's Adventures in Wonderland*. (New York: Entertainment Co., 1912). Williams & Madan 729.

**28**     "Scenes From Alice in Wonderland." In Nixon, Lillian Edith, *Fairy Tales a Child Can Read and Act* (Garden City, N.Y.: Doubleday, Page & Company, 1912), 87-147.

**29**     Tidmarsh, Albert G. *Scenes from Alice in Wonderland. Adapted for use at Public Schools*. (London: J.M. Dent & Sons, Ltd., [1912]). Williams & Madan 726.

**30**     Thompson, Fred. *Alice Up-To-Date*. Presented at the London Pavilion, 29 Dec. 1913. Apparently only very loosely related to *Alice*.

**31**     Adams, Marion L. *Alice in Wonderland. A Fairy Tale Play in Three Scenes*. Music by Stephen R. Philpot. (London: Stead's Publishing House, Oct. 1915). 232 in the *Books for Bairns* series. Williams & Madan 754.

**32**     Leutkenhaus, Anna M. (ed.) *Plays for School Children*. (New York: The Century Co., 1915). Includes "Through the Looking-Glass" (51-81), with author's name given as "Lewis Carroll." Williams & Madan 734.

In Grady, William E. and Paul Klapper, *Reading for Appreciation* (New York: Charles Scribner's Sons, 1935), credited to Leutkenhaus.

**33**     Gerstenberg, Alice. *Alice in Wonderland*. Music by Eric De Lamarter. Presented by the Players Producing Company at the Fine Arts Theater, Chicago, beginning on 11 Feb. 1915.

Published: as *Alice in Wonderland; a dramatization of Lewis Carroll's* Alice's Adventures in Wonderland *and* Through the Looking-Glass. (Chicago: McClurg, 1915). Williams & Madan 735.

Also published in paperback by Longmans, Green & Co., NY 1929; in *A Treasury of Plays for Children* (Boston: Little Brown, 1921); and in *Plays Old and New* (Allyn & Bacon, 1929).

Original production presented at the Booth Theatre, New York, beginning 23 March 1915. Rev: *NY Times* 3/24/15. Transferred to the Hudson Theater on 5 April.

Presented by the Junior League of Chicago in 1921, and subsequently by numerous Junior Leagues nationwide.

Presented by the Syracuse Drama League at the Little Theatre, Syracuse, N.Y., from 19 to 20 Jan. 1923.

Presented by the Union High School of Bakersfield, Cal., mid-1920's.

Presented by the Cornell Dramatic Club, Ithaca, N.Y., from 16-17 March 1928 with music selected, arranged, and played by Miss Gertrude Nye. Also presented by the same group with the same music from 16 to 17 Jan. 1931; 28 April to 12 May 1934; and 12 March 1937.

Presented at the Repertory Theatre of Boston, Mass., Dec. 1928.

Presented by the Rochester, N.Y., Community Playhouse, ca. 1930.

Presented at the Pasadena Community Playhouse, Pasadena, Cal., from 26 Dec. 1932 to 7 Jan. 1933 with music by Sally Linley.

Presented by the Wesleyan Players at the Little Theatre, Middletown, Conn., on 17 Feb. 1933 with music by John Ansell.

An adapted version (adapted and directed by Edward P. Mangum) was presented by the Mount Vernon Methodist Church Department of Drama (The Mount Vernon Players), Baltimore, Md. Probably 1940's.

**34**     *Alice in Wonderland.* Presented by the Community Theater of San Francisco during their 1915 season (this was their first season). The theater was founded by Mrs. D. E. F. Easton and Garnet Holme under the auspices of the Recreation League.

**35**     Dunn, Fannie Wyche. "Tweedledum and Tweedledee." In Dunn's *What Shall We Play?* (New York: Macmillan Company, 1916), 21-35, 180.

**36**     Wickes, Frances G. "Scenes from Alice in Wonderland." In Mee, Arthur and Holland Thompson (eds.), *Plays, Pictures and Poems* (New York: The Grolier Society, 1916), 40-54.

**37**    *Alice in Wonderland.* Directed by Gilmor Brown. Presented at the Pasadena (Cal.) Playhouse from 16 to 20 April 1918. This may have been the Gerstenberg script (see number 33), which this theatre produced in 1932.

**38**    Findlay, Maud I. *Alice in Wonderland dramatized for school use.* (London: Oxford University Press, [1919]). Williams & Madan 738.

**39**    *Alice in Wonderland.* Presented by the Children's Theatre of Emerson College, Boston, on 18 Oct. 1919. Adaptation probably by Emerson College students.
       Presented by the same group on 21 May (probably 1920) and during the 1924–25 season.

**40**    Debenham, Mrs. L. *Alice in Wonderland.* (Manchester: Abel Heywood & Son, [ca. 1920's]).

**41**    Smith, Evelyn. "Alice in Wonderland." In *Form-room Plays; Junior Book Compiled from English Literature* (London: J.M. Dent, 1920).

**42**    Butler, Rachel Burton. *Alice in Wonderland.* Originally presented at the Little Theatre, New York, from 12 to 17 April 1920.
       Subsequently presented at Hunter College (New York) in 1931, and in Cincinnati, Ohio, in 1931. Wiliams & Madan 753.

**43**    "A Mad Tea Party." In Elson, William H. and Edna R. Kelly, *Child Library Readers, Book Four* (Chicago: Scott, Foresman, 1924), 239-48.

**44**    *Alice in Wonderland.* Original production supervised by Gertrude Royster. Presented by the Meredith College faculty at Meredith College, Raleigh, N.C., on 15 March 1924. Since the initial performance, this production has been presented by the faculty every four years, the most recent presentation having been in 1988.

**45**    *Music Box Revue.* Songs by Irving Berlin. Presented at the Music Box Theater, New York, beginning on 1 Dec. 1924. This revue included a song titled "Alice in Wonderland" and a pageant of Alice's adventures including the Mad Tea-party and "The Walrus and the Carpenter."

**46**      Headland, A.R. and H.A. Treble. "Tweedledum & Tweedledee." Adapted from *Through the Looking Glass*. In Headland, A.R. and H.A. Treble, *Dramatic Reader I* (Oxford: Clarendon Press, 1925).

**47**      von Vollenhoven, Hanna. *Alice in Movieland. Operetta in one act and three scenes*. (Cincinnati: Willis Music Co., 1925?). Williams & Madan 748.

**48**      Smith, Evelyn. "Tweedledum and Tweedledee." In *Form-room Plays; Intermediate Book Compiled from English Literature* (London: J.M. Dent, 1926).

**49**      Phipps, May E. and Marjorie van Horn. *Alice in Wonderland; a dance pantomime*. (New York: Womans Press, 1927). Williams & Madan 749.

**50**      Van Delden, Egbert H. "Alice in Everydayland." *Poet Lore,* 38 (1927), 96-105. Play which features Alice (the daughter of the Head Prohibition Officer), the Madd Hattere (a bootlegger), Humpti Dumpti, Queenie Hartes, and other characters with Carrollian names. The action is vaguely reminiscent of the Mad Tea-party, and concerns "modern" society.

**51**      Forrest, Belford. *Alice in Movieland*. Presented by the Children's Theatre of Emerson College, Boston, during their 1927–28 season. The play follows the form of the Lewis Carroll tales, except that the land through the looking-glass is Hollywood.

**52**      *Alice in Wonderland*. Presented at the Hart House Theatre, Toronto, Canada, from 26 Dec. 1927 to 7 Jan. 1928.

**53**      "Alice in Wonderland." In Finney, Stella B. (ed.), *Plays Old and New* (London: Allyn and Bacon, 1928).

**54**      *Alice in Wonderland*. Directed by Edith D. Nancrede. Presented by the Hull-House Children's Dramatic Club at the Hull-House Theatre, Chicago, from 19 to 27 April ca. 1930.

**55**   *Alice in Wonderland.*   Puppet play presented by Tony Sarg's Marionette Theatre at the Belmont Theatre, New York, Dec. 1930. Rev: *NY Times* 12/25/30.

**56**   Todt, William and Rylla Martin. *Alice in Wonderland.* Presented by the Reginald Travers Repertory Players at the Columbia Theatre (San Francisco?) for three matinees in April 1931 (?).
     Presented in the Fox-California Theater, Salinas, Cal., on 1 June 1933.

**57**   O'Neil, Randall. *Alice in Wonderland.* A musical adaptation presented by the Pupils of The Gardner School at the Heckscher Theatre on 2 & 5 May 1931.

**58**   Leonard, Della. "Alice in Wonderland." *Grade Teacher*, 48 (June 1931), 822ff.

**59**   Major, Clare Tree. *Alice in Wonderland.* Presented by the Clare Tree Major Company at the Westchester Theatre, Mount Vernon, N.Y., on 18 Dec. 1931. This production toured the U.S.A. during 1941.

**60**   Beagle, Maud S. "Alice in Bookland." In Sanford, Anne Putnam (ed.), *Little Plays for Everybody Short Plays for Grammar and High Schools* (New York: Dodd Mead & Company, 1932), 179-206. Alice and the White Rabbit get caught outside their book and visit several other children's stories. The final scene is the Mad Tea-party.

**61**   Kerr, Frances M. "Alice in Ireland (with apologies to Lewis Carroll)." *Instructor*, 41 (March 1932), 59, 80. One-act play in which Alice, The Mad Hatter, and March Hare learn about Ireland for St. Patrick's Day.

**62**   Le Gallienne, Eva and Florida Friebus. *Alice in Wonderland.* Presented at the Civic Repertory Theater, New York, beginning 12 Dec. 1932. Transferred to the New Amsterdam Theater on Broadway on 3 Feb. 1933. This production subsequently toured parts of the U.S.A. Rev: *NY Times* 12/12/32, *NY Sun* 12/12/32, *NY Evening Post* 12/16/32.
     Frequently produced in the U.S.A.

Published: New York: Samuel French, 1932. Published in both cloth and paper bindings. Frequently reprinted.

Presented by the Play-Likers, University of North Carolina Women's College, Greensboro, N.C., in Aycock Auditorium on 27 Feb. 1943.

Presented by the American Repertory Theater at the International Theatre, New York, beginning April 4, 1947. Rev: *NY Times* 4/7/47.

Presented by the Montreal West Summer Theatre, Montreal, Canada in the summer of 1969.

Presented at the Alley Theater Arena Stage, Houston, Tex., from 11 Nov. to 17 Dec. 1978.

Presented at the Virginia Theatre, New York, beginning 23 Dec. 1982. Rev: *NY Times* 12/24/82.

A scene from this script titled "The Mad Hatter's Tea Party" was presented by the Royal Crown Players at the Bryant Library, Roslyn, N.Y., on 20 March 1983 under the direction of Stan Marx.

Presented by the North Carolina School of the Arts at the Stevens Center, Winston-Salem, N.C., from 5 to 8 Nov. 1987.

**63**     Price, Nancy. *Alice in Wonderland*. Presented at the Little Theatre, London, beginning 21 Dec. 1932. Rev: *Times* 12/22/32.

Presented at the Duke of York's Theatre, London, beginning 22 Dec. 1933. Rev: *Times* 12/23/33.

**64**     Prentice, Herbert. *Alice in Wonderland*. Presented by the Repertory Theatre Workshops, Birmingham, England, beginning 23 Dec. 1932.

Presented at the Festival Theatre (Cambridge, England) from 8 to 20 Jan. 1934, with music by Walter Slaughter and Alfred Scott Gatty.

Presented at the Opera House, Coventry, England, from 26 Dec. 1934 to early Jan. 1935.

Presented at the Theatre Royal, Nottingham, on 18 Feb. 1935. This version was produced by Ronald Kerr. Kerr's production was later presented at the Q Theatre, London, beginning 23 Dec. 1938. Rev: *Times* 12/27/38.

**65**     Findlay, Maud I. *Through the Looking-Glass  A Play in ten scenes*. (London:  Oxford University Press, 1933).

**66**     "Mad Tea Party." In Kenny, Ernest J. (ed.), *Golden Tales (The Westminster Readers) First Series, Book 3*   (Published 1933).

**67**     Pearn, Violet A. *A Play in One Scene from* Alice's Adventures in Wonderland. Dramatized for the centenary production. Music by Henry Cyphus. (London: Macmillan, 1933).
       A play titled *Alice in Wonderland*, credited to Pearn, was presented at the Dominion Drama Festival, Hamilton, Ontario, Canada in 1954.

**68**     Pearn, Violet A. *A Play in One Scene from* Through the Looking Glass. Dramatized for a centenary production. Music by Henry Cyphus. (London: Macmillan, 1933).
       Presented, with additional text by Denis Crutch, by the Glenlyn School of Dance at the Lewisham Leisure Centre, England, on 25 Jan. 1981.

**69**     Parker, Mary M. "Alice in Wonderland." In Parker, M. M., *Happy Plays for Happy Days* (Boston: Play Fair Publishing Co., 1934).

**70**     Williams, Bertha. "Through the Magnifying Glass." In *Easy Plays for Children* (New York: Fitzgerald Pub. Co., 1934), 99-111. Play in which Rose-Ellen meets "Excellent," "Good," and "Ordinary" in Wonderland. Though set in Wonderland, this play has no Carrollian characters or scenes.

**71**     Cauman, Sarah. "Alice in Bookland." *Wilson Library Journal*, 9 (Oct. 1934), 81-5, 95. Play in which Lewis Carroll's Alice journeys through the world of classic books.

**72**     Pitcher, W. E. "Alice in Dozenland." *Math Teacher*, 27 (Dec. 1934), 390-96. Alice, having trouble with her math, finds herself in a schoolroom in Dozenland, where math is complicated by being in base 12.

**73**     *Alice in Wonderland*. A P. N. T. production presented at the Duke of York's Theatre, London, beginning 19 Dec. 1934.

**74**     Bennett, Rodney. "Hiawatha's Photographing." In Bennett, R., *Let's Do a Play!* (London, Nelson, 1935), 177-181.

**75**      Ely, Grace D. *Alice in Wonderland*. Presented at the Kendall School in April 1935.

Published, together with a description of the original production, in *Volta Review* 39 (June 1937), 330-32.

**76**      Wickard, Beulah Jo.    "Alice in Blunderland Meets the Tax Protesters." *School Activities*, 7 (Oct. 1935), 25-6. Alice and the Mad Hatter show a Tax Protester that his taxes are put to good use.

*Note*: Ms. Wickard also wrote a play titled "Alice Becomes a Good Neighbor" published in *Grade Teacher*, 57 (May 1940), 36; 62-4. This play is unrelated to the works of Lewis Carroll. See also number 84.

**77**      Rigdon, Edna May.    *Alice in Wonderland*. Presented by school children of Westchester County, N.Y., at the Little Theater in White Plains in Nov. 1935.

**78**      Price, Nancy. *Alice Through the Looking Glass*. Presented at the Little Theatre, London, beginning 23 Dec. 1935. Rev: *Times* (12/24/35).

Presented at the Little Theatre, London, Christmas, 1936. Rev: *Times* 12/23/36.

Presented at the Playhouse, London, beginning 21 Dec. 1938. Rev: *Times* 12/22/38.

Presented at the Q Theatre, London,  Dec. 1947.

**79**      Dickie, D. J.(compiler) and May Cameron (ed.). *Enchanted Paths*. (Toronto: J.M. Dent, 1936). Includes dramatic sketches of "The Trial of the Knave of Hearts" (101-106) and "The Mad Hatter" (170-75). This volume also contains a printing of "Father William" (184-86).

**80**      *Alice in Wonderland*. Adapted by the staff of the Federal Theater Project in New Haven, Conn. Presented by the Federal Theater Project, New Haven, from 3 March to 28 April 1936.

**81**      *Alice in Wonderland*. Directed by Brownlow Card. Presented by the Canadian Drama League at the Canadian National Exhibition, Toronto, in the fall of 1936.

**82**     Chesse, Ralph and Irene Phillips. *Alice in Wonderland.* Produced by the Federal Theatre and presented by the Theatre of the Magic Strings, Los Angeles, in 1937.

**83**     "Mad Tea Party." In Ratcliff, Nora (ed.), *Refresher Plays, Intermediate Book* (London: Thos. Nelson, 1937).

**84**     Wickard, Beulah Jo. "Alice Ambles through Alphabet Land." *School Activities*, 8 (Jan. 1937), 205-7. Political satire in which Alice and the Mad Hatter change the view of Mr. Tax Payer about the heavy taxes he pays because of the New Deal. See also number 76.

**85**     Schofield, Mary. *Alice in Wonderland.* (London: Thomas Nelson, July 1937).

**86**     Glover, W. J. "Mad Tea Party." In Glover, W. J., *Dramatic Prose for Reading and Acting: Book III Make Believe* (London: George Phillip & Son, Ltd., 1938).

**87**     Collins, Dean. *Alice in Wonderland.* Presented by the Federal Theater Project in Portland, Oregon, from 26 Dec. 1938 to 14 Jan. 1939.

**88**     Chorpenning, Charlotte B. *Alice in Wonderland.* Presented at the Goodman Theater, Chicago, from 4 Feb. to 8 April 1939.
       Published: (Chicago: The Dramatic Publishing Company, 1946). "A Play from the Library of the Association of the Junior Leagues of America." Reprinted several times.
       Presented by the Children's Theatre of Raleigh, N.C., at the Wiley School Auditorium from 5 to 12 Nov. 1954.

**89**     Carpenter, Miriam. "Alice in Waterland." *Journal of Health and Physical Education*, 10 (Sept. 1939), 380-83. Water pageant based on *Alice in Wonderland*.

**90**     *Alice in Wonderland.* Directed by Norma Sangiuliana. Presented by the Children's Theatre of Wilkes-Barre at the Bucknell University Junior College Theatre (Lewisburg, Pa.) on 25 May 1940.

**91**      Abbey, Denise. *Alice in Wonderland*. Presented by members of the Little Theatre Cooperative of the Central Branch YMCA, New York, from 4 to 5 Dec. 1942. Abbey was a winner of the N.C. State playwriting contest.

**92**      Dane, Clemence. *Alice's Adventures in Wonderland and Through the Looking-Glass*. Presented at the Scala Theatre, London, beginning 24 Dec. 1943, with music by Richard Addinsell. Rev: *Times* 12/28/43.
          Presented at the Palace Theatre, London, beginning 26 Dec. 1944. Rev: *Times* 12/27/44.
          Published: (London: Samuel French, 1948).
          Presented by the Junior Members of the All Saints' Fulham Drama Group, England, from 10 to 12 May 1984.

**93**      *Alice in Wonderland*. Presented at the Little Theatre, Nottingham, England, beginning 27 Dec. 1943.

**94**      White, J.R. "Alice Threw the Looking Glass." In White, J.R., *Three Way Plays* (New York: Harper & Brothers Publishers, 1944), 2-39. Play starring Alice and March Hare, but no other Carrollian characters or scenes.

**95**      *Alice in Wonderland and Through the Looking Glass*. Directed by Bettie Boyd. Presented by the Princeton Community Players at the High School Auditorium, Princeton, N.J., on 11 April 1944.

**96**      Green, Roger Lancelyn. *Sylvie and Bruno*. Mentioned in Green's edition of *The Lewis Carroll Handbook* as being written in 1945, but never published or performed.

**97**      Pole, Francis. *Alice in Wonderland*. Music by John Charles Sacco. Presented by the Cambridge Summer Theatre at Brattle Hall, Cambridge, Mass., from 10 to 21 July 1945.
          Presented in the Summer of 1951 as a touring show which played in many New England and Pennsylvania summer play houses.

**98**      Follen, Josephine P. "Alice in Queenland." In Follen, J.P., *Laugh and Learn* (Boston: Baker, 1946), 7-23. Alice Smith is taken by the White Rabbit to the Queen's Party where she meets several famous Queens.

**99**    Elias, George. *Alice in Wonderland*. Presented by Penthouse Productions at the Erie Theatre, Schenectady, N.Y., on 24 Sept. 1947.

**100**    Coles, Hylton. *Alice in Wonderland*. (London & Glasgow: Blackie & Son, 1948).

**101**    *Alice in Wonderland*. Directed by J. Ivan Holm. Presented by the Players Group Theatre in Frick Auditorium, Oakland, Pa., from 8 to 11 Aug. 1949.

**102**    *Alice in Wonderland*. Directed by José Quintero. Presented by the Loft Players of Woodstock, New York, in the summer of 1950.

**103**    Mangum, Edward and Zelda Fichandler. *Alice in Wonderland*. Presented at the Arena Stage, Washington, D.C., beginning 18 Dec. 1950.

**104**    Miller, Madge. *Alice in Wonderland*. Presented at the Pittsburg Children's Theater, ca. 1950–51.
    Presented at the Children's Theatre of Nashville, Tenn., during their 1951–52 season.
    Published: Anchorage, Ky.: The Children's Theatre Press, 1953.
    Presented by the Millikin University Children's Theatre, Decatur, Ill., on 26 Jan. 1963.
    Presented by the Drama Dept. of Skidmore College (Saratoga Springs, N.Y.) with music by Harvey Gaul.

**105**    Scarr, Kathleen. *Alice's Advenutres in Wonderland and Through the Looking-Glass*. Presented by the girls of Chesterton Secondary Modern School, Cambridge, England, ca. 1951.
    Published: London: Frederick Warne & Co., 1951.

**106**    Barry, Katharine V. *Alice in Wonderland*. Presented by the Brynglas Secondary School on the school grounds, Newport, England, as part of the Brynglas "Festival of Britain" from 12 to 13 June 1951.

**107**    Forman, Max L. "Alice in Educationland." In *Ideas That Work Pin-up Programs for School Occasions* (New York: Bloch Pub. Co., 1952).

**108**     Davis, Ossie. *Alice in Wonder*. Written in 1952–3. No production
details known.

**109**     *Alice in Wonderland*. Presented as the inaugural production of the
new Portland, Ore. theater for high school drama in 1953.

**110**     Wills, George. *Alice in Bibleland*. (New York: Philosophical
Library, Inc., 1953). Alice finds perplexing things in the Bible.

**111**     Horovitz, Joseph. *Alice in Wonderland*. Ballet with music by
Horovitz. Presented by the Royal Festival Ballet (choreography by Michael
Charnley) at Festival Hall, Bournemouth, beginning 9 July 1953.
        Presented in Vienna (choreographed by Mitterhuber) in 1970.
        Presented in Cassel (choreographed by André Doutreval) in 1973.
        Presented at the Cambridge Ballet Workshop 19 to 23 Dec. 1977.
        Presented by the Northern Ballet Theatre in various cities in England
in 1983, 1985, and 1988.
        Presented in Kiel, West Germany, with staging by Rosemary Hel-
liwell, beginning 15 June 1984.
        A production titled *Through the Looking-Glass* with music by Horo-
vitz was presented at the Theatre Royal, Bury St. Edmunds, England, from
18 to 23 July 1977.

**112**     *Alice in Wonderland*. Directed by Julia Farnsworth. Presented at the
Pasadena (Cal.) Playhouse  on 17 Dec. 1953.  This may have been the
Gerstenberg version (see number 33), which this theatre produced in 1932.

**113**     *Alice in Wonderland*. Presented at the Q Theatre, London,  beginning 23 Dec. 1953. Rev: *Times* 12/24/53.

**114**     Douglas, Felicity. *Alice Through the Looking-Glass*. Music by
David King and Raymond Leppard. Presented at Her Majesty's Theatre,
Brighton, on 24 Dec. 1953 where it ran for 5 weeks prior to opening in
London at the Prince's Theatre on 9 Feb. 1954. Rev: *Times* 2/10/54.
        Presented at the Palace Theatre, Chelsea, during Christmas 1955.
Rev: *Times* 12/28/55.

Presented at the Lyric Theatre, Hammersmith, beginning 21 Dec. 1961. Rev: *Times* 12/22/61.

Presented at the Ashcroft Theatre from 26 Dec. 1972 to 20 Jan. 1973.

Presented at the Mercury Theatre at Colchester Christmas, 1973. Rev: *Jabberwocky*, Spring 1974.

**115**    Fisher, Aileen & Olive Rabe. *Alice in Puzzleland.* In Fisher, A. & O. Rabe, *United Nations Plays and Programs* (Boston: Plays, Inc., 1954). Uses characters from Carroll's books. Alice figures out a puzzle which tells her about the activities of the United Nations.

Reprinted in *Plays*, 14 (Jan. 1955), 65-70.

**116**    Moulton, Robert. *Alice in Wonderland.* Presented by the University of Minnesota Young Persons Theatre in 1954.

**117**    Schofield, Mary. *Through the Looking Glass.* (London: T. Nelson, [1954]).

**118**    *Alice in Wonderland.* Directed by Mildred K. Gellendre. Presented by the members of the Sunday School and Young People's League of the New Church, New York, from 23 to 25 April 1954.

**119**    *Alice in Wonderland.* Directed by Albert Quinton. Presented by The Dramatic Arts Department of New York University in the Education Auditorium, New York, from 12 to 13 Nov. 1954.

**120**    Beresford, Philip. *Alice in Wonderland.* Music by Arthur Furby. Presented at the Palace Theatre, Chelsea, for a four-week run beginning on 26 Dec. 1956. Rev: *Times* 12/27/56.

Presented at the Winter Garden Theatre, London, beginning 26 Dec. 1959. Rev: *Times* 12/28/59.

**121**    Orr, William. *Alice in Wonderland.* Music by Dot Mendoza. Presented in Sydney, Australia, ca. 1957, possibly by Playgoers' Co-Operative Theatres, Ltd.

Presented at the Comedy Theatre, Melbourne, Aus., beginning 26 Dec. 1961.

**122**     Holroyd, George H. *Alice in Wonderland*. (London: George Philip & Son, Ltd., 1958).

**123**     *Alice in Wonderland*. Ballet by Glasstone (?). Presented in Amsterdam in late 1958 or early 1959.

**124**     Healy, Mary Barrett. *Alice in Wonderland*. Music by Anthony Scibetta. Presented at the Studio Theatre, Buffalo, N. Y., (dates unknown).
     Presented by the Footlight Players at the Dock Street Theatre in Charleston, S.C., in Dec. 1959.
     *Note*: The Studio Theatre of Buffalo presented a production of *Alice in Wonderland* in the late 1960's which may have been the same adaptation.

**125**     Siletti, Mario. *Alice in Wonderland*. Presented in the late 1950's and early 1960's by a company of professional adult actors in New York City whose productions were specifically for children.

**126**     *Alice in Wonderland* (?) Musical version including episodes from both books presented in Kuala Lumpur, Malaya, ca. 1960.

**127**     Doughty, Charles L. *Alice in Wonderland*. Presented by the Nashville Children's Theatre during their 1960–61 season.
     Presented by the same group in their 1966–67 season.

**128**     Brown, Regina. "Through the Looking-Glass and What Alice Found There." In Brown, R., *A Play at Your House* (New York: Ivan Oblensky, Inc., 1962).

**129**     Urban, Catherine. "Alice in Bookland." *Plays*, 22 (Nov. 1962), 72-4. Alice wants to talk to Betsy Ross in Bookland rather than go to Wonderland. The White Rabbit brings the Red Queen and Mad Hatter to fetch Alice back.

**130**     Davis, Ronald. *Alice in Wonderland*. Presented by E 52 University Theatre in Mitchell Hall of Delaware University from 2-3 May 1963. Toured the area from 4 to 18 May 1963.

**131**    Winslow, Richard (composer). *Alice*. Opera with libretto by Susan McAllester. Presented in Hartford, Conn. in 1964.

**132**    Blankenship, Joseph. *Alice With Kisses*. Presented at the Forty First Street Theatre, New York, in the Spring of 1964. A dramatic musical in three acts, featuring Alice and numerous other Carrollian characters.

**133**    Glennon, William. *Alice in Wonderland*. (Pittsburgh: The Pittsburgh Playhouse Press, 1965).

**134**    Martens, Anne Coulter. *Alice in Wonderland*. (Chicago: The Dramatic Publishing Company, 1965).
     Presented by the Stockton Civic Children's Theatre, Stockton, Cal., from 1 to 10 July 1983. The program refers to this as the fourth annual production.

**135**    Wagner, Jearnine. *Alice in Wonderland*. Production developed under the direction of Wagner and presented by the Children's Theatre of Trinity University (San Antonio, Texas) in the mid-1960's.
     An account of the development of this production, together with performance photos, appears in Wagner, Jearnine and Kitty Baker, *A Place for Our Ideas— Our Theatre* (San Antonio: Principia Press of Trinity University, 1965).

**136**    *Alice in Wonderland*. Production inspired and mounted by Adrian Benjamin to celebrate the centenary of *Alice*'s publication. Presented in Christ Church Meadow, Oxford, in June 1965, and later at the Minack Theatre in Cornwall and at an English theatre in Rome. Mounted mainly by Oxford undergraduates, including Nigel Rees and Tammy Ustinov. Christ Church performance rev: *Times* 6/26/65.

**137**    *Alice in Wonderland*. Presented by the Merri-Mimes at the Cricket Theatre, New York, from 19 Nov. to 17 Dec. 1966.

**138**    Minehart, Katherine. *Alice in Wonderland*. Presented by the Free Theatre of the Germantown (Pa.) Theatre Guild in 1967, and on four subsequent occasions, including a production in April of 1978 at the John B. Kelly School in Germantown, Pa., which included the first performance of the "Wasp in a Wig" episode.

The Wasp episode was also performed for the members of the Lewis Carroll Society at their Spring 1978 meeting on 13 May at the Sheraton Hotel, Philadelphia.

**139**    Hill, Rochelle. "Alice in Wonderland."*Plays* 26 (Jan. 1967), 81-97. Reprinted in *Plays* 31 (April 1972), 51-60; 36 (May 1977), 83-92.

**140**    Gardiner, John. *Alice Through the Looking Glass.* Operetta presented in Essex, England, in early 1967.

**141**    Sachs, Dr. Arieh. *Alice in Wonderland.* Presented by the students and faculty of the English Department of the Hebrew University, Jerusalem, Israel, in March 1967.

**142**    Myers, Catherine. *Alice in Wonderland.* Music by Paul Pocaro. Presented by the Brooklyn College Department of Theater and Speech at the George Gershwin Theater, Brooklyn, N.Y., in April 1967.

**143**    Place, Richard and Martin Kushner. *Alice in Wonder York.* Presented beginning 2 Aug. 1967 as part of the Mini-Mobile Theater's touring program in under-priviliged neighborhoods in the New York area. *Alice* adapted to the world of young New Yorkers. Rev: *NY Times* 8/3/67.

**144**    Neville, Oliver. *Alice in Wonderland and Through the Looking Glass.* Presented at the Ipswich Arts Theatre, Ipswich, England, during Christmas 1967.

**145**    Pisu, Silverio. *Alice Nel Paese Delle Meraviglie* [Alice in Wonderland]. (Milano: Fratelli Fabri Editori, 1968). 2 volumes. In Italian.

**146**    Ross, Dorothy. *Alice in Sunday School-land.* In Shakow, Z. (ed), *Curtain Time for Jewish Youth* (Middle Village, N.Y.: Jonathan David, 1968). Alice and Peter Rabbit attend a class at a Jewish Sunday school.

**147**    Worcester, N. S. "A Mad Tea Party." In Durrell, D. D. and B. A. Crossley (eds.), *Thirty Plays for Classroom Reading; a New Approach to the Reading Program in the Intermediate Grades* (Boston:  Plays, Inc., 1968).

**148**    Swortzell, Lowell. *An Afternoon with Lewis Carroll.* Presented by New York University at Town Hall, New York, on 9 March 1968.

**149**    Eyen, Tom. *Alice Through the Glass Lightly.* Presented by the Electric Circus Children's Theatre, New York, in April  1968.

**150**    Thompson, Evan and Joan Shepard. *Alice Through the Looking Glass.* Music by John Clifton. Presented by the Pixie Judy Troupe in Judson Hall, New York,  in Feb.  1969.

**151**    Carroll, Vinnette. *But Never Jam Today* (first version).  Music by Gershon Kingsley.  Presented as part of Black Expo at New York's City Center, 22 to 27 April 1969.
     Rewritten as *Alice* (1978), and *But Never Jam Today* (1979); see numbers 227 and 241.

**152**    Bantleman, L. *Alice (Alfresco).*  Presented in Montreal, Canada, from 15 June to 19 July 1969.

**153**    Gash, Anthony. *The Hunting of the Snark.* Presented at Magdelan College, Oxford, ca. 1970.

**154**    Robbie, Dorothy. *Alice in Wonderland.* Music by Desmond Hand. (Dixon Cal.:  Procenium Press,  1970).

**155**    *Alice in Wonderland.*  Production created by the Manhattan Project under the direction of André Gregory and presented  at the Extension Theater, New York, beginning 8 Oct. 1970. Rev: *NY Times* 10/9/70, *Time* 10/26/70.
     This production toured internationally, including performances at the Edinburgh Festival (Cambridge St. Theatre) from 31 Aug. to 11 Sept. 1971. Rev: *Times* 9/3/71, *Jabberwocky*, no. 9 (Winter 1971).

Published: New York: Dramatists Play Services, Inc., 1972.

Presented at Ratner's, N.Y., beginning in April 1973 (Rev: *NY Times* 4/7/73); at the Loeb Theatre, Boston, beginning in Feb. 1974; and at the Performing Garage, N.Y., beginning in March 1974.

Presented (with additional material by Dave Sayer) by the Vagabond Players in New Westminster, B.C., Canada, from 10 to 21 Dec. (1986?).

Presented at the Nevada Theatre in Nevada City, Cal., from 20 June-7 July 1980's.

*Note*: An account of the original production, related by Gregory and the actors and illustrated with photographs, was published as *Alice in Wonderland The Forming of a Company and the Making of a Play*. (New York: Merlin House, 1973).

**156**    Barry, Stephen. *Alice in Wonderland*. Music and lyrics by Lionel Segal. Presented at the Yvonne Arnaud Theatre in Millbrook, Guildford, England, from 23 Dec. 1970 to 23 Jan. 1971. Rev: *Times* 12/28/70.

**157**    Hangerup, Klaus. *Alice i Underverdenen* [Alice in Wonderland]. Norwegian adaptation presented in late 1970. Rev: *Dagbladet*, 1/1/71.

**158**    Grove, I. Van (composer) *Alice in the Garden*. Ballet choreographed by Ruth Page, and presented at the Jacob's Pillow Dance Festival, near Lee, Mass., in 1971.

**159**    Koste, Virginia. *Alice in Wonder*. (Rowayton, Conn.: New Plays for Children, 1971). Dramatization of several scenes from Carroll's books.

Presented at the Studio Theater, California State University at Hayward, in the winter of 1982.

Presented at the Dallas Theater Center, Dallas, Tex., in the summer of 1987.

**160**    Racina, Thom. *Alice in Wonderland*. Music and lyrics by the author. Presented by the Goodman Children's Theatre Company (sponsored by The Art Institute of Chicago) at The Goodman Theatre, Chicago, from 3 Jan. to 21 March 1971. Described in the program as "a mod, mad musical based on the famous Lewis Carroll tale."

Published as *Allison Wonderland* (New York: Samuel French, 1972).

**161**    *Alice in Wonderland.* Presented by the Fort Knox Arts Complex as part of the Edinburgh Festival Fringe in Sept. 1971.

**162**    Tchakirides, Bill. *The Hunting of the Snark.* Music by Edwin Roberts. Operatic version, presented by Systems Theater at the Whitney Museum, New York, Sept. 1971. Rev: *NY Times* 9/10/71.

**163**    Brind'amour, Yvette. *Alice au Pays des Merveilles.* Presented at Le Théâtre du Rideau Vert, Montreal, from Dec. 1971 to Jan. 1972.

**164**    *The Hunting of the Snark.* Pantomime presented by the Tavistock Repertory Company at the Tower Theatre, Cononbury, England, Christmas 1971. Rev: *Jabberwocky* (Spring 1972).

**165**    Douglas, Felicity. *Alice in Wonderland.* Presented at the Ashcroft Theatre, Croyden, England, from 27 Dec. 1971 to 22 Jan. 1972.
          Presented by Triumph Theatre Productions at the Royal Shakespeare Theatre, Stratford, England, from 23 Dec. 1972 to 6 Jan. 1973. Rev: *Jabberwocky* vol. 2, no. 1 (Spring 1973).

**166**    Brandreth, Gyles. *Lewis Carroll Through the Looking-Glass.* One-person show starring Cyril Fletcher as Lewis Carroll presented at the Ipswich Arts Centre. Toured England during 1972. Rev: *Jabberwocky* (Autumn 1972).

**167**    Rose, Helen. *Alice in Healthland.* In Rose, H., *"Out of the mouths . . ." Readings and Recitations for Young Actors* (Boston, Bakers Plays, 1972). Alice learns about health from nursery rhyme characters.

**168**    Williams, Ellen Virginia (choreographer). *Alice in Wonderland.* Ballet presented in Boston in 1972.

**169**    *A Come Alice* [A Is for Alice]. Presented by the Space Re (v) action Company of Theater le Fede, Rome, Italy. Toured in the U.S. during 1972, including a performance at the University of California, Los Angeles, on 19 Jan. The play is an adaptation of Carroll's *Alice* with an insertion from Rabelais' *Gargantua and Pantagruel.*

**170**    *Alice in Wonderland.* Presented by the Pip Simmons Group at the Cockpit, London. Rev: *Jabberwocky* (Spring 1972).

**171**    Green, Roger Lancelyn. *Alice Through the Looking Glass.* Presented in the garden at Poulton Hall, England, 23 June to 1 July 1972 to celebrate the centennial of the publication of *Through the Looking-Glass.* Rev: *Jabberwocky* (Autumn 1972).

**172**    Pettaway, Marc and Mary Jane Malus. *Alice in Wonderland.* Presented by the Cotton Candy Players at the Arcade Theatre on the Mall in Lake Charles, Louisiana, from 21 to 29 Oct. 1972.

**173**    Barton, James. *Alice.* Presented at the County Hall, London, from 11 to 15 Dec. 1972. Billed as "A Victorian Alice in the Eastern Style." Rev: *Jabberwocky* (Spring 1973).

**174**    Jackson, Elizabeth. *Alice in Wonderland.* Music by June Woods. (London: Heinemann Educational Books, 1973).

**175**    *The Adventures of Alice.* Presented by the Dulwich Players in late January, 1973. Rev: *Jabberwocky* (Spring 1973).

**176**    *Alice in Wonderland.* Ice show presented by the North Toronto Skating Club, Toronto, Canada, from 14 to 15 April 1973.

**177**    Geoly, John, Carol Harris, and Lucy Taylor. *Alice in Wonderland.* Presented at Roslyn High School, Roslyn, New York, on 29 April 1973.

**178**    *Alice in Wonderland.* Company developed production presented by the Florida Studio Theatre in the Summer of 1973. Toured Florida and the East Coast during 1973–5.

**179**    *Edith Evans and Friends: William Shakespeare, George Bernard Shaw, Christopher Fry, John Betjeman, and Lewis Carroll.* Presented by Dame Edith Evans at the Richmond Theatre in Nov. 1973. Parts of this entertainment were issued in a live recording (RCA Red Seal LR15037).

**180** Joffe, Maryann and Susan Mainzer. *Alice in Wonderland*. Presented by Big Time Productions in Montreal, Canada, Dec. 1973.

**181** Kersey, Donald. *Alice in Wonderland*. Songs by Kersey. Presented by the Theater Arts for Youth at Carnegie Hall, N. Y., 10 to 14 Dec. 1973.

**182** Butlin, Jan. *Alice in Wonderland*. Music and lyrics by Norman Newell and Phil Green. Presented at the Theatre Royal, Brighton, England, from 26 Dec. 1973 to 19 Jan 1974. Costumes inspired by Arthur Rackham's illustrations.

**183** *Alice in Wonderland*. Presented by 1400 children in a park in Montreal, Canada, in 1974.

**184** Hardwick, Mollie. *Alice in Wonderland*. (London: Davis Poynter, Ltd., 1974).

**185** Rosen, Richard. *Alice and Wonderland-A Rock Opera*. Music by Wink Kelso; lyrics and stage direction by Richard Rosen. Presented at the San Antonio Theatre Club, San Antonio, Texas, and performed 36 weeks to 135 sold-out performances during 1974. Rev: *Knight Letter* (Aug. 1974).

Presented in rewritten form at the Alice and Wonderland Theatre, Houston, Texas, in 1974.

**186** Mahlmann, Lewis. "Alice's Adventures in Wonderland." *Plays*, 33 (March 1974), 77-83. A puppet play.

Also published in Mahlmann, Lewis and David Cadwalader Jones, *Puppet Plays for Young Players 12 Royalty Free Plays for Hand Puppets, Rod Puppets, or Marionettes* (Boston: Plays, Inc., 1974).

**187** *Alice in Wonderland*. A marionette version presented at the John Sherman Junior High School, Mansfield, Ohio, Spring 1974. An account of this production was published in *School Arts*, 73, no. 10 (June 1974), 14-15.

**188** Krepchin, Ira. *Alice!* Music and lyrics by T. Gilligan and L. Barton. Presented by the M.I.T. Community Players (Boston) at the M.I.T. Student Center, 26 July to 2 Aug. 1974.

**189**    Katzman, Don. *Hurrah! It's Lewis Carroll Day!* Presented by The Highland Players in Boulder and Denver, Col., Dec. 1974.   Reviewed in *Boulder Daily Camera* 12/7/74, rept. in *Knight Letter* (Feb. 1975); and in *The Colorado Daily* 12/6/74.

**190**    Simms, Willard. *Alice in Wonderland.* A participation play for children. (Denver, Col.: Pioneer Drama Service, 1975).

**191**    Russell, A. J., Joseph Raposo, and Sheldon Harnick. *Alice in Wonderland.* Music and lyrics by Joe Raposo and Sheldon Harnick. Presented by Bil Baird's Marionettes at the Bil Baird Theater, New York, from Feb. to April 1975.

**192**    *Alice in Wonderland.* Music by Pat & Clark Burson.  Directed by Bob Soares.  Presented at the Fountain Valley Community Theater, Cal., July 1975.

**193**    *Through the Looking Glass.* Ballet presented by the children of the Arts Educational School at Tring Park, England, in the Elizabethan Gardens of the Park from 4 to 5 July 1975. "A series of episodes from the books interspersed with ballet sequences."

**194**    *Wonderland.* Presented at Kidbrooke School, England.  This production was described in an illustrated article 'Alice' by E. Mantle, in *Ilea 'Contact,'* issue 12 (12 Sept. 1975): 32-3.

**195**    Jacobson, Leslie. *Lewis Dreamchild.*   Music by Jonathan Firstenberg, lyrics by Judy Daley.  Presented at Cedar Knolls Dinner Theatre in Virginia in Nov. 1975. "Alice's musical journey through Wonderland in 1975 in search of the real Lewis Carroll." Rev: *Knight Letter* (Feb. 1976).

**196**    Dias, Susan and Meridee Stein. *Alice Through the Looking Glass.* Lyrics by Susan Dias. Music by Philip Namanworth. Presented at The First All Children's Theater Company, New York, during their 1975–76 season.
　　　Presented by the same company for their 1978–79 season.
　　　Presented at the Florida Studio Theatre, Sarasota during their 1979–80 season.

**197** Billman, Larry. *Alice in Wonderland.* (Winona, Minn.: Hal Leonard Publishing Co., 1976). A Disney Youth Musical, with music from the Disney film.

This script was written primarily for school use and has been widely produced by schools and amateur groups throughout the U.S.

**198** Reiter, Seymour. *Alice Through the Looking Glass.* A full length musical with music by Lor Crane and book and lyrics by Reiter. (Chicago: Dramatic Publishing Co., 1976).

**199** Waters, Maryla and Anne Elbourne. *Once Upon a Dream.* Presented by the Children of Roslyn Home and School Drama Group, Montreal, Canada, April 1976. Adapted from the stories of Lewis Carroll.

**200** *Alice in Wonderland.* Text by Lewis Carroll, music by Harry Freedman, and puppetry by Andrew Tarjan. Presented by the Toronto Arts Production as part of the Canadian Sound series, May 1976. Rev: *The Globe and Mail* (Toronto), 5/22/76.

**201** Horlock, David and Michael Rothwell. *Crocodiles in Cream.* A one-man Lewis Carroll show, starring Michael Rothwell. Presented at the Bristol Old Vic from 18 May to 12 June 1976 and at the Mermaid Theatre, London, from 4 to 28 Aug. 1976. Rev: *Times* 8/5/76, *Daily Telegraph* 8/5/76, *Evening Standard* 8/5/76.

Mr. Rothwell toured extensively with the show for several years, including a U.S. tour in Sept. 1978.

The play was later retitled *The World of Lewis Carroll*, and toured North and South America during 1980, returning to the Bristol Old Vic from 6-11 Oct. 1980. Mr. Rothwell continued to present the play after this engagement.

Performed by Kevin Moore at the Salisbury Playhouse in March 1983. Mr. Moore then toured England with his performance and travelled to Norway to do a television version of the play.

**202** Taylor, Brenda (choreographer). *Alice.* Presented by the Brenda Taylor School of Ballet at the Playhouse, Harlow, England, from 23 to 26 June 1976. Dance, music, and dialogue from Carroll's stories.

**203**    *Alice Through the Looking-Glass*. Presented in the Provost Garden, Queens College, Oxford, July 5 to 10, 1976.

**204**    Heath, Peter. *Alice*. Music by Anthony Filby and Josephine Collins. Rock version presented by The Chicken Shed at the Intimate Theatre, Palmers Green, England, 8 to 10 & 15 to 17 July 1976. Rev: *Bandersnatch* (Oct. 1976).

On 10 Nov. 1977, The Chicken Shed presented a pot-pourri for the Silver Jubilee *Queens in Fantasy* production at the East Barnet Senior High School which included excerpts from their *Alice* production.

**205**    *Alice in Wonderland*. Musical version presented by the Ariel Theatre Company (the BBC's amateur dramatic society) at the Half Moon Theatre, London, from 14 to 17 July 1976. This production combined both *Alice* books. Rev: *Bandersnatch* (Oct. 1976).

**206**    Lloyd, Mervyn. *Alice in Wonderland*. Presented by the Hertfordshire Players, Minack Theatre, Cornwall, from 9 to 13 Aug. 1976. Rev. *Jabberwocky* (Spring 1977).

**207**    *Alice in Wonderland Trilogy*. Presented by the Bijuberti Puppet Players at the Creek Theater in Austin, Texas, 11 & 18 Sept. 1976. The three scenes were "Pig and Pepper," "Humpty Dumpty," and "Tweedledum & Tweedledee." Rev: *Knight Letter* (Jan. 1977).

This same company had previously presented "The Walrus and the Carpenter" as part of their repertory.

**208**    Wilkerson, Jack. *Alice Who?* Presented at the Alcazar Theater, San Francisco, on 17 Nov. 1976.

**209**    Schevill, James. *Alice in the American Wonderland*. Music by Shep Shapiro. Presented by the Looking Glass Theater, Providence, Rhode Island, during their 1976–77 season. *Alice* set in the American West.

**210**    Hoover, Ralph. *Jabberwocky*. (London & Sydney: Pan Books, 1977).

CHECKLIST 135

**211** Sewell, Byron. *At 38.* (Chicken Little Press, 1977). Play in which Alice is now 38 years old. Action takes place at her home Cuffnells, on a train, and in Wonderland revisited. Not produced.

**212** Sircom, Malcolm. *Alice in Wonderland.* Musical adaptation presented at the Round House, London, Feb. 1977. Rev: *Times* 2/8/77.
    Presented at the Dundee Repertory Theatre from 6 Dec. 1984 to 5 Jan. 1985.
    Presented at the Octagon Theatre, Bolton, from 27 Nov. 1985 to 11 Jan. 1986.
    Presented at the Birmingham Repertory Theatre from 6 Dec. 1988 to 28 Jan. 1989.
    Presented by the Worcester Repertory Company, dates unknown.
    *Note*: Sircom also wrote a play titled *Jabberwocky* which was presented at the Polka Children's Theatre, London, from 27 June to 28 July (year not known).

**213** Thomas, Gordon and Margaret Becker. *Alice in Wonderland.* Music by Robert "Dude" Skiles. Presented by the Fun Theatre of the Zachary Scott Theatre (Austin, Texas, Community Theatre), in the spring/summer of 1977. Production combined live action and video projection. Rev: *Knight Letter* (June 1977).

**214** The Roadshow. *Alice in Wonderland* Original production developed by the Roadshow (based in New York) which toured the New York area in summer of 1977.

**215** *Alice in Wonderland.* Presented by The Fourth Wall at the Provincetown Playhouse, N. Y., June 1977. Rev. *Village Voice* 6/20/77.

**216** *Jabberwock.* Directed by Matt Chait and produced by Laurence Becker. Presented at the Truck & Warehouse Theater [New York?], from 9 to 19 June 1977.

**217** *Alice.* Presented by Summer Stages at St. Lawrence College, Ontario, Canada, from 29 July to 7 Aug. 1977.

**218**    Duteil, Jeff. *The Snark Was a Boojum, You See*. Music by Stan Smith. Presented by the Nettle Creek Players at the Nat Horne Musical Theatre, New York, Aug. 1977. "Based on the dual life of Lewis Carroll/ Charles Dodgson." Rev: *Knight Letter* (Nov. 1977).

**219**    Josephs, Wilfred. *Through the Looking-Glass, And What Alice Found There*. Operatic version presented by the Leeds Opera Group at the Lounge Hall, Harrogate, England, from 3 to 5 Aug. 1977. Rev: *Bandersnatch* (Autumn 1978).

**220**    *Through the Looking-Glass*. Presented by Diorama (a group of art students, teachers, and social workers) at the 1977 Edinburgh Festival (Aug.–Sept.). A multi-media production. Rev: *Bandersnatch* (Oct. 1977).

**221**    Jennings, Alex and Tessa Panter. *Alice: Adapted from the Stories of Lewis Carroll*. Score by Adam Glasser. Presented at Warwick University Arts Centre, Warwick, England, Dec. 1977.
    Presented by Alice Productions at the Collegiate Theatre, London, from 13 to 24 May 1980 with a slightly modified script and with the original score augmented and adapted by Simon Lowe.

**222**    Turnbull, Keith. *Alice Through the Looking-Glass*. Music by Walter Buczynski and Alan Laing. Presented at the Theatre London, London, Ontario, from 30 Dec. 1977 to 22 Jan. 1978.

**223**    Kelly, Tim. *Alice's Adventures in Wonderland*. (Denver, Col.: Pioneer Drama Service, 1978).

**224**    *Alice in Wonderland*. Directed by Shirley Cox. Presented by the Islip Arts Theatre at Suffolk County Community College, Selden, N.Y., from 10 to 18 March 1978.

**225**    Laderman, Ezra. *The Hunting of the Snark*. Operatic version presented by the Queens College Departments of Music & Drama and Theatre at the Queens College Theatre, Queens, N.Y., from 13 to 16 April 1978.

**226** Kalliel, J. Sean and Paul Gadebusch. *Alice: A Musical Fantasy.* Presented by the Washington Square Players at New York University from 19 to 21 May 1978.

**227** Carroll, Vinnette. *Alice.* Music by Micki Grant. Production developed at the Actors Studio and the Urban Arts Corps in the 1970's. The Broadway production premiered at the Forrest Theater, Philadelphia, 31 May 1978, following a week of previews, and closed on 27 July 1978 during out-of-town tryouts.

*Note*: This was the second version of an *Alice* musical by Vinnette Carroll (see also numbers 151 and 241).

**228** Hodges, Constance. *Alice in Danceland.* Ballet presented at Pat's School of the Dance, Newport, Oregon, June 1978. Choreography by Pat Grimstad.

*Note*: A pamphlet titled *Alice in Danceland*, published by the Delcon Corporation in 1979, gives Hodges' account of the mounting of this ballet.

**229** Beechey, Alan. *Alice's Adventures in Wonderland.* Music by Julian Slot. Open-air performance presented at Magdelan College, Oxford, from 26 June to 2 July 1978.

**230** Scrivener, George F. *Alice in Wonderland.* Open-air, floodlit performance presented as part of the Saffron Walden Trienniel Carnival Celebrations in the Bridge End Gardens, Walden, Essex, England, from 4 to 7 July 1978. Music composed by members of the local County High School. Adapted from both books.

Presented by the Castle Keep Company on the grounds of Saffron Castle, Walden, on 17 May 1985.

**231** Indick, Ben. *Theatre—A Celebration.* Presented by the Bag-a-tale Players at the 13th St. Theatre, New York, Dec. 1978. A five minute excerpt from *Looking-Glass* is part of the show.

**232** Swados, Elizabeth. *Alice in Concert.* Production partially staged at the Public Theatre, N.Y., from 27 to 29 Dec. 1978. Rev: *NY Times* 12/29/78.

Presented in complete form beginning 7 Jan. 1981 at the Public Theater. This was an all musical version featuring Meryl Streep as Alice. Rev: *NY Times* 1/8/81, *NY Post* 1/8/81, *Time* 1/19/81.

Libretto published: New York: Samuel French, 1987.

**233**     Eiler, Jim. *Alice in Wonderland.* Music by Eiler and Jeanne Bargy. Presented by the Prince Street Players at Town Hall, New York, from 21 Dec. 1978 to 1 Jan. 1979. This production later toured the country. Rev: *Daily News* (NY) 12/28/78.

**234**     Hendrie, Bill and James McCue. *Alice in Wonderland.* (London: Macmillan, 1979). Published in the Dramascripts series.

**235**     Johnson, Christine. *Alice.* Music by Barbara Politeau. (Colorado Springs, Col.: Contemporary Drama Service, 1979).

Also published by Hanbury Plays, Keeper's Lodge, Broughton Green, Droitwich, in 1986.

**236**     *Alice in Wonderland.* A play with music presented at the Lakewood Little Theater School, Lakewood, Cleveland, Ohio, from 26 Jan. to 3 Feb. 1979.

**237**     Guillemette, Ron. *Alice in Wonderland.* A musical presented by the Performing Arts Collective of Alberquerque, N.M., from 24 Feb. to 18 March 1979. With music by the members of the Performing Arts Collective.

**238**     *Alice in Wonderland.* Presented by the Eighth Street Middle School of Milwaukee, Wisc., 5 April 1979.

**239**     Venezia, Gregory P. *Alice in Wonderland.* Presented by the Philaletheis Society of Vassar College in Rockefeller Hall, Vassar College, Poughkeepsie, N.Y., from 19 to 21 April 1979.

**240**     Miller, Norma. *Alice in Wonderland and Through the Looking Glass.* Presented by the Shadowplayers at the Lighthouse for the Blind, San Francisco, from 9 to 10 June 1979.

**241**    Carroll, Vinnette. *But Never Jam Today.* Music and lyrics by Bert Keyes and Bob Larimer. Presented at the Urban Arts Corps, New York, and on Broadway at the Longacre Theater, where it opened 31 July 1979. Rev: *NY Times* 8/1/79, *NY Post* 8/1/79, *Wall Street Journal* 8/7/79.

*Note*: This was the third version of an *Alice* musical by Vinnette Carroll (see also numbers 151 & 227).

**242**    Millward, Richard. *Wonderland.* Musical production presented by the Cabaret for Kids of Norfolk, Conn., Aug. 1979.

**243**    Wakeling, Edward. *Euclid and His Modern Rivals.* Abridgement presented at the County Hall, Westminster, for a meeting of the Lewis Carroll Society (Great Britain) on 31 Aug. 1979. Performed by various members of the Society.

**244**    Frank, Lee. *The Alice-In-Wonderland Game.* Music by Jerry Markoe. Presented by On Stage, Children! at the Hartley House Theatre, New York, from 7 Oct. to 18 Nov. 1979. Audience participation play in the form of a game show. Rev: *Show Business*, 10/19/78.

**245**    Francy, Paul. French version of *Alice* enacted in Liege, Belgium, on 19 Oct. 1979.

**246**    McGuinness, Joan. *Looking-Glass Garden.* A Christmas pantomime presented at the Bellerby Theatre, Guildford, England, from 11 to 29 Dec. 1979. Rev: *Bandersnatch* (Jan. 1980).

**247**    *Alice in Wonderland.* Music and lyrics by A. Paul Johnson. Developed by the Palisades Theater Company, St. Petersburg, Fla., and presented during their 1979–80 season.

**248**    Cook, Jon Paul. *Alice in "I Really Wonderland."* Presented by the Denver Center Theatre Company, Denver, Col., as part of their 1979–80 season.

**249**    Flament, Ludovic. *La Chasse au Snark* [The Hunting of the Snark]. French version presented in 1980.

**250**     Turner, Charles. *Alice in Wonderland*. Lyrics and music by Steven Moore. (Boston:  Baker's Plays, 1980).

**251**     Crowther, Carol. *Alice in Wonderland*. British touring production presented by Clown Cavalcade. This production mixed music hall, panto-mime, and clowning. Rev: *Bandersnatch* (May 1980).

**252**     Suffran, Michel and Martine de Breteuil. *Lewis et Alice* [Lewis and Alice]. Presented at Théâtre Petit Forum, Paris, from 8 April to 3 May 1980.

**253**     Graham, Ross. *Alice in Wonderland*. Music by Lou Ann Graham. Presented by the San Francisco Attic Theater from 2 to 10 May 1980, and again from 19 to 30 Dec. 1980.

**254**     Underhill, Linda. *Alice in Wonderland*. Presented by the Riverside Children's Theatre at the Ramona High School Auditorium, Riverside, N.Y.,  from 16 to 17 May 1980.

**255**     Abbs, Keith. *Alice*. Music by Abbs. Presented at Our Lady's Convent High School, Amhurst Park,  England, from 10 to 12 July 1980. Rev: *Bandersnatch* (Sept. 1980).
        Presented in a new version for narrator and mixed choir as part of *Song & Carroll*, presented as  part of the Camden Fringe Festival (London) by the Primrose Hill Singers at Hampstead Theatre from 14 to 15 Nov. 1983.

**256**     Yarnell, Gwen. *Adventures in Wonderland*. Music by Rita Klaus-ner. Presented by the Harlequin Players' Summer Theatre Company, Willoughby, Ohio, from 23 to 27 July 1980.

**257**     *Alice in Wonderland*. Directed by Micheal Dimond and Eric Hamburger. Multi-media rock production presented by the Youth Arts Summer Project, Mamaroneck, N.Y., Aug. 1980.

**258**     *Through the Looking-Glass*. Presented by the Philadelphia Com-pany in a two-by-four theatre on Philadelphia's Broad St., Dec. 1980. Rev: *Knight Letter* (March 1981).

**259**  Farrell, Gordon. *A Lewis Carroll Evening*. Presented by City Theatre, San Francisco, for two weeks beginning 11 Dec. 1980. Includes several scenes from *Alice*.

**260**  Bayer, Marijan and Howard Crabtree. *Alice in Wonderland*. Ballet presented at Harbourfront, Toronto, Canada, from 20 Dec. 1980 to 2 Jan. 1981.
   Presented at the same theatre from 26 to 30 Dec. 1981.
   Presented at the same theatre from 26 Dec. 1982 to 2 Jan. 1983.

**261**  *Alice in Wonderland*. Presented at the Manitoba Theatre Centre, Winnipeg, Canada, from 20 Dec. 1980 to 3 Jan. 1981.

**262**  Carp, Richard. *Alice in Wonderland and Through the Looking Glass*. Music by Jim Baldwin and Vance Thom. Presented by the Bay Theater Collective (Oakland, Cal.) as part of the Arts in Process series, from 27 Dec. 1980 to 21 Jan. 1981.
   Presented by the same group on 27 May 1979 at the meeting of the West Coast Chapter of the Lewis Carroll Society of North America.

**263**  Stephens, John. *Alice in Wonderland*. Music by John F. Ferguson and company. Presented at the Academy Theater, Atlanta, Ga., during their 1980–81 season.

**264**  Cowell, David. *Through the Looking-Glass*. Presented by the Thalian Theatre Group at the Towngate Theatre, Basildon, Essex, England, from 26 to 28 March 1981.

**265**  Lee, Shelly (choreographer). *Alice*. Music by Robert Pettigrew. Presented by the Basic Space Dance Theatre at The Workshop, Edinburgh, 26 March 1981. The production described as ". . . down a rabbit-hole into the world of sinister and surreal visions . . ."

**266**  *Alice Through the Looking-Glass*. Presented by the Junior Theater of Marin (California) through its Masque Unit in April 1981.

**267**     van Noort, Lenie. *Alice in Wonderland*. Dutch language adaptation presented by the Toneelgroep Arti Speelt (Theatre Arts Players) at the Theater de Engelenbak, Amsterdam, May 1981.

**268**     *Alice in Wonderland*. Children's Ballet presented at the Kenya National Theatre from 14 to 16 May 1982.

**269**     *Alice in Wonderland*. Production developed by The MimeAct troup of the Dallas Theatre Center under the direction of Robyn Flatt and James Stephens. Presented in the summer of 1981 and toured Texas during 1981–83.

**270**     Tucker, Patrick. *A Carroll for Alice: A Play drawn from the Words of Lewis Carroll*. Presented at the New End Theatre, Hampstead, England, from 1 to 4 July 1981.

**271**     Leopold-Kimm, Paul, Sue Passmore, and John Harrison. *Alice: A Ballet Fantasy in Three Acts*. Presented by Bush Davies Dance Company at the Adeline Genee Theatre, East Grinstead, England, from 16 to 25 July 1981. Adaptation from both books.

**272**     *Alice Through the Looking-Glass*. Presented by the Abercromby Theatre Group, Liverpool University, at St. Columba's by the Castle, Edinburgh, from 17 to 29 Aug. 1981 as part of the Edinburgh Festival Fringe.

**273**     Yeger, Sheila. *Alice in The Looking-Glass and Other Reflections*. Presented by the Insight Out Theatre Company at Buster Brown's, Edinburgh, from 17 to 29 Aug. 1981 as part of the Edinburgh Festival Fringe. A one-woman show performed by Marlene Sideaway which includes two short pieces, plus the longer "Alice" segment. "Alice is now long out of Wonderland . . . even she must grow old and the dream fade."

Performed (as *Alice in the Looking-Glass*) as part of the Richmond Festival from 28 May to 12 June 1983.

Performed (As *Alice—And Other Reflections*) at the Theatre West End, Edinburgh, from 20 Aug. to 1 Sept. 1984 as part of the Edinburgh Festival Fringe.

**274**    *Alice Through the Telescope*. Presented by the Good Company at Church Hill Little Theatre, Edinburgh, from 17 Aug. to 5 Sept. 1981 as part of the Edinburgh Festival Fringe.

**275**    Chaul, Robert. *Alice in Wonderland*. A modern opera presented at the Cubberly High School Auditorium, Palo Alto, Cal., 25 Oct. 1981, and at the Spangenberg Theater, Palo Alto, from 17 Oct. to 8 Nov. 1981.

Presented at the Broque Opera's Triplex Theatre, New York, beginning 19 May 1985.

**276**    *Alice*. Presented at the Ashburton High School, Croydon, England, from 2 to 5 Dec. 1981. This production combined *Alice* and *Looking-Glass*.

**277**    De Rita, Maria Luisa. *Alice nel teatrino delle Meraviglie* [Alice in the Theatre of Wonders]. (Rome:  Nuove Edizioni Romane, 1982).

**278**    Haverkamp, Friso. *Alice in Wonderland*. Dutch version translated and adapted by Haverkamp. Presented at the RO Theatre, Rotterdam, in 1982. Text developed in close cooperation with Franz Marijnen.

**279**    Graves, Warren. *Alice The Tea Party*. (Toronto:  Playwrights Canada, 1982).

Presented (under the title *Alice*) at the Young People's Theatre, Toronto, from 8 March to 15 April 1984.

**280**    Lemoine, R. *Heureux Qui Comme Alice* [Happy like Alice]. Unpublished script dated 1982. Adapted from translations by Henri Parisot and Jean Gattégno. Unproduced.

**281**    Snee, Dennis. *Alice in America-land; or Through the Picture Tube and What Alice Found There*. (Boston:  Baker Plays, 1982). Adaptation in which Alice meets characters who are concerned about contemporary American issues.

**282**    Holland, Sharon. *Alice in Wonderland*. Presented by the Children's Theater Company of Minneapolis from 23 April to 13 June 1982.

Presented by the same group from 24 April to 14 June 1987.

**283**    *Poets' and Storytellers' Theatre.* Presented at a Cavalier Days celebration in Prince Frederick, Md., May 1982. Included Alan Booth showing
slides of Christ Church, Oxford, and narrating "The Wasp in a Wig." This
production also included the showing of some *Alice* films from the collection of David and Maxine Schaefer.

**284**    DeFrange, Tim and Tom. *Alice in Blunderland.* A musical anti-
nuclear play. Production sponsored by Legacy, Inc. presented in several
cities in Ohio during summer of 1982.
      Published: Kent, Ohio: Legacy, Inc., 1983.
      *Note*: This play was widely performed during the mid-1980's. In May
of 1984 there were no fewer than 62 groups in 29 states preparing or
performing the play.

**285**    Sutton, Michael and Cynthia Mandelberg. *Looking-Glass.*   Presented at the Entermedia Theater, New York, beginning 4 June 1982. Rev:
*NY Times* (6/15/82).
      Published:   New York: Broadway Play Publishing, 1983.
      Presented at the Studio Theater, Los Angeles, beginning 7 July 1983.
      Presented at the Woolly Mammoth Theatre Company during their
1985 season.
      Presented at the College Theatre, City College of San Francisco, from
10 to 14 Dec. 1986.

**286**    Boyer, Jean-Marie. *La Chasse au Snark.* [The Hunting of the
Snark]. Music by Denis Lefebvre du Prey. Presented at the Théâtre Atelier
du Luxembourg, Paris, as part of the  Festival Foire St-Germain from 11
June to 2 July 1982.

**287**    *The Hunting of the Snark.* Presented by June Alleyn's School in
South London from 8 to 9 July 1982.  An operetta with music especially
written for the production with some traditional tunes added.

**288**    *Through the Looking Glass.* Open-air production presented by the
Pranksters Drama Group on the grounds of Guildford Castle from 24 to 13
July 1982

**289**     Morton, Tony. *The Artful Dodgson*. Portrayal of Lewis Carroll performed by Morton, with help from another actor and four members of the National Portrait Gallery staff, at the National Portrait Gallery, London, from 2 to 7 Aug.1982.

**290**     *The Adventures of Alice*. Presented by Theatr Powys. This production toured Wales from 18 Aug. to 17 Sept. 1982.

**291**     *Alice Through the Looking Glass*. Presented by the Leicestershire Youth Theatre at St. Ann's Community Centre, Edinburgh, from 23 to 28 Aug. 1982 as part of the Edinburgh Festival Fringe.

**292**     *Alice in Wonderland*. Ballet presented by The Western Association of Ballet Schools at the Pavilion Theatre, Bournemouth, England, from 12 to 13 Nov. 1982. Narrated by Johnny Morris.

**293**     *Alice's Adventures in Wonderland*. Presented daily by the San Francisco Shakespeare Company in Levi Plaza at the end of Dec. 1982.

**294**     Asselin, Jean. *Alice*. Production developed for Omnibus, a touring Canadian repertory group based in Montreal. Presented in Montreal from 8 Dec. 1982 to 9 Jan. 1983 prior to touring. Returned to Montreal in Dec. 1983. Based on the translation of *Alice* by Henri Parisot.

**295**     *Alice in Wonderland*. A musical version presented at the Georgian Theatre, Richmond, England, for two weeks beginning 20 Dec. 1982.

**296**     Ginman, John. *The Adventures of Alice*. Presented at The Nuffield Theatre, Southampton, during Christmas 1982. Music (mainly from Gilbert & Sullivan) arranged by Paul Herbert.

**297**     *Alice in Wonderland*. Presented by the DaSilva Puppets in Norwich from Dec. 1982 to Jan 1983. This production toured England during 1983.

**298**     *Alice's Adventures Through the Looking Glass*. Ballet choreographed by Wendy Robinson. Presented by the Baltimore (Md.) Ballet during their 1982–83 season.

**299** Endersky, Clive. *Alice*. (Toronto: Playwrights Canada, 1983). Bound with *The Wizard of Oz*.

**300** Surette, Roy. *Alice: A Wonderland*. Music and lyrics by Sandra Head. (Toronto: Playwrights Canada, 1983).

**301** *Alice in Winter Wonderland*. Presented by the Carshalton Panto-mime Company, England, in aid of Queen Mary's Hospital for Children from 14 to 29 Jan. 1983. Adapted from the *Alice* books.

**302** Leisy, James. *Alice*. Songs by James Leisy and Carol Eberhart. Presented by the Holy Child School, Old Westbury, N.Y., from 28 to 29 Jan. 1983.

**303** Chater-Robinson, Piers. *Through the Looking Glass*. Music, book, and lyrics by Robinson; additional lyrics by Ursula Macdonald. Presented by the Plymouth Theatre Company, Plymouth, England, from March to April, 1983. Rev: *Bandersnatch* (July 1983).

**304** Schaap, Barbara. *Alice's Adventures in Wonderland*. Presented by the Theatre Workshop of Lynbrook, N.Y., a family production company, May 1983.

**305** *Alice at the Palace*. Presented by the San Francisco Dancers' Repertory Theater on 21 May 1983.
　　　Presented by the same group on 2 June 1984.

**306** Gibbs, Patrick. *Alice*. Music by Jo Cooke. Presented by the Christ Church Dramatic Society in the Cathedral Garden, Christ Church, Oxford, at the end of May and beginning of June 1983 (closed 4 June). Rev: *Bandersnatch* (July 1983).

**307** Bobrow, Morris. *Alice in Levi's Land*. Presented at Levi's Plaza, San Francisco, in the summer of 1983. Full of Alician themes, but primarily about the Levi Corp.'s 1984 U.S. Olympic Team uniforms.

**308**    Goodman, Tim. *Alice in Wonderland*. Presented by the Arts Educational School, Tring Park, Herts., England, as their annual summer show from 1 to 4 July 1983. A series of dramatic episodes interspersed with ballet sequences. Rev: *Bandersnatch* (Oct. 1983).

**309**    *Alice's Adventures in Wonderland*. Presented at the London Regional Children's Museum, London, Ontario, Canada, Aug. 1983.

**310**    *Alice in Wonderland*. Directed by Caryl Green (?). Presented by The Happy Times Children's Theatre of Newark, N.J., in the Newark Museum Sculpture Garden, 22 Aug. 1983.

**311**    *Alice in Wonderland*. A water ballet presented by the San Francisco Merionnettes Synco Swim Club on 13 Nov. 1983.

**312**    Butchart, Graham, et al. *Alice in Wonderland*. Presented at the The Burton Hospital, Burton-on-Trent, as their Christmas Show, Dec. 1983.

**313**    Jackson, R. E. *The Hunting of the Snark*. Music by David Ellis. Presented by The Children's Musical Theatre of Mobile, Alabama, as their 1984 touring production.

**314**    Landes, William-Alan. *Alice 'n Wonderland*. (Studio City, Cal.: Players Press, ca. 1984).

**315**    Thomas, Gareth. *Alice: A Musical Fantasy*. Music by Mike Smith. Lyrics and narration by Gareth Thomas. (Tamworth, Staffs.: G.T.M.S. Productions Ltd., 1984).

**316**    *Conversations with Alice*. Presented Off-Broadway in New York City in January 1984.

**317**    Darby, Roy. *Alice in Wonderland*. Presented by the Silsoe Drama Club, Beds., England, from 26 to 28 Jan. 1984.
       The same group presented a production of *Alice in Wonderland* (possibly the same adaptation) from 4 Dec. 1986 to 10 Jan. 1987.

**318**    Perlman, Arthur. *Dodgson.* (later titled *Once on a Summer's Day*).
Presented by the Ensemble Studio Theater, New York, from 2–4 Feb. 1984,
and (as *Once on a Summer's Day*) from 7 to 23 Dec. 1984.

**319**    *Wonderland: And What Alice Found There.* Presented at the U.C.
Playhouse, Toronto, from 7 to 10 March 1984.

**320**    Scott, Richard. *Alice.* A new rock musical with music by Anthony
Phillips. Presented at the Leeds Playhouse from 22 March to 14 April 1984.

**321**    *Alice Through a Prism.* Directed by Jane Barrell. Presented in
Riverside Park, New York, on 19 May 1984. An outdoor performance with
dance, music, and song.

**322**    *Alice.* A musical presented by the San Francisco Children's Chorus
at the Community Music Center, San Francisco, on 2 June 1984

**323**    *Alice in Wonderland . . . The Play.* Directed by Margrit Roma.
Presented by The New Shakespeare Company at San Francisco's Golden
Gate Park, from 4 to 23 July 1984.

**324**    *Alice Down Under.* Presented by the Sydney Puppet Theatre,
Sydney, Australia, from 26 Aug. to 9 Sept. (probably 1984).

**325**    Blackman, Charles and Barry Moreland. *Alice in Wonderland.* A
Musical Fantasy presented at His Majesty's Theatre, Perth, for the West
Australian Ballet Company, from 29 Nov. to 22 Dec. 1984.

**326**    Martin, Christopher. *Alice in Wonderland.* Music by Stephanie
Nunn. Presented by the Phoenix Theatre Company at the Phoenix Arts
Centre, Leicester, England, from 29 Nov. 1984 to 19 Jan. 1985.
       Presented at  the New Victoria Theatre, Newcastle-under-Lyme,
beginning 10 Dec. 1986.

**327**    *Jabber the Rock.* Presented by the Meridian Secondary School,
Royston, Herts., England, 6 Dec. 1984. Loosely based on "Jabberwocky."

**328** Reinicke, Ehrhard. *Alice im Wunderland* [Alice in Wonderland]. Music by Herbert Baumann, libretto by Reinicke, choreography by Roberto Trinchero. German ballet presented at the Staatstheater, Wiesbaden, West Germany, beginning 23 Dec. 1984.

Presented in Lucerne in April 1985.

**329** *Alice in Wonderland.* Presented by the Pleasure Guild of the Children's Hospital Auxillary of Columbus, Ohio, for 11 performances late in 1984.

**330** *Alice in Wonderland* (?). Adaptation of both books directed by Helen Karpow. Presented at the Passage Theatre, Chicago in 1985.

**331** Raum, Elizabeth. *The Garden of Alice.* Operatic version of *Alice* presented at the Globe Theatre, Regina, Canada, beginning 19 Jan. 1985.

**332** *Alice in Wonderland.* Presented by the Bankside Theatre Company at the Bear Gardens Museum of the Shakespearean Stage, England, from 21–27 Jan. 1985 and at Chelsea Community Centre from 1 to 2 Feb. 1985.

**333** Cummings, Greg. *Jabberwocky.* Dance-play for children presented at the Shelter Rook Public Library, Albertson, N.Y., 26 Jan. 1985.

**334** Cohen, Phillipe. *Alice '85.* French adaptation. Directed by Olivier Ding. Presented at the Théâtre Saint-Gervais, Geneva, Switzerland, from 17 April to 5 May 1985.

**335** Togni, Andrej. *Alice im Wunderland* [Alice in Wonderland]. Music and lyrics by Togni. Presented by the Theater-Zum group in Lucerne, Switzerland in May 1985. This production consisted of mostly mime, followed by an audience participation tea-party.

**336** Collins, Regina. *Alice in Wonderland.* Ballet presented by the Oyster Bay Ballet at the Nassau County Center of the Fine Arts, 16 June 1985. This production was previewed at the Westbury Music Fair in April.

**337**    *Oxford in Wonderland*. Directed by Pascal Crantelle. Presented by The Old Fire Station Theatre Group, Oxford, from 1 to 13 July 1985. A Promenade Theatre Production in which the town of Oxford was the setting. This production consisted mainly of audience participation and improvisation.

**338**    *Alice in Wonderland*. Directed by Cathy Lawson. Presented at the Straw Hat Theater, Ashtabula, Ohio, from 2 to 11 Aug. 1985.

**339**    *Alice in Wonderland*. Presented by the G.C.T. Theatre Group at Buster Brown's, Edinburgh, from 12 to 17 Aug. 1985 as part of the Edinburgh Festival Fringe.

**340**    *Alice in Wonderland*. Presented by the Cambridge Floodlight Theatre Co. at Cat's Pyjamas, Edinburgh, from 12 to 24 Aug. 1985 as part of the Edinburgh Festival Fringe.

**341**    Crutch, Denis and Brian Sibley. *Dodge-Podge: A Carrollian Gallimaufry*. Presented by the authors at the County Hall, Westminster, for a meeting of the Lewis Carroll Society (Great Britain) on 18 Oct. 1985.
       *Note*: This production was originally scheduled for a Society meeting on 24 April 1981 (under the title *Dodge-Podge: A Carrollian Catch-All*) but was cancelled due to unforeseen circumstances.

**342**    Pengilly, Gordon. *Alice on Stage*. Presented by Theatre Calgary, Calgary, Canada, from 29 Nov. to 29 Dec. 1985.

**343**    Graves, Warren. *Alice*. Presented at the D.B. Clarke Theatre, Montreal, Dec. 1985.

**344**    Révérand, Frédéric. *Le Sacre d'Alice* [The Crowning of Alice]. Presented at the Théâtre de La Ville, Paris, from 10 to 14 Dec. 1985. Play with original 19th-century musical settings to Carroll's poems depicting an imaginary encounter between Carroll and five little girls at Eastbourne.

**345**    Gross, Gerry. *Alice Underground*. Presented at Concordia University, Montreal, from 10 to 15 Dec. 1985.

**346** *Alice in Wonderland.* Presented at the Malvern Festival Theatre from 26 Dec. 1985 to 4 Jan. 1986.

**347** Montley, Dr. Patricia. *Alice in Collegeland.* Presented by the Chatham Players Touring Company of Chatham College, Pittsburgh, Pa., during their 1985–86 touring season. A parody of Lewis Carroll's fantasy which dramatizes the dilemma of high school students trying to choose a college.

Published: Pittsburgh: Theatre Department, Chatham College, 1986.

**348** Tetley, Glen. *Alice.* Ballet set to music by David del Tredici. Presented by the National Ballet of Canada, Toronto, beginning on 19 Feb. 1986. This production later toured internationally.

**349** Spencer, Dennis. *Alice in Wonderland.* Presented at the Richmond Theatre, Richmond, England, from 24 Feb. to 1 March 1986.

**350** Wesley-Smith, Peter & Martin. *Boojum!* Presented by The State Opera of South Australia at the Scott Theatre, Adelaide, from 10 to 22 March 1986.

**351** *Alice in Wonderland.* Presented by the Civic Arts Junior Theater, Walnut Creek, Cal., from 6 to 8 June 1986.

**352** *Alice!* Presented by the Nichiren Shoshu of the United Kingdom (a Buddhist cult) at the Hammersmith Odeon from 21 to 22 June 1986. A sequel to the adventures in Wonderland, directed by Sue Thornton, with songs by members of NSUK.

Presented again from 17 to 18 Jan. 1987.

**353** Barnes, Peter Morgan. *Alice in Wonderland.* Presented by the Nasty Dog Theatre Company at the Bedlam Theatre, Edinburgh, from 10 to 23 Aug. 1986 as part of the Edinburgh Festival Fringe.

**354** Buchanan, Pat. *Alice's Adventures in Wonderland and Through the Looking-Glass.* Presented by the Theatre of Youth of the Lothian Players in the South Leith Parrish Hall, Edinburgh, from 11 to 16 Aug. 1986 as part of the Edinburgh Festival Fringe.

**355**    Turner, Kathryn.  *Alice*.  Ballet directed and choreographed by
Turner.  Premiered at the Queen Mother Theatre, Woodside, Hitchin, North
Hertfordshire, from 20 to 22 Oct. 1986.

**356**    Sandford, Christopher and Anthony Ingle.  *Alice Through the
Looking Glass*.  Presented at the Theatr Clwyd, Mold, Clwyd, Wales, from
4 Dec. 1986 to 24 Jan. 1987.
       A production of an adaptation credited only to Sandford was presented
in Williamson Park, Lancaster, England, from 14 June to 23 July 1988.

**357**    *Alice in Wonderland*.  Puppet play presented by the Center for
Puppetry Arts, Atlanta, Ga., beginning 12 Dec. 1986.  This production
toured the East during the 1987–88 season.

**358**    Wells, John. *Alice in Wonderland*.  Music by Carl Davis. Presented
at the Lyric Theatre, Hammersmith, from 18 Dec. 1986 to 31 Jan. 1987. Rev:
*Evening Standard* (12/19/86), *Daily Telegraph* (12/20/86), *Guardian* (12/
20/86).

**359**    Williams, Cindy (?). *The Adventures of Alice*. Presented at the Swan
Theatre during Christmas 1986.

**360**    *Alice in Wonderland*.  Presented at the Royal Lyceum Theatre,
Edinburgh, during Christmas 1986.

**361**    Martin, Christopher.  *The White Rabbit*.  A play for five to seven-
year-olds adapted from Martin's *Alice in Wonderland* (see number 326)
presented at the New Victoria Theatre, Newcastle-Under-Lyme, during
Christmas 1986.

**362**    Adams, Maryline Poole.  *Jabberwocky arranged as a Play With
Music*.  (Berkeley, Cal.:  Poole Press, 1987).  Limited edition of 75 copies.

**363**    *Through the Looking Glass (And What Alice Found There)*. Puppet
play presented by the Puppet Company as a touring production in winter of
1987 beginning at The Capital Children's Museum, Washington, D.C., on
2 Jan. 1987.

**364**    *Alice in Wonderland*. Directed by Adrianne Moore. Presented at the Bondi Pavillion Theatre, Bondi Beach, Australia, from 19 to 31 Jan. 1987. Choreographed by Michael Huxley.

**365**    *With Alice in Wonderland*. A dramatic reading performed by James R. Winkler at the Mark Taper Forum, Los Angeles, during January and February of 1987 and at the Itchey Foot Ristorante in Los Angeles, on Sundays during the same period. Rev: *LA Herald Examiner* (2/3/87).
    Presented as part of the Classics in Context series at the Actors Theatre of Louisville (Ky.) in Oct. 1988.

**366**    Mars, Tanya. *Pure Nonsense*. Presented in Toronto, Canada, April 1987. Only vaguely related to *Alice*. One character appears as Freud and the White Rabbit and another as Jung and the Mad Hatter.

**367**    Harrold, David. *Alice*. Music by Adam Collins. Produced by Young Idea and presented by the Hertford Dramatic & Operatic Society, England, 27 to 30 May 1987. Rev: *Bandersnatch* (July 1987).

**368**    Dorsey, Jaz. *Alice in America*. Presented by the Atlanta Playwright's Theatre at the Performance Gallery, Atlanta, Ga., June 1987. The play brings Alice to America where she has more dream adventures.
    Presented by the Café Players in New York City in Oct. 1987.

**369**    *Toltec in Decoland & Through the Smoking Glass*. A "Shamanic solo performance" performed by White Cloud Hawk Xochipillillama (an American Indian) at the Hatley Martin Art Gallery, San Francisco, from 26 to 27 June 1987. This was the third presentation of this Indian interpretation of the *Alice* story; dates for the first two unknown.

**370**    *Alice in Wonderland*. Presented by Upton's St. Monica School, England, to celebrate its diamond jubilee in early July 1987.

**371**    *A Groovy Alice in Wonderland*. A shadow puppet play presented by the Dragonfly Puppet Theatre (Betty Polus, Artistic Director) in the San Francisco area from 26 July to 2 Aug. 1987.

**372**     Gill, Richard (creator).  *Alice in Wonderland*.  Presented by the Polka Children's Theatre at the Brentford Arts Centre, England, from 30 Nov. to 19 Dec. 1987.  A play using 30 puppets and a live Alice.
    Presented at the Nuffield Theatre from 21 Dec. 1987 to 2 Jan. 1988.

**373**     del Tredici, David.  *Haddock's Eyes*.  A chamber musical presented at St. Clement's Episcopal Church, New York, by Lyn Austin's Music-Theatre Group during Dec. 1987. "Presents a picture of Carroll's obsession with words, mathematics, and little girls."  Rev: *NY Times* (12/22/87).

**374**     Kunin, Matilda.  *Alice in Wonderland*.  Presented by  Young Performers Theatre, Ft. Mason Center, San Francisco, from 4 to 10 Dec. 1987.

**375**     Ende, Michael.  *Die Jagd Dem Schlarg* [The Hunting of the Snark]. Music by Wilfried Hiller.  Performed at the Staatstheater am Gärtnerplatz, Munich, West Germany,  16 Jan. 1988.

**376**     Field, Alan.  *Alice in Wonderland*.  Music and lyrics by Mick Smith and Wilf Tudor.  Originally presented at the Gatehouse Theatre, Stafford, England (dates unknown).
    Presented by Act II, Leicst., England, 11 to 13 Feb. 1988.

**377**     *Alice in Wonderland*.  Presented by Pendle Productions around England Feb. to March  1988.  An up-tempo musical.

**378**     Kemp, Lindsay.  *Alice*.  Music by Arturo Annechino and Sergio Rendine.  Presented at the Teatro Gayarre, Pamplona, Spain, May 1988.

**379**     Chambers, Bettye.  *Le Avventure D'Alice Nel Paese Delle Meraviigle* [Alice's Adventures in Wonderland].  Italian language version adapted by Chambers from the translation by T. Pietrocola-Rossetti.  Performed by first-year Italian students at Georgetown University on  2 May 1988.

**380**     Lee, Levi & Rebecca Wackler.  *Alice*. Presented at the Center for Puppetry Arts, Atlanta, Ga., from 9 to 18 June 1988.  Modern retelling with puppets and live actors.

**381** *Alice Through the Looking-Glass.* Presented by The Dukes Air Theatre, in Association with the Lancaster City Council in Lancaster's Williamson Park (England) beginning in late June 1988.

**382** *Alice at Belsay Hall.* Presented at Belsay Hall, Castle & Gardens, near Newcastle, England, from 10 to 25 Sept. 1988. Participatory production in which the audience was invited to dress as Alice or a Playing Card and to join in the Caucas Race and the Lobster Quadrille.

**383** *Alice in Santaland.* Presented during Dec. 1988 by the Manhattan Savings Bank, New York City. "A Musical fantasy for the Christmas season."

**Works in Progress:**

**384** Forman, Joanne. *Picnic in July.* Work in progress which features a live actor in the role of Lewis Carroll and puppets in other roles (including Punch, Judy, the Tum-Tum Tree, etc.). Music by Forman.

**385** Meecham, Margaret. Multi-media theatre piece using the text of *Alice in Wonderland* in a condensed form. Ms. Meecham has written music and libretto for portions of this operatic adaptation. A portion of this piece, including the Prologue, Transition, and Scenes I & II, was performed at the Tawes Recital Hall of the University of Maryland, College Park, on 1 May 1982.

This same portion was also performed with dancers as part of a Margaret Meecham retrospective at the Sterling and Francine Clark Art Institute of Williamstown, Mass., on 4 Feb. 1984, and again at the same venue as part of *Margaret Meecham and Friends* on 21 Aug. 1986.

**386** The Idea Workshop of Trinity University, San Antonio, Tex., annually presents a Mad Hatter's Tea Party, an improvisational workshop with the Mad Hatter and the March Hare.

**Undated Adaptations**:

**387**    *Alice in Wonderland.*  Presented by the Colchester Youth Theatre, England.

**388**    *Alice in Wonderland.*  Presented at Eaton Auditorium, Toronto, from 19 to 22 April (year unknown).

**389**    *Alice in Wonderland.*  Presented at Greenwich House in New York (founded by Helen Murphy in the mid-1920's).

**390**    *Alice in Wonderland.*  Presented by the Port Washington Children's Theatre in Port Washington, Long Island, N.Y.  (Theatre started in 1947).

**391**    *An Alice in Wonderland Playlet.*  (New York: The American Home, nd.)

**392**    *Alicja w krainie Carow.*  Polish version of *Alice in Wonderland* presented at the  Teatr Groteska.  Possibly adapted by Jan Polewka.

**393**    A British acting team resident in Tokyo in the early 1980's frequently performed adaptations of Carroll's works.  *Alice* was presented around Easter most years.

**394**    *The Hunting of the Snark.* Translated into Portuguese and presented in Lisbon.  Ca. 1986.

**395**    *La Chasse au Snark.*  French version of *The Hunting of the Snark* presented at the Théâtre de Plaisance, Paris (dates unknown).

**396**    *Through the Looking Glass.*  Presented at the residence of Mrs. Bernard S. Clark in Shadow Lane, South Street (city and dates unknown). "In aid of the Red Cross."

**397**     Barney, Mrs. *The Dream of Alice in Wonderland—A Burlesque.* Consisting of a Prologue and Two Acts. Most likely presented as private theatricals at a summer resort early in the twentieth century.

**398**     DuPage, Florence. *Alice in Wonderland.* Operetta.

**399**     Edwards, Caroline E.H. "Alice's Adventures: Scenes from 'Alice in Wonderland'." In *Our Children's Book of Plays, II.* No date.

**400**     Gould, Katherine Kanvanagh. *Alice in Wonderland.* Unpublished script.

**401**     Masters, Raymond. *Alice Underground.* Presented by Theatre Arts of West Virginia, Beckley, W. Va. Year unknown.

**402**     Pasqualetti, John (choreographer). *Alice in Wonderland.* Presented by the Pacific Ballet. Music from Bach to Britten. Year unknown.

**403**     Seiler, Ludwig. Alice in Wonderland. Presented by the Orchard Park Secondary School Drama Club, Ontario, Canada.

**404**     Sheldon, Edward Brewster. *Alice in Wonderland (a dream in two parts).* Typescript in the New York Public Library.

**405**     Sherwood, William. *Alice in Wonderland.* Unpublished manuscript in the Library of the British Drama League.

# Appendix B
## Henry Savile Clarke's Dream-Play
### *Alice in Wonderland*
### Script and Bibliography

The text which follows is that of the first printing of Savile Clarke's script in 1886. Songs have been omitted, as those which are not taken from the *Alice* books are printed in Chapter IV. Revisions made in subsequent editions of the script are noted in the bibliography and in Chapters V and VI. The original text has been copied as closely as possible, including typographical errors, illogical punctuation, etc.

ACT I.

———

SCENE.— *A Forest in Autumn. Alice asleep at foot of tree and Fairies dancing round her.*

CHORUS OF FAIRIES.

['Sleep, maiden sleep!']

[*Fairies troop off at each side, the Chorus dying softly away in the distance. Scene changes to Wonderland, Garden set. The* CATERPILLAR *discovered smoking on gigantic mushroom at side.* ALICE *wakes up, and goes up and down stage in great bewilderment. The white* RABBIT *crosses the stage hurriedly.*

RABBIT. Oh! the Duchess, the Duchess! Oh, won't she be savage if I've kept her waiting!

ALICE. If you please, Sir— (RABBIT *starts and exit dropping white kid gloves and fan.*) Dear! Dear! How queer everything is to-day. And yesterday things went on just as usual. I wonder if I've been changed in the night. Let me think, was I the same when I got up this morning. But if I'm not the same who am I? Ah! that's the puzzle. I'll try if I know all the things I used to know. Let me see four times five is twelve, and four times six is thirteen, and four times seven— Oh dear, I shall never get to twenty at that rate. I'll try "How doth the little busy bee."

———

## SONG.—"HOW DOTH THE LITTLE CROCODILE."

AL. Oh! dear I'm sure those are not the right words, and I'm so very tired of being all alone here.

[*Comes opposite* CATER.

CATER. Who are you?

AL. I—I hardly know, Sir, just at present. At least I knew who I was when I got up this morning, but I think I must have been changed several times since then.

CATER. What do you mean by that? explain yourself.

AL. I can't explain *myself*, I'm afraid, Sir, because I'm not myself, you see.

CATER. I don't see.

AL. I'm afraid I can't put it more clearly, for I can't understand it myself to begin with.

CATER. You. Who are *you*?

AL. I think you ought to tell me who you are first.

CATER. Why? (ALICE *tosses her head and is going off*) Come back! I've something important to say. (AL. *returns to him*) Keep your temper.

AL. (*indignantly*) Is that all?

CATER. No. So you think you're changed, do you?

AL. I'm afraid I am, Sir. I can't remember things as I used.

CATER. Can't remember *what* things?

AL. Well I've tried "How doth the little busy bee," but it all came different.

CATER. Try "You are old, Father William."

AL. With pleasure, Sir.

———

## SONG.—"YOU ARE OLD, FATHER WILLIAM."

CATER.  That is not right.

AL.  Not *quite* right, I'm afraid.  Some of the words have got altered.

CATER.  It's wrong from beginning to end.  Good day.

[CATERPILLAR *and Mushroom are drawn off.  Enter* WHITE RABBIT.

RAB.  The Duchess!  The Duchess!  Oh my dear paws!  Oh!  my fur and whiskers.  She'll get me executed as sure as ferrets are ferrets.  Where can I have dropped them I wonder?

AL.  (*aside*)  He's looking for his fan and gloves.

[*She also looks for them.  The* RABBIT *then notices her.*

RAB.  Why, Mary Ann, what *are* you doing out here?  Run home this moment and fetch me a pair of gloves and a fan.  Quick now!

AL.  (*aside*)  He takes me for his housemaid.  How surprised he'll be when he finds out who I am.  But I'd better get him his fan and gloves.

[*picks up fan and gloves and gives them to* RABBIT.

RAB.  Thank you, Mary Ann, thank you.  Now wait for the Duchess, she's coming here with the baby and the cook.                    [*exit* RABBIT.

AL.  Oh dear me!  I'm Mary Ann now, and the Duchess is coming and the baby, and the cook.  Are they going to cook the baby, I wonder?

*Enter* DUCHESS *carrying child.* COOK *with a saucepan and pepper castor, and* CHESHIRE CAT.

AL.  Please would you tell me why your cat grins like that?

DUC.  It's a Cheshire Cat, and that's why.  (*to baby*)  Pig!

AL.  I didn't know that Cheshire Cats always grinned: in fact I didn't know that cats *could* grin.

DUC.  They all can and most of 'em do.

AL.  I don't know of any that do.

DUC.  You don't know much and that's a fact.

COOK.  There's nothing like pepper say I.  There's not half enough yet!  Nor a quarter enough.

> Boil it so easily.
> Mix it so greasily,
> Stir it so sneezily,
>   One, two, three.

One for the Missis, two for the cat, and three for the baby.

> [*The* COOK *peppers soup and baby alternately.*

AL. Oh, *please* mind what you're doing?  Oh, there goes his *precious* nose!

DUC. If everybody minded their own business, the world would go round a great deal faster than it does.

AL. Which would *not* be an advantage.  Just think what work it would make with the day and night.  You see the earth takes twenty-four hours to turn round on its axis—

DUC. Talking of axes, chop off her head.

AL. Twenty-four hours, I think—or is it twelve—

DUC. Oh don't bother me.  I never could abide figures.

---

## SONG.— "SPEAK ROUGHLY."

DUC. (*to* COOK) Off with you. (*exit* COOK) Here catch! (*throws baby off stage*) *I'm* going to the Queen.

> [*exeunt* DUCHESS, CAT, *and* RABBIT.

AL. And I wonder what I'm going to do.  I hope the cook caught the baby.

> [*The head of* CHESHIRE CAT *appears in tree.*

AL. Cheshire Puss.  Would you tell me please which way I ought to go from here?

CAT. That depends a good deal on where you want to get to.

AL. I don't much care where.

CAT. Then it doesn't matter which way you go.

AL. So long as I get *somewhere*.

CAT. Oh you're sure to do that, if you only walk long enough.

AL. What sort of people live about here?

CAT. In one direction lives a hatter, and in the other a March Hare.  Visit either you like— they're both mad.

AL. But I don't want to go among mad people.

CAT. Oh you can't help that.  We're all mad here. I'm mad. You're mad.

AL. How do you know I'm mad?

CAT. You must be, or you wouldn't have come here.

AL. And how do you know that you're mad?

CAT.  To begin with a dog's not mad.  You grant that?

AL.  I suppose so.

CAT.  Well then.  You see a dog growls when it's angry, and wags its tail when it's pleased.  Now I growl when I'm pleased and wag my tail when I'm angry.  Therefore I'm mad.

AL.  I call it *purring* not growling.

CAT.  Call it what you like:  and say "thank you for the information."

————

DUET.

['Cheshire Puss, my thanks to thee']

[*dance and exeunt.*

————

*Enter* HATTER, MARCH HARE, *and* DORMOUSE *with tea-table which they set and seat themselves at it.  Enter* ALICE.

HATTER *and* HARE.  No room!  No room!

AL.  There's plenty of room.

[*sits in chair at head of table.*

HARE.  Have some wine.

AL.  I don't see any wine.

HARE.  There isn't any.

AL.  (*angrily*)  Then it wasn't very civil of you to offer it.

HARE.  It wasn't very civil of you to sit down without being invited.

AL.  I didn't know it was your table.  It's laid for a great many more than three.

HAT.  Your hair wants cutting.

AL.  (*severely*)  You should learn not to make personal remarks.

HAT.  (*looking astonished*)  Why is a raven like a writing-desk?

AL.  I believe I can guess that.

HARE.  Do you mean that you think you can find out the answer to it?

AL.  Exactly so.

HARE.  Then you should say what you mean.

AL.  I do— at least I mean what I say; that's the same thing you know.

HAT.  Not the same thing a bit.  You might just as well say that "I see what I eat" is the same thing as "I eat what I see."

HARE.  You might just as well say that, "I like what I get" is the same thing as "I get what I like."

DOR.  You might just as well say, that "I breathe when I sleep" is the thing [sic] as "I sleep when I breathe."

HAT.  It *is* the same thing with you.  (*to* AL., *taking out his watch*.)  What day of the month is it?

AL.  The fourth.

HAT.  Two days wrong.  (*to* HARE)  I told you butter wouldn't suit the works.

HARE.  It was the best butter.

HAT.  Yes, but some crumbs must have got in as well, you shouldn't have put it in with the bread-knife.

[HARE *takes watch and dips it in cup.*

HARE.  It was the *best* butter you know.

AL.  What a funny watch!  It tells the day of the month, and doesn't tell what o'clock it is.

HAT.  Why should it.  Does *your* watch tell you what *year* it is?

AL.  Of course not, but that's because it stays the same year for such a long time together.

HAT.  Which is just the case with mine.  Have you guessed the riddle yet?

AL.  No I give it up.  What's the answer?

HAT.  I haven't the slightest idea.

HARE.  Nor I.

AL.  I think you might do something better with the time than wasting it in asking riddles that have no answers.

HAT.  If you knew Time as well as I do: you wouldn't talk about wasting *it*.  It's *him*.

AL.  I don't know what you mean.

HAT.  Of course you don't, I dare say you never spoke to Time.

AL.  Perhaps not, but I know I have to beat time when I learn music.

HAT.  Ah! that accounts for it.  He won't stand beating.  Now, if you only kept on good terms with him, he'd do almost anything you liked with the clock.  For instance, suppose that it were nine o'clock in the morning— just time to begin lessons, you'll only have to whisper a hint to Time, and round goes the clock in a twinkling:  Half-past one— time for dinner!

HARE.  I only wish it was.

AL. That would be grand certainly, but then I shouldn't be hungry for it, you know.

HAT. Not at first perhaps, but you could keep it to half-past one as long as you liked.

AL. Is that the way you manage?

HAT. Not I. We quarrelled last March, just before he went mad, you know (*points at* HARE) it was at the great concert given by the Queen of Hearts, and I had to sing

> Twinkle, twinkle little bat,
> How I wonder what you're at!
> Up above the world you fly
> Like a tea-tray in the sky.

Well I'd hardly finished the first verse when the Queen bawled out, "He's murdering the time, off with his head."

AL. How dreadfully savage!

HAT. And ever since that he won't do a thing I ask. It's always six o'clock now.

AL. Is that the reason so many tea-things are put out here?

HAT. (*sighing*) Yes, that's it. It's always tea-time, and we've not time to wash the things between whiles.

AL. Then you keep moving round, I suppose?

HAT. Exactly so, as the things get used up.

AL. But what happens when you come to the beginning again?

HARE. Suppose we change the subject. Wake up, Dormouse, and tell us a story.

DOR. Once upon a time there were three little sisters, and their names were Elsie, Lacie, and Tillie, and they lived at the bottom of a well—

AL. What did they live on?

DOR. They lived on treacle.

AL. They couldn't have done that, you know, they'd have been ill.

DOR. So they were— *very* ill.

HARE. Take some more tea.

AL. I've had nothing yet: so I can't take more.

HAT. You mean you can't take less. It's very easy to take more than nothing.

AL. Nobody asked your opinion.

HAT.  Who's making personal remarks now?

AL.  (*to* DORMOUSE)  Why did they live at the bottom of a well?

DOR.  It was a treacle well.

AL.  There's no such thing.

HAT. *and* HARE.  Hush!  Hush!

DOR.  And so these three little sisters, they were learning to draw you know—

AL.  What  did they draw?

DOR.  Treacle.

HAT.  I want a clean cup, let's all move one place on.

> [HAT. *moves, followed by* DOR. *and* MARCH HARE,
> AL. *into* MARCH HARE'S *place.*

AL.  But I don't understand.  Where did they draw the treacle from?

HAT.  You can draw water out of a water-well, so I should think you could draw treacle out of a treacle-well— Eh, stupid?

AL.  But they were *in* the well.

DOR.  Of course they were, well in— they were learning to draw everything that begins with an M—

AL.  Why with an M?

HARE.  Why not?

DOR.  (*half asleep, and pinched by* HAT. *gives a little shriek and goes on*)—that begins with an M; such as mouse-traps, and moon, and memory, and muchness, you know you say things are "much of a muchness," did you ever see such a thing as a drawing of a muchness.

AL.  Really now you ask me, I don't think—

HAT.  Then you shouldn't talk.

AL.  (*jumping up*)  How rude you are!

> [*all rise from table and come down stage.*

———

COUPLETS AND CHORUS.— "SO THEY SAY."

> [*All dance off—* HARE *and* HATTER *taking table away.*
> *Enter Two, Five and Seven of Clubs,*) *then* KING, QUEEN *and*

KNAVE *of Hearts and other Cards, also* ALICE.—*Procession goes round the stage. Two, Five and Seven lie down at sides.*

QUEEN. (*to* KNAVE) Who is this? (KNAVE *only bows*) Idiot! (*to* ALICE) What's your name, child?

AL. My name is Alice, so please you majesty. (*aside*) Why they're only a pack of cards; I needn't be afraid of them.

QUEEN. (*pointing to Two, Five and Seven*) And who are *these?*

AL. How should *I* know? It's no business of mine.

QUEEN. (*glares at* ALICE *and then shouts*) Off with her head! off—

KING. Consider, my dear, she is only a child.

QUEEN. (*to* KNAVE) Turn them over. (*Two, Five and Seven get up and bow rapidly to everyone*) Leave off that, you make me giddy. Off with their heads!

AL. You shan't be beheaded.                     [*shows them off stage.*

RAB. (*to* ALICE) It's—it's a very fine day.

AL. Very! where's the Duchess?

RAB. Hush! Hush! She's under sentence of execution.

AL. What for?

RAB. Did you say what a pity?

AL. No I didn't. I don't think it at all a pity— I said what for?

RAB. She boxed the Queen's ears.

AL. Oh what fun!

RAB. Oh hush, the Queen will hear you.

QUEEN. Are their heads off?

KNAVE. Their heads are off, so please your Majesty.

QUEEN. Get to your places!

[KING *gives* ALICE *his hand*— KNAVE *with* QUEEN. *Grand Gavotte of Court Cards. At end head of* CHESHIRE CAT *appears in tree.*

CAT. (*to* AL.) How do you like the Queen?

AL. Not at all. She's extremely— (QUEEN *comes behind her*) polite.

[QUEEN *smiles and passes on*

KING. Who *are* you talking to?

AL. It's a friend of mine, a Cheshire Cat.

KING. A Cheshire Cat?

AL.  Allow me to introduce it.

KING.  I don't like the look of it at all.  However it may kiss my hand if it likes.

CAT.  I'd rather not.

KING.  Don't be impertinent, and don't look at me like that.          [*gets behind* QUEEN.

AL.  A cat may look at a King.

KING.  Well it must be removed.  (*to* QUEEN)  My dear, I wish you would have this cat removed.

QUEEN.  Off with his head.

KING.  Hi!  Executioner.

KNAVE.  Here he is.

*Enter* EXECUTIONER.

KING.  Off with that cat's head.

EX.  Can't be done.

QUEEN.  What!

EX.  You can't cut a head off unless there's a body to cut it off from.  I never had to do such a thing before and I'm not going to begin at my time of life.

——

TRIO & CHORUS.—"HE IS THE EXECUTIONER."

——

[*All go off to end of song.*  QUEEN *stops to say to* AL.

QUEEN.  Have you seen the Mock Turtle yet?

AL.  No, I don't even know what a Mock Turtle is.

QUEEN.  It's the thing Mock Turtle soup is made from.

AL.  I never saw one or heard of one.

QUEEN.  The Gryphon shall show you.

*Enter* GRYPHON.

Here Gryphon, introduce this young lady to the Mock Turtle.  I must go and see after some executions I have ordered.

[*exit* QUEEN.

GRY.  What fun!

AL.  What *is* the fun?

GRY. Why *she*. It's all her fancy that, they never executes nobody you know. Hi! Mock Turtle.

*Enter* MOCK TURTLE *weeping*.

AL. What is his sorrow?

GRY. It's all his fancy—that; he hasn't got no sorrow you know. This here young lady she wants for to know your history, she do.

MOCK. I'll tell it her. Sit down both of you. Once I was a real turtle!

GRY. Hjckrrh.

MOCK. When we were little we went to school in the Sea. The Master was an old Turtle, we used to call him Tortoise.

AL. Why did you call him tortoise if he wasn't one?

MOCK. We called him tortoise because he taught us. Really you are very dull.

GRY. You ought to be ashamed of yourself for asking such a simple question.

MOCK. Yes, we went to school in the Sea; though you mayn't believe it—

AL. I never said I didn't.

MOCK. You did.

GRY. Hold your tongue.

MOCK. We had the best of educations, in fact we went to school every day.

AL. *I've* been to a day school too. You needn't be so proud as all that.

MOCK. With extras?

AL. Yes. We learned French and music.

MOCK. And washing?

AL. Certainly not.

MOCK. Ah! then yours wasn't a really good school. Now at ours they had at the end of the bill, French, music *and washing* extra.

AL. You couldn't have wanted it much, living at the bottom of the sea.

MOCK. I couldn't afford to learn it. I only took the regular course.

AL. What was that?

MOCK. Reeling and writhing, of course, to begin with, and then the different branches of arithmetic. Ambition, Distraction, Uglification, and Derision.

AL. I never heard of Uglification. What is it?

GRY. Never heard of uglifying. You know what to beautify is, I suppose.

AL. Yes. It means to make anything prettier.

GRY. Well then, if you don't know what to uglify is, you *are* a simpleton.

AL. What else had you to learn?

MOCK. Well there was Mystery, ancient and modern, with Seaography, then Drawling— the Drawling-master was an old conger-eel that used to come once a week, he taught us Drawling and Stretching, and Fainting in Coils,

AL. What was *that* like.

MOCK. Well I can't show it you myself. I'm too stiff and the Gryphon never learned it.

GRY. Hadn't time. I went to the Classical master though, he was an old crab, *he* was.

MOCK. I never went to him, he taught laughing and grief they used to say.

GRY. So he did. So he did.

　　　　　　　[*both creatures hide faces in their paws in sorrow.*

AL. And how many hours a day did you do lessons.

MOCK. Ten hours the first day, nine the next and so on.

AL. What a curious plan.

GRY. That's the reason they're called lessons because they lessen from day to day.

AL. Then the eleventh day must have been a holiday.

MOCK. Of course it was.

AL. And how did you manage on the twelfth.

GRY. That's enough about lessons, sing her a song.

---

## SONG AND CHORUS

['Beautiful soup so rich and green']

---

MOCK. You may not have lived under the sea.

AL. I haven't.

MOCK. And perhaps you were never even introduced to a lobster?

AL. I once tasted— (*checks herself*) No never!

MOCK. So you can have no idea what a delightful thing a Lobster Quadrille is?

AL.  No indeed!  What sort of dance is it?

GRY.  Why, you first form into a line along the sea-shore—

MOCK.  Two lines!  Seals, turtles, salmon and so on;  then when you've cleared all the jelly-fish out of the way—

GRY.  *That* generally takes some time!

MOCK.  You advance twice—

GRY.  Each with a lobster for a partner—

MOCK.  Of course, advance twice, set to partners!

GRY.  Change lobsters and retire in same order.

MOCK.  Then you throw the—

GRY.  The Lobsters!  [*with a shout and bound into the air.*

MOCK.  As far out to sea as you can.

GRY.  Swim after them!

MOCK.  Turn a somersault in the sea!  [*capering about.*

GRY.  (*loudly*)  Change lobsters again?

MOCK.  Back to land again and that's all the first figure.

[*The two creatures who have been jumping about like mad things, now sit down again and look at* ALICE.

AL.  It must be a very pretty dance!

MOCK.  Would you like to see a bit more of it?

AL.  Very much indeed!

MOCK.  (*to* GRYPHON)  Come let's try the first figure.  We can do it without lobsters you know.  You sing.

———

SOLO AND CHORUS.

["'Will you walk a little faster?'"]

AL.  Thank you!  It's a very interesting dance; and I do so like that curious song about the whiting.

MOCK.  Oh, as to the whiting— you've seen them of course?

AL.  Yes.  I've often seen them at dinn—

MOCK.  I don't know where Dinn may be, but if you've seen them so often of course you know what they're like.

AL.  I believe so, they have their tails in their mouths, and they're all over crumbs.

MOCK. You're wrong about the crumbs, crumbs would all wash off in the sea; but they *have* their tails in their mouths.

GRY. The reason is they would go with the lobsters to the dance. So they got thrown out to sea So they had to fall a long way. So they got their tails fast in their mouths. So they couldn't get them out again.

AL. Thank you, it's very interesting. I never knew so much about a whiting before.

GRY. Do you know why it's called a whiting?

AL. I never thought about it. Why?

GRY. It does the boots and shoes. [*solemnly.*

AL. *Does* the boots and shoes?

GRY. Why, what are *your* shoes done with— I mean what makes them so shiny?

AL. They're done with *blacking*, I believe.

GRY. Boots and shoes under the sea are done with *whiting*. Now you know.

AL. And what are they made of?

GRY. Soles and eels, of course, any shrimp could have told you that.

AL. If I'd been the whiting, I'd have said to the porpoise, keep back please, we don't want *you* with us.

MOCK. They were obliged to have him with them. No fish would go anywhere without a porpoise.

AL. Wouldn't it really?

MOCK. Of course not. Why if a fish came to me, and told me he was going on a journey— I should say, with what porpoise?

AL. Don't you mean "purpose?"

MOCK. I mean what I say. Now let's hear some of *your* adventures.

AL. The queerest thing that happened to me to-day was singing "You are old, Father William" to the caterpillar, and all the words came different.

MOCK. That's very curious.

GRY. Its about as curious as it can be.

MOCK. The words all came different. I should like to hear her try and sing something now.

GRY. Stand up and sing "'Tis the voice of the sluggard."

———

SONG.— "TIS THE VOICE OF THE LOBSTER."

GRY.  It is time for the trial.

AL.  What trial.

MOCK.  The trial of the Knave of Hearts.

> [*Trumpets and March music.  Enter* KING *and* QUEEN *of Hearts,*
> *Court Cards &c.*  WHITE RABBIT *attired as Herald.*  KNAVE *in*
> *chains guarded by soldiers.*

KING.  Herald, read the accusation.

> [WHITE RABBIT *blows three blasts on trumpet, unrolls a scroll and*
> *reads.*

RAB.  The Queen of Hearts she made some tarts
>           All on a summer day,
>      The knave of Hearts he stole those tarts
>           And took them quite away.

KING.  Call the first witness.

RAB.  (*blows trumpet*)  First witness.

> *Enter* HATTER *with teacup, and bread and butter.  Also* MARCH
> HARE *and* DORMOUSE *arm in arm.*

HAT.  I beg your pardon, your Majesty, for bringing these in, but I hadn't quite finished my tea when I was sent for.

KING.  You ought to have finished.  When did you begin?

HAT.  Fourteenth of March I *think* it was.

KING.  Take off your hat.

HAT.  It isn't mine.

KING.  Stolen!

HAT.  I keep them to sell.  I've none of my own.  I'm a hatter.

> [QUEEN *puts on spectacles and glares at him and he fidgets.*

KING.  Give your evidence and don't be nervous, or I'll have you executed on the spot.

> [HATTER *fidgets and bites a piece out of his teacup instead of the bread*
> *and butter.*

QUEEN.  Bring me the list of the singers at the last concert.

> [HATTER *trembles so that he shakes his shoes off.*

KING.  Give your evidence or I'll have you executed whether you're nervous or not.

HAT.  I'm a poor man, your Majesty, and I hadn't begun my tea— not above a week or so, and what with the bread and butter getting so thin, and the twinkling of the tea—

KING.  The twinkling of *what?*

HAT.  It *began* with the tea.

KING.  Of course twinking [sic] begins with a T.  Do you take me for a dunce?  Go on.

HAT.  I'm a poor man and most things twinkled after that— only the March Hare said—

HARE  I didn't !

HAT.  You did!

HARE.  I deny it !

KING.  He denies it, leave out that part !

HAT.  Well at any rate the Dormouse said—

DOR.  I didn't

HAT.  You did !

DOR.  I deny it !

HAT.  And after that I cut some more bread and butter.

KING.  But *what* did the Dormouse say?

HAT.  That I can't remember.

KING.  You must remember or I'll have you executed !

      [HAT. *drops teacup, and bread and butter, and goes on his knees.*

HAT.  I'm a poor man, your Majesty.

KING.  You're a very poor speaker! (*applause in Court*)  and if that's all you know about it you may stand down.

HAT.  I can't go no lower.  I'm on the floor as it is.

KING.  Then you may *sit* down !

HAT.  I'd rather finish my tea.

KING.  You may go—                                    [HAT. *rushes out.*

QUEEN.  And just take his head off outside?

KING.  Call the next witness!

    [*Enter the* DUCHESS'S COOK *with pepper pot— one or two sneezes heard near her.*

KING.  Be good enough to take the time from me.  Now all together. (*All sneeze. To* COOK)  Give your evidence.

COOK.  Shan't!

KING.  What are these tarts made of?

COOK.  Pepper mostly.

DOR. Treacle!

QUEEN. Collar that Dormouse! Behead that Dormouse! Turn that Dormouse out of court! Suppress him! Pinch him! Off with his whiskers!

[COOK *stands back.*

KING. Next witness?

RAB. (*Blows trumpet*) Alice!

KING. What do you know about this business?

AL. Nothing!

KING. Nothing *whatever* ?

AL. Nothing whatever!

KING. That's very important! In that case consider your verdict.

QUEEN. No, no, sentence first, verdict afterwards.

AL. Stuff and nonsense.

QUEEN. Hold your tongue.

AL. I won't.

QUEEN. Off with her head.

AL. Who cares for you! My verdict is "Not Guilty, but the Knave mustn't steal the tarts again."

*All.* Not guilty! Hurrah!


FINALE.

['Not guilty I declare']

ACT-DROP.


ACT II.

———

"THROUGH THE LOOKING-GLASS."
SCENE I.— *The Looking-glass.*

AL. How nice it would be if we could only get through into Looking-Glass Land. I'm sure it's got such beautiful things in it. Let's pretend there's a way of getting through it somehow. Let's pretend the glass has got all soft gauze.

So that we can get through.  Why it's turning into a sort of dimness I declare. It'll be easy enough to get through.

> [*Climbs on to mantlepiece, and goes through Looking-glass.*

SCENE II.  *Looking-glass Land.  The garden of Live Flowers.  Chessmen discovered on stage.*

### CHESS CHORUS

['Here ranged in due order of battle we stand']

––––

[*Dance:  at the end of which one of the white pawns falls down, and the* WHITE QUEEN *rushes to her to pick her up, knocking the* WHITE KING *down in her haste.*

WHITE KING *and* QUEEN *on floor.  Enter* ALICE.

AL.  Why the chessmen are walking about!

WHITE Q.  My Precious Lily!  My Imperial kitten!

> [*tries to get up.*

WHITE K.  (*sitting up and rubbing his nose*)  Imperial fiddlestick.

[ALICE *lifts* WHITE QUEEN *up to a standing position :  also the pawn.*

WHITE Q.  (*to* KING)  Mind the Volcano!

WHITE K.  What Volcano?

WHITE Q.  It blew me up on to my legs.  Mind you get up in the regular way, don't get blown up!

AL.  (*lifting the* KING *up*)  Why you'll be hours and hours getting up at that rate. (*the* KING *is struggling to rise*) I'd far better help you! Hadn't I? (*helps the* KING *up hastily and dusts him.  He makes faces*) Oh please don't make such faces, my dear! You make me laugh so that I can hardly hold you. And don't keep your mouth so wide open! All the dust will get into it ! There, now I think you're tidy. (*Holds the* KING *upright, the moment she lets him go he falls flat on his back.*) Oh! he's fainted.

WHITE K.  (*to* QUEEN) I assure you, my dear, I turned cold to the very ends of my whiskers!

WHITE Q.  You haven't got any whiskers?

WHITE K.  The horror of that moment I shall never, *never* forget!

WHITE Q.  You will though, if you don't make a memorandum of it?

[KING *gets up takes out memorandum book and tries to write.* ALICE
*takes hold of his hand and pencil and helps him.*

WHITE K.  My dear, I really must get a thinner pencil? I can't manage this
one a bit—it writes all manner of things I don't intend.

WHITE Q.  (*taking it*)  What manner of things?  *That's* not a memorandum
of your feelings!  (*to* ALICE)  Here you read it, or sing it?

AL.  Dear me!  It's all in some language I don't know.

WHITE Q.  (*to* WHITE KNIGHT)  Then you read it!

———

SONG.—"JABBERWOCKY."

[*all rush off.* ALICE *alone.*

AL.  Dear me I wish they had stayed!  (*To* LILY)  Oh Tiger-Lily, I wish you
could talk?

LILY.  We *can* talk, when there's anybody worth talking to!

AL.  (*almost in a whisper*)  And can *all* the flowers talk?

LILY.  As well as *you* can and a great deal louder.

ROSE.  It isn't manners for us to begin, you know, and really was [sic]
wondering when you'd speak. Said I to myself, "her face has got some sense
in it, though it's not a clever one." Still you're the right colour and that goes
a long way.

LILY.  I don't care about the colour! If only her petals curled up a little
more she'd be all right!

AL.  Aren't you sometimes frightened at being planted out here with
nobody to take care of you?

ROSE.  There's a tree, what else is it good for?

AL.  But what could it do if any danger came?

ROSE.  It could bark. It says "Bough-wough," and that's why its branches
are called boughs.

AL.  How is it that you can talk so nicely? I've been in many gardens before
but none of the flowers could talk!

LILY. Put your hand down and feel the ground, then you'll know why!

AL. (*feeling the ground*) It's very hard, but I don't see what that has to do with it.

LILY. In most gardens they make the beds too soft, so that the flowers are always asleep.

AL. I never thought of that before! Are there any more people in the garden besides me?

ROSE. There's one other flower in the garden that can move about like you, I wonder how you do it, but she's more bushy than you are.

AL. Is she like me? (*aside*) There's another little girl in the garden somewhere.

ROSE. Well she has the same awkward shape as you, but she's redder, and her petals are shorter, I think.

LILY. Her petals are done up close, almost like a Dahlia— not tumbled about anyhow like yours!

AL. Does she ever come out here?

ROSE. I daresay you'll see her soon. She's one of the thorny kind!

AL. Where does she wear the thorns?

ROSE. Why all round her head of course! I was wondering *you* hadn't got some too. I thought it was the regular rule!

LILY. She's coming, I can hear her footstep thump, thump, along the gravel walk.

*Enter* RED QUEEN.

RED Q. Where do you come from? And where are you going? Look up, speak nicely; and don't twiddle you fingers all the time.

AL. I've lost my way.

RED Q. I don't know what you mean by *your* way— all the ways about here belong to me,— but why did you come here at all? Curtsey while you're thinking what to say, it saves time.

AL. Indeed— I'll try it when I go home, the next time I'm a little late for dinner.

RED Q. It's time for you to answer now, open your mouth a *little* wider when you speak, and always say "Your Majesty."

AL. I wanted to see what the garden was like, your Majesty.

RED Q. (*patting* ALICE'S *head.*) That's right, though when you say garden, *I've* seen gardens compared with which, this would be a wilderness.

AL. And I thought I'd try and find my way to the top that hill.

RED Q. When you say "hill," *I* could show you hills in comparison with which you would call that a valley.

AL. No I shouldn't, a hill *can't* be a valley you know. That would be nonsense.

RED Q. (*shaking her head*) You may call it nonsense, but *I've* heard nonsense compared with which that would be as sensible as a dictionary. Would you like to play Chess?

AL. (*curtseying*) Oh yes, your Majesty. What fun it would be. How I wish I was one of you. I wouldn't mind being a pawn if only I might join— though of course I should *like* to be a Queen best.

RED Q. That's easily managed. You can be White Queen's Pawn, if you like, as Lily's too young to play, and you're in the second square to begin with, when you get to the eighth square you'll be a Queen, come along! You'll see Tweedledum and Tweedledee.

[*Takes* ALICE *by the hand and both run off. Enter* TWEEDLEDUM *and* TWEEDLEDEE *solemnly, and take up position side by side, umbrella behind.*

———

DUET.

['Tweedledum and Tweedledee']

———

*Enter* ALICE.

AL. Here they are! I suppose they've each got TWEEDLE round at the back of the collar.

[*They stand still and* ALICE *is going round to inspect the back of their collars.*

DUM. If you think we're waxworks you ought to pay, you know. Waxworks weren't made to be looked at for nothing. Nohow!

DEE. Contrariwise, if you think we're alive you ought to speak.

AL. I'm sure I'm very sorry.

DUM. I know what you're thinking about, but it isn't so, nohow.

DEE. Contrariwise, if it was so, it might be; and if it were so, it would be; but as it isn't, it aint. That's logic.

AL. I was thinking which is the best way out of this wood. Would you tell me, please? (*They only look at each other and at her, and grin.* ALICE *points her finger at* TWEEEDLEDUM.) First Boy!

DUM. Nohow!

AL. Next Boy!

DEE. Contrariwise!

DUM. You've begun wrong. The first thing in a visit is to say "How d'ye do," and shake hands.

[*They shake hands with each other and then each give a hand to her. Then the music of* "Here we go round the mulberry bush" *commences, and all sing and dance round.*

———

TRIO.— "HERE WE GO ROUND THE MULBERRY
BUSH."

———

DUM. That's enough for one dance!

[*Both stop suddenly out of breath, music also stops suddenly and they drop her hands.*

AL. (*aside*) It would never do to say, "How d'ye do" *now*; we seem to have got beyond that somehow. (*aloud*) I hope you're not much tired!

DUM. Nohow! And thank you very much for asking.

DEE. Contrariwise! So *much* obliged! Can you repeat us some poetry?

AL. (*doubtfully*) Perhaps I could!

DUM. Nohow!

DEE. Contrariwise! Repeat "The Walrus and the Carpenter?"

AL, I'm afraid I don't know it!

DUM. Then we'll tell it you.

[*Scene opens and discloses sea-shore, and* WALRUS *and* CARPENTER.

## "THE WALRUS AND THE CARPENTER."

[*Scene closes back to garden.*

———

AL. I like the Walrus best, because you see he was a *little* sorry for the poor oysters.

DEE. He ate more than the carpenter though. You see he held his handkerchief in front so that the carpenter couldn't count how many he took: Contrariwise!

AL. That was mean, then I like the Carpenter best— if he didn't eat so many as the Walrus.

DUM. But he ate as many as he could get.

AL. (*lights rather down*) It's getting dark! Do you thing it's going to rain?
        [TWEEDLEDUM *spreads large umbrella over himself and brother.*

DUM. No! I don't think it is, at least, not under *here*! Nohow!

AL. But it may outside!

DEE. It may if it chooses, we've no objection. Contrariwise.

AL. Selfish things! I shall say good-bye.
[*turns to go when* TWEEDLEDUM *rushes from under umbrella and seizes her by the wrist.*

DUM. (*in a rage—pointing to small white rattle under tree*) Do you see *that?*

AL. It's only a rattle— not a rattle-*snake*, you know— only an old rattle, quite old and broken.

DUM. (*dancing about in a rage, tearing his hair, &c.*) I knew it was, it's spoilt of course.

AL. You needn't be so angry about an old rattle.

DUM. But it isn't old! It's new, I tell you! I bought it yesterday. (*screaming*) My nice new rattle!
[*during this* TWEEDLEDEE *tries to fold himself up in the umbrella with only his head out, in a fright.*

(*to him*) Of course you agree to have a battle!

DEE. (*sulkily, crawling out of umbrella*) I suppose so : only *she* must help us to dress up, you know.

[*run off at opposite sides and bring on bolsters, blankets, hearthrugs, and coalscuttles.*

DUM. I hope you're a good hand at pinning and tying strings. Everyone of these things has got to go on somehow or other!

[*they bustle about and dress up,* ALICE *helping them.*

AL. (*aside*) Really they'll be more like bundles of old clothes by the time they're ready.

DEE. Now for the bolster to keep my head from being cut off! (ALICE *ties it on*) You know it's one of the most serious things that can possibly happen to one in a battle— to get one's head cut off!

DEE. (*coming up to her to have coalscuttle tied on*) Do I look very pale?

AL. Well— yes— a *little.*

DUM. I'm very brave generally, only to-day I happen to have a headache!

DEE. And I've got a toothache, I'm far worse than you!

AL. Then you'd better not fight to-day!

DUM. We *must* have a bit of a fight, but I don't care about going on long! What's the time now?

DEE. Half past four.

DUM. Let's fight till six and then have dinner!

DEE. Very well and *she* can watch us, only you'd better not come *very* close, I generally hit everything I can see when I get really excited.

DUM. And *I* hit everything within reach whether I see it or not!

AL. (*laughing*) You must hit the trees pretty often I should think.

DUM. I don't suppose there'll be a tree left standing for ever so far round by the time we've finished.

AL. And all about a rattle.

DUM. I shouldn't have minded it so much if it hadn't been a new one.

AL. (*aside*) I wish the monstrous crow would come.

DUM. (*to his brother*) There's only one sword. (*takes up wooden toy sword*) butyou [sic] can have the umbrella. It's quite as sharp. (*Stage darker*) Only we must begin quick. It's getting as dark as it can.

[*they fence up to each other.*

DEE. And darker.

AL. What a thick black cloud that is, and how fast it comes! why I do believe it's got wings.

DUM. It's the crow.

[*Both rush off frantically. Stage light again,* WHITE QUEEN'S *shawl flies across to* ALICE *who catches it.*

AL. Dear me. Here's somebody's shawl being blown away.

*Enter* WHITE Q. *and* AL. *puts the shawl on.*

Am I addressing the White Queen?

WHITE Q. Well yes: if you call that a-dressing. It isn't my notion of the thing at all.

AL. If your Majesty will only tell me the right way to begin. I'll do it as well as I can.

WHITE Q. But I don't want it done at all, I've been a-dressing myself for the last two hours.

AL. (*aside*) Every single thing's crooked and she's all over pins. (*aloud*) May I put your shawl straight for you?

WHITE Q. I don't know what's the matter with it. It's out of temper, I think. I've pinned it here and pinned it there, but there's no pleasing it.

AL. (*putting the* QUEEN *to rights*) Come you look rather better now, but really you should have a lady's-maid.

WHITE Q. I'm sure I'll take you with pleasure. Two-pence a week and jam every other day.

AL. (*laughing*) I don't want you to hire *me*, and I don't care for jam.

WHITE Q. It's very good jam.

AL. Well I don't want any *to-day* at any rate.

WHITE Q. You couldn't have it if you *did* want it. The rule is jam to-morrow and jam yesterday, but never jam to-day.

AL. It must sometimes come to jam to-day.

WHITE Q. No it can't! It's jam every *other* day, and to-day isn't any *other* day you know.

AL. I don't understand you! It's dreadfully confusing!

WHITE Q. That's the effect of living backwards! It always makes one a little giddy at first.

AL. Living backwards— I never heard of such a thing!

WHITE Q. But there's one great advantage in it, that one's memory works both ways.

AL. I'm sure *mine* works only one way, I can't remember things before they happen!

WHITE Q. It's a poor sort of memory that only works backwards. Try the other way, sing "Humpty Dumpty" and you'll see what will happen— Ta-ta! [*exit* WHITE Q.

AL. Sing "Humpty Dumpty?" I wonder what will happen!

———

### SONG.— "HUMPTY DUMPTY."

[*as she finishes*, HUMPTY DUMPTY *seats himself on the wall at back.*

AL. Why, there he is I declare! And how exactly like an egg he is!

HUM. It's very provoking to be called an egg! Very!

AL. I said you *looked* like an egg, sir! And some eggs are very pretty you know.

HUM. Some people have no more sense than a baby! What's your name and business?

AL. My name is Alice!

HUM. It's a stupid name, what does it mean?

AL. *Must* a name mean something?

HUM. Of course it must! *my* name means the shape I am, and a good handsome shape it is too! With a name like yours you might be any shape almost.

AL. Why do you sit out here all alone?

HUM. Why, because there's nobody with me! Did you think I didn't know the answer to that? Ask another.

AL. Don't you think you'd be safer down on the ground?

HUM. What tremendously easy riddles you ask! Of course I don't think so! Why if ever I *did* fall— which there's no chance of— the King has promised me, with his very own mouth—

AL. To send all his horses and all his men.

HUM. Now I declare that's too bad, you've been listening at doors, and behind trees, and down chimneys, or you couldn't have known it.

AL. I haven't indeed! It's in a book.

HUM. Ah well! They may write such things in a book. That's what you call a History of England that is! Now take a good look at me? I'm one that has spoken to a king, *I* am: mayhap you'll never see such another; and to show I'm not proud you may shake hands with me.

[*shakes hands with* ALICE.

AL.  What a beautiful belt you've got on!

HUM.  (*in a deep growl*) It is a *most provoking thing* when a person does not know a cravat from a belt!  It's a cravat, child, and the White King and Queen gave it me as an un-birthday present!

AL.  I beg your pardon?

HUM.  I'm not offended!

AL.  I mean, what *is* an un-birthday present?

HUM.  A present given when it isn't your birthday, of course.

AL.  I like birthday presents best!

HUM.  You don't know what you're talking about!  How many days are there in a year?

AL.  Three-hundred and sixty-five.

HUM.  And how many birthdays have you?

AL.  One.

HUM.  And if you take one from 365, what remains?

AL.  364, of course.

HUM.  Well, that shows that there are 364 days when you might get un-birthday presents.

AL.  Certainly.

HUM.  And only one for birthday presents, That's all, good-bye.

AL.  Good-bye till we meet again.

HUM.  I shouldn't know you again if we *did* meet, you're so exactly like other people.

AL.  The face is what one generally goes by.

HUM.  That's just what I complain of.  Your face is the same as everybody has—the two eyes—so, (*marking the places in the air with his thumb*) nose in the middle, mouth under.  It's always the same.  Now if you had two eyes on the same side of the nose for instance— or the mouth at the top— that would be *some* help,

AL.  It wouldn't look nice.

HUM.  Wait till you've tried.

AL.  Good-bye. (*going off*) Of all the unsatisfactory people I ever met—

[*Starts and runs off—for* HUMPTY *falls with a fearful crash off the wall. Enter all the king's horses and all the king's men.*

—

CHORUS.— "HUMPTY DUMPTY'S FALLEN DOWN."

*Enter* RED KING *and* ALICE.

RED K. I've sent them all. I couldn't send all the horses, you know, because they're wanted; and I haven't sent the two messengers. They're both gone to the town. Just look along the road and tell me if you see either of them.

AL. I see nobody on the road.

RED K. I only wish I had such eyes. To be able to see Nobody! And at that distance too, why it is as much as I can do to see real people.

AL. (*looking off*) I see somebody coming now; but what curious attitudes!

RED K. Not at all; He's an Anglo-Saxon messenger and those are Anglo-Saxon attitudes. (*Enter Messenger*) His name is Hare, and the other is Hatter. I must have two you know, one to come and one to go.

AL. I beg your pardon!

RED K. It isn't respectable to beg.

AL. I only meant I didn't understand.

RED K. Didn't I tell you I must have two; one to fetch and one to carry. (*To Messenger*) What's the matter? you alarm me— I feel faint! Give me a ham sandwich. (*Messenger hands one out of bag*, KING *eats it*.) Another sandwich.

HARE. There's nothing but hay left now.

RED. Hay then. (*Hay is handed him and he munches it*) (*to* AL.) There's nothing like eating hay when you're faint. (*to messenger*) Who did you pass on the road.

HARE. Nobody!

RED K. Quite right, this young lady saw him too. So of course nobody walks slower than you.

HARE. I do my best. I'm sure nobody walks faster than I do.

RED K. He can't do that, or he'd have been here first. However, tell us what's going to happen.

HARE. I'll whisper it. (HARE *makes a trumpet of his hands, and puts them to* KING'S *ear, then shouts loudly*) They're at it again.

RED K. (*jumps*) Do you call *that* a whisper? If you do such a thing again, I'll have you buttered. It went through and through my head like an earthquake.

AL. Who are at it again?

RED K. Why the Lion and the Unicorn fighting for the Crown, and the best of the joke is that it's *my* crown all the time. Here they come!

*Enter* LION *and* UNICORN *fighting*.

UNI. (*to* KING) I had the best of it that time.

RED K. A little, a little!

UNI. Come fetch out the plum cake, old man, none of your brown bread for me. (HARE *offers cake to* LION, *looking at* KING) What a fight we must have for the crown now!                              [KING *trembles*.

LION. I should win easy.

UNI. I'm not so sure of that.

LION. Why I beat you all round the town, you know. Didn't I?

*All*. Yes! Yes!

––––

CHORUS.—"THE LION AND THE UNICORN."

[*Exeunt all but* AL.

AL. If that doesn't drum them out of town nothing ever will.

*Enter* WHITE KNIGHT *brandishing club*.

WHITE KNT. Ahoy! Ahoy! Check! you're my prisoner.

AL. I don't want to be anybody's prisoner. I want to be a Queen.

WHITE KNT. So you shall presently. Now I'll say good-bye! You'll be a Queen presently.

AL. Good-bye. (*Exit* KNIGHT. *She follows him off stage, returning at once with crown on her head*) And now to be Queen! But what *is* this on my head?  A golden crown!  How *can* it have got there without my knowing it?  (*takes it off, sits down and examines it and puts it on again*  Well this *is* grand!                                                    [*Struts up and down.*

*Enter* RED *and* WHITE QUEENS.

If I really am a Queen I shall be able to manage it quite well in time (*to* RED Q.)  Please would you tell me—

RED Q.  Speak when you're spoken to.

AL.  But if everybody obeyed that rule, and if you only spoke when you were spoken to, and the other person always waited for you to begin, you see nobody would ever say anything.

RED Q.  Ridiculous!  what right have you to call yourself a Queen?  You can't be a Queen till you've passed the proper examination.  And the sooner we begin it the better.

WHITE Q.  Can you do addition?  What's one and one, and one and one, and one and one, and one and one, and one and one.

AL.  I don't know.  I lost count.

RED Q.  She can't do addition.  Can you do subtraction— Take nine from eight.

AL.  Nine from eight I can't, you know, but—

WHITE Q.  She can't do subtraction.  Can you do Division.  Divide a loaf by a knife, what's the answer to that.

AL.  I suppose—

RED Q.  Bread and butter of course.  Try another subtraction sum.  Take a bone from a dog what remains?

AL.  The bone wouldn't remain of course if I took it, and the dog wouldn't remain; it would come to bite me, and I'm sure I shouldn't remain.

RED Q.  Then you think nothing would remain.

AL.  I think that's the answer.

RED Q.  Wrong as usual.  The dog's temper would remain.  The dog would lose its temper, wouldn't it?

AL.  Perhaps it would.

RED Q.  Then if the dog went away— its temper would remain.

AL.  They might go different ways.

RED Q.  Of course you'll invite us to your party to-night.

AL.  I didn't know I was to have a party at all.
RED Q.  Of course you are.

*Grand procession for the feast— King's men and chessmen.  Trumpets
sound.*

————

SOLO AND CHORUS.— "TO THE LOOKING-GLASS WORLD."

(*Old Tune.*)

————

ALICE *and* QUEENS *take up position.  Joint and Pudding set before them.*

RED Q.  We always miss the soup and fish.  Put on the joint.  (ALICE *takes
knife and fork, and hesitates*)  You look a little shy, let me introduce you to
that leg of mutton.  Alice— mutton!  mutton— Alice.
[*Leg of mutton gets up and bows.*
AL.  May I give you a slice?
RED Q.  Certainly not!  It isn't etiquette to cut anyone you've been
introduced to.  Remove the joint!
[*Mutton taken off by head and legs.  Large plum-pudding brought on.*
AL.  I won't be introduced to the pudding please, or we shall get no dinner
at all!  May I give you some?
RED Q. (*sulkily, growling*) Pudding— Alice! Alice— pudding! Remove
the pudding!
[*they are taking it out.*

AL.  Waiter, bring back the pudding!  (*it is brought back,* ALICE *cuts a slice
and hands it to* QUEEN)  Let me help you!
PUD.  What impertinence!  I wonder how you'd like it if I were to cut a slice
out of *you*, you creature!
RED Q.  Now we'll drink you're health.  Queen Alice's health!
*All.*  Queen Alice's health!

CHORUS.—"ALICE'S HEALTH."

[*Gauzes down, and stage dark.*

FINAL CHORUS.

['Wake! Alice! wake! now no longer a rover']

[ALICE *discovered at foot of tree asleep as in first Act. Slow music, she wakes and rubs her eyes.*

AL.  Oh, I've had such a curious dream!

CURTAIN.

## Alice in Wonderland:  A Dream-Play

## A Bibliography of Editions

The identification and description of the various issues and editions of Savile Clarke's play has proved a great difficulty for bibliographers, owing not only to the scarcity of copies, but also to the fact that surviving copies are scattered on both sides of the Atlantic.  Though the following bibliography still leaves some unanswered questions, it is hoped that it will provide a more complete picture than has heretofore been available.

The author is indebted to Selwyn Goodacre and Jeffrey Stern for their article "Savile Clarke's Alice in Wonderland:  A Dream Play, or The Case of the Crucial Comma," *Jabberwocky*, vol. 15, nos. 1-2 (Winter/Spring 1986), 7-13, which gives a detailed comparison of the first and second editions.

**1**.  First Edition (1886):

ALICE IN WONDERLAND.  |  A DREAM PLAY FOR CHILDREN,  |  IN TWO ACTS.  |  FOUNDED UPON  |  MR. LEWIS CARROLL'S  |  "Alice's Adventures in Wonderland," and "Through  |  the Looking-Glass," with the express sanc on  |  of the Author.  |  BY  |  H. Savile Clarke.  |  MUSIC BY  |  Walter Slaughter.  |  [ornamental line]  |  London:  |  PUBLISHED AT "THE COURT CIRCULAR" OFFICE,  |  2, SOUTHAMPTON STREET, STRAND.  |  1886.

55pp.  Stitched in cream wrappers with the legend *"First edition, under revision."* at the head of the front wrapper.  Advertisements on inside covers (the one on the inside rear cover being for the issue of *The Court Circular* which contains a revision of Carroll's *Mischmasch*).

Text as printed above, with four pages of Tenniel drawings blank on versos, and with cast list on pp. [2-3] and dedicatory verses on p. [4].

Published in late 1886, probably in December in time to go on sale in the theatre when the play opened on the twenty-third.

Copies in the Parrish Collection (Princeton University), Weaver Collection (University of Texas, Austin) and in the collections of Charles & Stephanie Lovett, and Jeffrey Stern.

*Note*: Two variants of this edition have been noted. One, with the wrappers printed in brown (also described as reddish grey) and with advertisements on the inside wrappers only (Lovett, Stern, and Parrish copies); and one with wrappers printed in black and advertisements on the rear outside wrapper as well (Weaver copy).

**2**. Second Edition [1887]:

Title page identical to number 1, except "san on" on line 7 of title page changed to "sanction."

54pp. Stitched in brown wrappers with the legend *"First edition, under revision."* absent from the front wrapper.

Textual changes include the elimination of Scene 1 of Act II, the addition of the extra verses at the end of "The Walrus and the Carpenter," the addition of roughly 1 1/2 pages of dialogue between Alice and the White Knight, and the addition of "The Waits" for the White Knight to sing. Text is printed on the versos of the pages which carry Tenniel drawings, so that the text ends on p. 54. The *Court Circular* advertisement appears on p. [55].

Though dated 1886, this edition was published in early 1887, probably in mid-January, as it includes additional material which Dodgson did not finish until January 3. The Weaver copy has an inscription dated Feb. 3, 1887.

Copies in the Warren Weaver collection and in the collection of Selwyn Goodacre.

**3**. Third edition (1888):

Title page dated 1888.

Text ends on p. 56.

Textual changes include: Page [2] blank; cast list on p. [3] only; dedicatory verses dropped from p. [4]; "To the Looking-Glass World" replaced with "Sound the Festal Trumpets;" dialogue concerning fish poetry added; and "First the Fish Must be Caught" added. In addition to these major changes, there are numerous minor ones, including added lines for the Dormouse and more words set in italics for proper emphasis. Inside covers are blank, rear outside wrapper has advertisement for "Ridge's Food."

Published in 1888, probably in time to be sold in the theatre when the play opened on December 26.

Copies in the Parrish Collection, Weaver Collection, and the Houghton Collection (Pierpont Morgan Library), the latter lacking cover and title page, but with notations on emphasis made for Isa Bowman by Charles Dodgson.

**4**. Third edition, second issue (1889):

Identical to first issue, but with date on front wrapper changed to 1889.

No copy examined. Though various editions of the *Lewis Carroll Handbook* state that the Parrish collection possesses a copy of this edition, and a copy is mentioned in the *Parrish Catalogue*, librarians at the collection were unable to locate such a copy in the Fall of 1988. The description here is based on a description in the 1970 edition of the *Handbook*, which states that Mr. Derek Hudson possessed a copy of an earlier edition of the *Handbook* which had a notation concerning this edition reading "My 1889 cover has 1888 title page. Identical inside."

Probably issued in early 1889. As the play closed in early February, it is unlikely that this issue was published much later than mid-January.

**5**. Fourth edition, songs only, no music [1898]:

ALICE IN WONDERLAND | A DREAM PLAY FOR CHILDREN | IN TWO ACTS | FOUNDED UPON | MR. LEWIS CARROLL'S | "Alice's Adventures in Wonderland," and "Through the Looking- | Glass," with the express sanction of the Author | BY | H. SAVILE CLARKE | MUSIC BY WALTER SLAUGHTER | [rule] | Performed at the Opera Comique Theatre under the Management | of Mr. ARTHUR ELIOT by arrangement with Mr. EDGAR BRUCE.

20pp. Wire stitched grey wrappers. No publisher given, but imprint reads "PRINTED BY RICHARD CLAY AND SONS, LIMITED | LONDON AND BUNGAY"

Contents: "Chorus of Fairies," "How Doth the Little Crocodile," "You Are Old, Father William," "Speak Roughly," Duet [Alice & Cheshire Cat]," "So They Say," "I Am the Executioner," "Song and Chorus [Beautiful Soup]," "Solo and Chorus ['Will you walk a little faster']," "'Tis the Voice of the Lobster," "Chess Chorus," "Jabberwocky," "Duet [Tweedledum & Tweedledee]," "Here We Go Round the Mulberry Bush," "The Walrus and the Carpenter"[including the stage direction for the entry of the first Oyster Ghost, but not including the extra stanzas], "Humpty Dumpty," "Humpty Dumpty's Fallen Down," and "I'll Tell Thee Everything I Can." With four Tenniel illustrations. Words only, no music.

Published in December 1898 (the play opened on December 22).

Copies in the Parrish, Weaver, and Goodacre collections.

*Note*: This edition had been mis-dated as 1889 in some editions of the *Handbook*. This mistake may stem from an error in dating in the *Parrish Catalogue* which gives the date of this edition as 1889.

**6**.  Fourth edition, variant issue [1899?]:

Identical to number 6, but with mention of Edgar Bruce dropped from the title page.

Probably published in early 1899.

Copy in the Parrish collection.

*Note*:  The priority given here is based on the fact that Edgar Bruce is mentioned prominently in a program from early in the run of the play, but not at all in another program issued specially for the 100th performance.


**7**.  Fifth edition, words and music (1906), first issue:

Not examined, but described in Williams and Madan, no. 716, and presumably identical to second issue with the exception that the price is only 3s.


**8**.  Fifth edition, second issue:

[against a decorative floral device] ALICE  |  IN WONDERLAND  | [within a double ruled border] A  Dream Play  |  for Children.  |  [below border] Written by  |  H. Saville  Clarke  |  [ornamental rule]  |  Music by  |  WALTER SLAUGHTER.  |  [ornamental rule]  |  [on left side] COPYRIGHT MCMVI BY  |  ASCHERBERG, HOPWOOD & CREW LTD.  |  [opposite copyright notice on right side]  PRICE 6/- NET  | ASCHERBERG, HOPWOOD & CREW, LTD,  |  16, Mortimer Street, London, W.1.  |  SOLE AGENTS:  |  U.S.A. and Canada: Chappell-Harms, Inc., 185, Madison Avenue. New York.  |  Australasia and New Zealand. Chappell & Co., Ltd., 250, Pitt Street, Sydney.

99pp.  Wrappers.  Front wrapper with title and an illustration of Alice peering from behind a tree at a group of Wonderland characters (signed W.E. EG).

Contents: Act I: "Sleep, Alice, Sleep," Entrance of White Rabbit, "How doth the little Crocodile," "Father William," Entrance of Duchess, "Speak roughly to your little Boy," Entrance of Alice and Cat, "Cheshire Pussy," "So they say," March, "Gavotte of Cards," Entrance of Executioner, Executioner's Chorus, "Beautiful Soup," "Will you join the Dance?," "'Tis the voice of the Lobster," Entrance, "'Not Guilty,' I declare!"

Act II: "Arranged in due order," "Jabberwock," Entrance of Lily and Rose, Entrance, Exit, "Alice and Flowers," Hatter's Entrance, "Tell me, Hatter," "Tweedledum and Tweedledee," "The Mulberry Bush," Entrance of the Walrus and Carpenter, Oyster Scene, "Humpty Dumpty," "Humpty Dumpty fallen Down," "Lion and Unicorn," "When the Wind is in the East," Change of Scene, "Sound the festal trumpets," "Drink to our Alice."

Also includes two supplementary songs, not related to Alice: "Flower-land," and "Naughty Little Bunny," (lyrics by Aubrey Hopwood).

Copies in the Goodacre collection and the New York Public Library.

*Note 1*: As mentioned above (p. 43) the original airs which Dodgson was parodying were used for "Beautiful Soup" and "'Will you walk a little faster?'" Though the music in this volume is credited to Walter Slaughter, the tunes for these two numbers are the originals: "Beautiful Star" by J. M. Sayles and "'Will you walk into my parlour?'" by Marry Howitts.

*Note 2*: This edition includes three songs which were not in previous editions—"Gavotte of Cards," "Tell Me Hatter," and "When the Wind is in the East." The lyrics to these songs are printed below.

## GAVOTTE OF CARDS

King, Queen and Knave, Here are we seen.
Dancing, Dancing So gaily on the green.
King Queen and Knave Here we are seen
So gay today, so gay today on the green.

Dance a-right in the good old way,
Hearts are light on this our natal day,
Tread a measure here in this glade,
King, Queen and Alice, young man and maid,
In the woodland fair is one lot,
Gaily dance the old Gavotte.


## TELL ME HATTER

(Alice)

Tell me why you look so wild and strange,
Won't you try to smile just for a change?
For I'm not ashamed to own,
Half afraid of you I've grown.
Tell me Hatter, What's the matter.
Now that we're alone.

Say you only meant to tease me,
For you've made me sad.
Won't you whisper just to please me,
You're not really mad.

I'm afraid your work is all in vain,
For I'm sure you really can't be sane.
All these antics you go thro'
All the foolish things you do
Can't deceive me, Only leave me,
More distress'd for you.

Let me sooth you, poor Mad Hatter,
Do please, let me try.
Poor mad Hatter, what's the matter?
You'll be better bye and bye.

## WHEN THE WIND IS IN THE EAST

(Hatter)

When the wind is in the East
On new-laid eggs I always feast!
When the wind is in the West,
I steal them from the Dodo's nest.
When the wind is in the South,
I place a dozen in my mouth!
When the wind is in the North,
On wintry nights I sally forth.

All the animals in the Ark,
Come to life when the house is dark,
Cocks and hens, and the owl and crow.
Flap their wings and away they go!
Up the passage and down the stairs.
Over tables and under chairs,
Pigs and puppies and polar bears,
They follow their leader round.

Refrain

Up the middle and down again.
Follow my leader round.
Out in the snow and hail and rain.
Follow my leader round.
Shut in a wooden ark all day,
Night is the only time to play,
Over the hill and far away,
Follow my leader round.

# Appendix C
## Selected Writings of Charles Dodgson
## Relating to the Theatre

**Excerpt from a letter to Tom Taylor, January 25, 1866.**

Seeing the performance of Percy Roselle in the Pantomime the other day suggested to me the idea how well he might succeed in a domestic drama, the interest of which might mainly centre in him, and forthwith uprose before my mind's eye the shadowy outline of a play, which I think might have the merit of novelty, now that the public has been fed to satiety with dramas whose interest depends on love and murder. I will give you a sketch of it, and would try to elaborate it further, should you give me any encouragement to hope that you might ultimately adopt it as part of the basis of a drama. It would contain a capital part for Miss Terry, I think.

The main idea is that the boy should be of gentle birth, and stolen away, and (of course) restored at the end. This would exhibit him in scenes of low life, with thieves, in which he should show heroism worthy of his birth. This part would be something like Oliver Twist, though it would be easy to avoid too close a resemblance. Before giving you the general outline, I will sketch 2 individual scenes, which took my fancy much, as being pathetic and picturesque.

In one, the boy is wandering in London in the winter's night (snow falling), never dreaming that his mother has come up to town to search for him, and he sits down on the door-step of the very house she is in. You might give him a very touching little soliloquy, ending by his singing a little child's song he had learnt at home, and so wandering off into the dark night, still singing. Then the scene changes to the warm, bright interior, where the mother is sitting with her little girl (I want Polly or Flo to take this part), and while they are talking they hear the little gentle voice singing outside. The little girl at once thinks it is her brother's voice, and wants to open the window. The mother prevents her at first, but afterwards, moved by a sudden instinct, hurriedly and excitedly sends her to the window. But it is too late—nothing is to be seen but the dark might and the driving snow, and she returns to the fireside consoling herself with the idea of the wild improbability of its having been her own boy.

The other is the concluding scene, which (I have great hope you will agree with me in thinking) might make a beautiful ending for the play, and would be in marked contrast with the popular wind-up, in which all the characters are brought in, in utter defiance of all probability, to form a grand tableaux.

It is a firelight scene, a group of 4 (there is nothing more picturesque, I think, than a group lit by a ruddy light, thrown upwards)— the mother (who, by the way, is a widow), her aged father, and her little boy and girl. All the storms of the drama are blown over— the villain has met his reward— and she is left in peace, with her recovered child, to cheer her father's last days. Something is said of happiness, and then the old man asks that the children should sing to him (the same little ditty I mentioned before). He is in an easy chair, and she on a low seat at his side. The children get up from the floor (they have been sitting at their mother's feet, looking over a picture-book together) and come and stand at her side, that all three may look over the song-book. After a verse or two, sung very low (it should be a plaintive, wailing ditty), she glances round and sees that the old man has fallen asleep, and silences the children by laying her finger on her lips. They noiselessly return to their places at her feet, and she resumes her former attitude, leaning her head on her hand, and gazing dreamily into the fire. There is silence for a few moments, and then the curtain glides quietly down.

I only wish this scene could be put upon the stage as I see it now in my mind's eye: I feel sure it would succeed.

I want the same little ditty to come in 3 times, and I *think* it should be an original one- the words yours, the music Mrs. Taylor's.

Now for the general plot: it has many hiatuses at present.

An old baronet has 2 sons. The eldest has died, leaving a widow and 2 children, girl and boy (the latter of course heir to the title and estate). The younger is the villain of the piece, and an associate of coiners and thieves; but he keeps all this in the background, and acts the upright and affectionate son. He steals the boy, and hands him over to a gang of thieves, on condition of their keeping him out of the way, and assists with a great show of zeal in trying to find him again. The widow sees through his hypocrisy, but conceals her feelings, and watches him. When the boy has been missing for

years, and is given up— the old man failing— and the villain's plans nearly
reaching their goal, the gang try a burglary on the house, not knowing that
their old "pal" is there. And they put the boy in at a window to open the door
for them. The uncle recognizes him, and his first idea is to shoot him (under
the pretence of defending the house), but the widow interposes and strikes
down the pistol, from mere motives of humanity at first, but directly
afterwards she finds it is her boy whose life she has thus saved.

I have no very distinct idea what ought to become of the villain.

As a comic element for the piece, it occurs to me you might make a
good deal of fun of a "Private Enquiry Office," "a la Pollaky."

I doubt if this sketch includes characters and plot enough for a whole
drama. You would probably find it necessary to work a second thread into
the web, throughout. But I think the main interest of the piece would be
interfered with by any love-story thrown in as an under-plot. I should much
like to see a piece without any lovers at all: it would be a feat in dramatic
writing, and a bone for the critics.

In conclusion, I will give you a list of the scenes, so far as I have
arranged them at present.

## ACT I

### Scene 1

Conservatory at a country house (the widow's house), an artist finishing off
a portrait of the boy (represented as a child of 8). The grandfather has come
down from town on a visit, and is admiring the picture. News of disappear-
ance of child.

### Scene 2

The villain going off with his little nephew, who suspects nothing wrong,
hands him over to the gang (the scene might be laid at a public house).

### Scene 3

Drawing-room at the country-house. The uncle joins with zeal in laying
plans for recovering the child. The little girl sings the ditty.

## ACT II

### *Scene 1*

London, street by night, snow falling. Boy seats himself on door-step, and finally wanders off, singing, into the dark.

### *Scene 2*

Interior, widow and little girl. Messenger arrives from "Private Enquiry Office." Singing heard outside; they open the window but see nothing.

### *Scene 3*

(not planned)

(An interval of 3 years)

## ACT III

### *Scene 1*

Thieves' cellar; burglary planned (on the baronet's town-house). Enter the uncle; they tell him of the plan, but without mentioning the house.

### *Scene 2*

(not planned)

### *Scene 3*

Library at the town-house. The widow has come down to nurse her father. The uncle is also there. All go to bed, leaving the uncle alone. Noise at window. Uncle recognises boy, and prepares to shoot him. Widow interposes. Meeting of mother and child.

## ACT IV

*Scenes 1, 2*

(not planned)

*Scene 3*

Library as before, fire-light only.  Children sing as already described.

## CURTAIN

I should be much gratified if you should think this plot, meagre as it is, worthy of further consideration— and still more, if you should think it worth while to show it to Miss Terry, to see whether she thought that the part of the widow could be made into one worthy of her powers of acting.

———————

**Prologue to a Play (Nov. 1871):**

*Curtain rises and discovers the Speaker who comes forward, thinking aloud,*

'Ladies and Gentlemen' seems stiffened cold.
There's something personal in 'Young and Old,;
I'll try 'Dear Friends' [*addresses audience*] Oh! let me call you so.
Dear friends, look kindly on our little show.
Contrast us not with giants in the Art,
Nor say 'You should see Southern in that part';
Nor yet, unkindest cut of all, in fact,
Condemn the actors while you praise the Act.
Having by coming proved you find charm it in,
Don't go away and hint there may be harm in it.

. . . . . . . . .

*Miss Crabb*. My dear Miss Verjuice, can it really be?
    You're just in time, love, for a cup of tea;
    And so, you went to see those people play.
*Miss Verjuice*. Well! yes, Miss Crabb, and I may truly say
    You showed your wisdom when you stayed *away*.
*Miss C*. Doubtless! Theatricals in *our* quiet town!
    I've always said 'The law should put them down',
    They mean no harm, tho' I begin to doubt it—
    But now sit down and tell me all about it.
*Miss V*. Well then, Miss Crabb, I won't deceive you, dear;
    I heard some things I— did'nt like to hear:
*Miss C*. But don't omit them now.
*Miss V*. Well! No! I'll try
    To tell you all the painful history
    [*They whisper alternately behind a small fan.*]
*Miss V*. And then my dear Miss Asterisk and he
    Pretended they were lovers!! *Miss C*. Gracious me!!'
    [*More whispering behind fan.*]

.    .    .    .    .    .    .    .

*Speaker*.
    What! *Acting* love!! And, hast that ne'er been seen
    Save with a row of footlights placed between?
    My gentle censors, let me roundly ask,
    Do none but actors ever wear a mask?
    Or have we reached at last that golden age
    That finds deception only on the Stage?
    Come, let's confess all round before we budge,
    When all are guilty, none should play the Judge.
    We're actors all, a motley company,
    Some on the Stage, and others—on the sly—
    And guiltiest he who paints so well his phiz
    His brother actors scarce know what he is.
    A truce to moralizing; we invite
    The goodly company we see to-night

To have the little banquet we have got,
Well dressed, we hope, and served up *hot & hot*.
'Loan of a Lover' is the leading dish,
Concluding with a dainty course of fish;
'Whitebait at Greenwich' in the best condition
(By Mr. Gladstone's very kind permission).
Before the courses will be handed round
And *Entree* made of Children, nicely browned.

                                                            *Bell rings.*

But hark!  The bell to summon me away;
They're anxious to begin their little Play.
One word before I go— We'll do our best,
And crave your kind indulgence for the rest;
Own that at least we've striven to succeed,
And take the good intention for the deed.

---

**Prologue to a Play (Feb. 1873):**

[Enter Beatrice, leading Wilfred.  She leaves him at centre (front), and after going round on tip-toe, to make sure they are not overheard, returns and takes his arm.]

B.  'Wiffie! I'm *sure* that something *is* the matter!
   All day there's been— oh, *such* a fuss and clatter!
   Mamma's been trying on a funny dress—
   I never *saw* the house in such a mess!
        (puts her arm round his neck)
   *Is* there a secret, Wiffie?'
                W. (shaking her off) 'Yes, of course!'
B. 'And you won't tell it?  (whimpers) Then you're very cross!
   (turns away from [him], and clasps her hands, looking
     up ecstatically)
   I'm sure of *this*!  It's something *quite* uncommon!'

W.  (stretching up his arms, with a mock-heroic air)
   'Oh, Curiosity!  Thy name is Woman!
     (puts his arm round her coaxingly)
   Well, Birdie, then I'll tell!  (mysteriously)  What should you
     say
   If they were going to act— a little play?
B.   (jumping and clapping her hands)
   I'd say "HOW NICE!"'
         W. (pointing to audience)
            'But will it please the rest?'
B. 'Oh *yes*!  Because, you know, they'll do their best!'
   [turns to audience]
   You'll praise them, won't you, when you've seen the play?
   Just say "HOW NICE!" before you go away!'
     [they run away hand in hand].

                         Feb. 14, 1873

---

**Circular to the Dramatic Profession (Feb. 1882):**

                         Ch. Ch. Oxford.
                               1882

    There is but little I can add to the arguments contained in the enclosed Prospectus*, beyond the expression of my own deep conviction that the whole tendency of the scheme is for good—first, to the Dramatic Profession itself; secondly, through them, to the Dramatic authors, who would surely be impelled to take higher and nobler aims, when they found that their plays were likely to be worthily and intelligently acted; and thirdly, through both

---

* No copies of this prospectus survive, but it described a scheme of Play-acting which apparently espoused the formation of a School of Dramatic Art.

these channels, to Society, whose moral tone is inseparably linked, both in action and reaction, with that of the Stage: neither the Play-actor, nor the Play-seer, can make any real step in an upward direction without insensibly raising the other.

The Stage is (as every play-goer can testify) an engine of incalculable power for influencing Society: and every effort to purify and ennoble its aims seems to me to deserve all the countenance that the great, and all the material help that the wealthy can give it: while even those who are neither great nor wealthy may yet do their part, and help to

> 'Ring out the darkness of the land,
> Ring in the Christ that is to be.'

> Believe me to be,

CHARLES L. DODGSON

---

**Circular about Shakespeare (April 1882):**

Ch. Ch., Oxford
1882

May I ask for your kind co-operation in a project of mine for editing a selection of the Plays of Shakespeare for the use of girls? What I want done will not, I hope, cost you more than a very small expenditure of time and trouble.

The first point to be settled is, *what* Plays are suitable for such a selection, and in this matter *experience* is the only trustworthy guide: and my wish is to collect opinions from ladies who, either by recollecting their own reading as girls, or by noticing which Plays prove most interesting to girls, are able to make out a list of Plays which they think should be included.

A mere list, arranged in the order usually adopted, will be of service: but one arranged *in order of merit*, the favourite Play being placed first, will be doubly valuable.

If several ladies in a family are willing to help, they can, if they prefer it, draw up *one* list only, by consultation. Such a list will be very useful: but, if each would draw up an *independent* list, and *complete* it before seeing what the others have written, much more evidence, of the kind I desire, would be thus obtained.

My hope is to produce a book which any English mother may put into the hands of her daughters. No edition, that I have yet seen, appears to me to meet this want: I have examined Bowdler's, Chambers', and Mr. Brandram's recently published 'Selected Plays.'

Believe me to be,

P.S. If you have any friends in London, who wish their children to have instruction in drawing, and would like to meet with a lady who would give them lessons in their own houses, I should be glad if you would let me know, as I have a friend whom I can cordially recommend for such a purpose.

---

**Letter on Girls' Shakespeare,** *Monthly Packet* **(June 1882):**

The Editor kindly allows me a little extra space to make a request to my lady readers. I am thinking of trying whether a selection of Shakespeare's Plays can be produced, in which many of the beauties should be preserved, and yet the whole made so absolutely free from objectionable matter, whether in plot or language, that any English mother might, without scruple, put it into the hands of her daughters from the age of 10 or 12 up to 16 or 18. Younger girls would not be likely to understand or appreciate the greatest of poets: and older ones may safely be left to read Shakespeare in any edition, expurgated or not, they may prefer: but it seems a pity that so many children should be debarred from a great enjoyment for want of an edition suitable to them. Neither Bowdler's, Chambers', Brandram's, nor

Cundell's 'Boudoir' Shakespeare, seems to me to meet the want: they are
not sufficiently expurgated to suit children.

I hope to produce a cheap and handy volume, containing about 15
plays, and shall be much obliged to any lady who will send a list (founded
on recollections of her own girlhood, or on observation of her daughters'
reading) of the plays she thinks suitable. When there are several ladies in
one family, if each would draw up an *independent* list, each such list would
have its own value as a separate piece of evidence. And a list arranged *in
order of merit* would be even more useful: but this, I fear, would entail some
trouble. Mistresses of girls' schools could give, probably, more information
than any private individual as to which plays are most liked by girls.

---

**"'Alice' on the Stage." *The Theatre*, (April 1, 1887), p. 179-184.**

"Look here; here's all this Judy's clothes falling to pieces again!"
Such were the pensive words of Mr. Thomas Codlin; and they may fitly
serve as motto for a writer who has set himself the unusual task of passing
in review a set of puppets that are virtually his own— the stage-embodi-
ments of his own dream-children.

Not that the play itself is in any sense mine. The arrangement, in
dramatic form, of a story written without the slightest idea that it would ever
be so adapted, was a task that demanded powers denied to me, but possessed
in an eminent degree, so far as I can judge, by Mr. Savile Clarke. I do not
feel myself qualified to criticise his play, as a play; nor shall I venture on any
criticism of the players, as players.

What is it, then, that I have set myself to do? And what possible claim
have I to be heard? My answer must be that, as the writer of the two stories
thus adapted, and the originator (as I believe, for at least I have not
*consciously* borrowed them) of the 'airy nothings' for which Mr. Savile
Clarke has so skillfully provided, if not a name, at least a 'local habitation,'
I may without boastfulness claim to have a special knowledge of what it was
I meant them to be, and so a special understanding of how far that intention
has been realised. And I fancied that there might be some readers of THE

THEATRE who would be interested in sharing that knowledge and that understanding.

Many a day had we rowed together on that quiet stream— the three little maidens and I— and many a fairy-tale had been extemporised for their benefit— whether it were at times when the narrator was 'i' the vein,' and fancies unsought came crowding thick upon him; or at times when the jaded Muse had to be goaded into action, and plodded meekly on, more because she had to say something than that she had something to say— yet none of those many tales got written down; they lived and died, like summer midges, each in its own 'golden afternoon,' until there came a day when, as it chanced, one of my little listeners petitioned that the tale might be written out for her. That was many a year ago, but I distinctly remember, now as I write, how, in a desperate attempt to strike out some new line of fairy-lore, I had sent my heroine straight down a rabbit-hole, to begin with, without the least idea what was to happen afterwards. And so, to please a child I loved (I don't remember having any other motive), I printed in manuscript, and illustrated with my own crude designs— designs that rebelled against every law of Anatomy or Art (for I had never had a lesson in drawing)— the book which I have just had reproduced in facsimile. In writing it out, I added many fresh ideas, which seemed to grow of themselves upon the original stock; and many more ideas added themselves when, years afterwards, I wrote it all over again for publication: but (this may perhaps interest some readers of 'Alice' to know) every such idea, and nearly every word of the dialogue, *came of itself.* Sometimes an idea comes at night, when I have had to get up and strike a light to note it down— sometimes when out on a lonely winter walk, when I have had to stop, and with half-frozen fingers jot down a few words which should keep the new-born idea from perishing— but, whenever or however it comes, *it comes of itself.* I cannot set invention going like a clock, by any voluntary winding-up: nor do I believe that any *original* writing (and what other writing is worth preserving?) was ever so produced. If you sit down, unimpassioned and uninspired, and *tell* yourself to write for so many hours, you will merely produce (at least I am sure *I* should merely produce) some of that article which fills, so far as I can judge, two-thirds of most magazines— most easy to write, most weary to read— men call it 'padding,' and it is, to my mind, one of the most detestable things in modern literature. 'Alice' and the 'Looking-Glass' are made up almost wholly of bits and scraps, single ideas which came of themselves. Poor they may have been; but at least they were the best I had to offer: and I can desire no higher praise to be written of me that the words of a Poet, written of a Poet,

> "He gave to people of his best:
> The worst he kept, the best he gave."

I have wandered from my subject, I know: yet grant me another minute to relate a little incident of my own experience. I was walking on a hill-side, alone, one bright summer day, when suddenly there came into my head one line of verse— one solitary line— 'For the Snark *was* a Boojum, you see.' I knew not what it meant then: I know not what it means now: but I wrote it down: and, some time afterwards, the rest of the stanza occurred to me, that being its last line: and so by degrees, at odd moments during the next year or two, the rest of the poem pieced itself together, that being its last stanza. And since then, periodically, I have received courteous letters from strangers, begging to know whether 'the Hunting of the Snark' is an allegory, or contains some hidden moral, or is a political satire: and for all such questions I have but one answer, "*I don't know!*" And now I return to my text, and will wander no more.

Stand forth, then, from the shadowy past, 'Alice,' the child of my dreams! Full many a year has slipped away, since that 'golden afternoon' that gave thee birth, but I can call it up almost as clearly as if it were yesterday— the cloudless blue above, the watery mirror below, the boat drifting idly on its way, the tinkle of the drops that fell from the oars, as they waved so sleepily to and fro, and (the one bright gleam of life in all this slumberous scene) the three eager faces, hungry for news of fairy-land, and who would not be said 'nay' to: from whose lips "tell us a story, please," had all the stern immutability of Fate!

What wert thou, dream-Alice, in thy foster-father's eyes? How shall he picture thee? Loving, first, loving and gentle: loving as a dog (forgive the prosaic simile, but I know of no earthly love so pure and perfect), and gentle as a fawn: then courteous— courteous to *all,* high or low, grand or grotesque, King or Caterpillar, even as though she were herself a King's daughter, and her clothing wrought of gold: then trustful, ready to accept the wildest impossibilities with all that utter trust that only dreamers know: and lastly, curious— wildly curious, and with the eager enjoyment of Life that comes only in the happy hours of childhood, when all is new and fair, and when Sin and Sorrow are but names— empty words, signifying nothing!

And the White Rabbit, what of *him*. Was *he* framed on the 'Alice' lines, or meant as a contrast? As a contrast, distinctly. For *her* 'youth,' 'audacity,' 'vigour,' and 'swift directness of purpose,' read 'elderly,' 'timid,' 'feeble,' and 'nervously shilly-shallying,' and you will get *something* of what I meant him to be. I *think* the White Rabbit should wear spectacles. I am sure his voice should quaver, and his knees quiver, and his whole air suggest a total inability to say 'Bo!' to a goose!

But I cannot hope to be allowed, even by the courteous editor of THE THEATRE, half the space I should need (even if my *reader's* patience would hold out) to discuss each of my puppets one by one. Let me cull from the two books a Royal Trio— the Queen of Hearts, the Red Queen, and the White Queen. It was certainly hard on my Muse, to expect her to sing of *three* Queens, within such brief compass, and yet to give each her own distinct individuality. Each, of course, had to preserve, through all her eccentricities, a certain queenly *dignity*. *That* was essential. And, for distinguishing traits, I pictured to myself the Queen of Hearts as a sort of embodiment of ungovernable passion— a blind and aimless Fury. The Red Queen I pictured also as a Fury, but of another type; *her* passion must be cold and calm; she must be formal and strict, yet not unkindly; pedantic to the tenth degree, the concentrated essence of all governesses! Lastly, the White Queen seemed, to my dreaming fancy, gentle, stupid, fat and pale; helpless as an infant; and with a slow, maundering, bewildered air about her, just *suggesting* imbecility, but never quite passing into it; *that* would be, I think, fatal to any comic effect she might otherwise produce. There is a character strangely like her in Mr. Wilkie Collins' novel 'No Name:' by two different yet converging paths we have somehow reached the same ideal, and Mrs. Wragg and the White Queen might have been twin-sisters.

As it is no part of my present purpose to find fault with any of those who have striven so zealously to make this 'dream-play' a waking success, I shall but name two or three who seemed to me specially successful in realising the characters of the story

None, I think, was better realised than the two undertaken by Mr.

Sydney Harcourt, 'the Hatter' and 'Tweedledum.' To see him enact the
Hatter was a weird and uncanny thing, as though some grotesque monster,
seen last night in a dream, should walk into the room in broad daylight, and
quietly say 'good morning!' I need not describe what I meant the hatter to
be, since, so far as I can now remember, it was exactly what Mr. Harcourt
has made him: and I may say nearly the same of Tweedledum: but the Hatter
surprised me most— perhaps only because it came first in the play.

    There were others who realised my ideas nearly as well; but I am not
attempting a complete review: I will conclude with a few words about the
two children who played 'Alice' and 'the Dormouse.'

    Of Miss Phoebe Carlo's performance it would be difficult to speak too
highly. As a mere effort of memory, it was surely a marvellous feat for so
young a child, to learn no less than two hundred and fifteen speeches—
nearly three times as many as Beatrice has in "Much Ado About Nothing"!
But what I admired most, as realising most nearly my ideal heroine, was her
perfect assumption of the high spirits, and readiness to enjoy *everything*, of
a child out for a holiday. I doubt if any grown actress, however experienced,
could have worn this air so perfectly: *we* 'look before and after, and sigh for
what is not': a child never does *this*: and it is only a child that can utter from
her heart the words poor Margaret Fuller Ossoli so longed to make her own,
'I am all happy *now* !'

    And last (I may for once omit the time-honoured addition 'not least,'
for surely no tinier maiden ever yet achieved so genuine a theatrical
success?) comes our dainty Dormouse. 'Dainty' is the only epithet that
seems to me exactly to suit her: with her beaming baby-face, the delicious
crispness of her speech, and the perfect realism with which she makes
herself the embodied essence of Sleep, she is surely the daintiest Dormouse
that ever yet told us 'I sleep when I breathe!' With the first words of that her
opening speech, a sudden silence falls on the house (at least it has been so
every time *I* have been there), and the baby-tones sound strangely clear in
the stillness. And yet I doubt if the charm is due only to the incisive clearness
of her articulation; to me there was an even greater charm in the utter self-
abandonment and conscientious *thoroughness* of her acting. If Dorothy
ever adopts a motto, it ought to be 'Thorough.' I hope the time may soon
come when she will have a better part than 'Dormouse' to play— when some

enterprising manager will revive the 'Midsummer Night's Dream,' and do his obvious duty to the Public by securing Miss Dorothy d'Alcourt as 'Puck'!

It would be well indeed for our churches if some of the clergy could take a lesson in enunciation from this little child; and better still, for 'our noble selves,' if *we* would lay to heart some things that she could teach us, and would learn by her example to realise, rather more than we do, the spirit of a maxim I once came across in an old book, "whatsoever thy hand findeth to do, *do it with thy might*."

---

### Excerpt from a letter to the *St. James Gazette* (19 July 1887):

I spent yesterday afternoon at Brighton where for five hours I enjoyed the society of three exceedingly happy and healthy little girls, ages twelve, ten, and seven. We paid three visits to the houses of friends; we spent a long time on the pier, where we vigorously applauded the marvellous underwater performance of Miss Louey Webb, and invested pennies in every mechanical device which invited such contributions and promised anything worth having, for body or mind, in return: we even made an excited raid on headquarters, like Shylock with three attendant Portias, to demand the 'pound of flesh'—in the form of a box of chocolate drops, which a dyspeptic machine had refused to render. I think that anyone who could have seen the vigour of *life* in those three children— the intensity with which they enjoyed everything, great or small, which came their way— who could have watched the young two running races on the Pier, or could have heard the fervent exclamation of the eldest at the end of the afternoon, We '*have* enjoyed ourselves!'— would have agreed with me that here at least was no excessive 'physical strain', nor any *imminent* danger of 'fatal results'!

But these, of course, were *not* stage children? They had never done anything more dangerous than Board school competition? Far from it: all three are on the stage— the eldest having acted for five years at least, and even the tiny creature of seven having already appeared in four dramas!

But, at any rate it is their holiday time, and they are not at present suffering the 'exceedingly heavy strain' of work on the stage?  On the contrary.  A drama, written by Mr. Savile Clarke, is now being played at Brighton; and in this (it is called *Alice in Wonderland*) all three children have been engaged, with only a month's interval, ever since Christmas:  the youngest being 'Dormouse', as well as three other characters— the second appearing, though not in a 'speaking' part— while the eldest plays the heroine, 'Alice'— quite the heaviest part in the whole play, and, I should think, the heaviest ever undertaken by a child:  she has no less than 215 speeches!  They had been acting every night this week, and *twice* on the day before I met them, the second performance lasting until after half past ten at night— after which they got up at seven next morning to bathe!...

----

### "The Stage and the Spirit of Reverence." *The Theatre* (June 1888), 285-94.

This article is *not* going to be a sermon in disguise.  This I protest at the outset, knowing how entirely usage— a mistaken usage, as I think— has limited the word to *religious* topics only, and that the reader is only too likely to turn this page hastily over, muttering *"Chacun son gout.*  This is meant for sectarians of *some* kind.  *I* have no such narrow sympathies.  Talk to me as a *man*, and I'll listen."

But that is exactly what I want to do.  I want to talk to the play-going, or play-writing, reader who may honour me with his attention, as a *man:* not as a churchman, not as a Christian, not even as a believer in God— but simply as a man who recognises (*this*, I admit, is essential) that there is a distinction between good and evil; who honours good men and good deeds, simply as being good; and who realises that from evil men and evil deeds comes much, if not all, of the sorrow of life.

And may not the word "good," also, have a broader meaning than usage has assigned to it?  May it not fairly include all that is brave, and manly, and true, in human nature?  Surely a man may honour *these* qualities, even though he own to no *religious* beliefs whatever?  A striking example of *this* kind of "reverence" is recorded of the robber-tribes of Upper Scinde, during Sir Charles Napier's campaign (I quote from a lecture by Robertson, of Brighton, on "The Influence of Poetry on the Working Classes"):—

"A detachment of troops was marching along a valley, the cliffs overhanging which were crested by the enemy. A sergeant, with eleven men, chanced to become separated from the rest by taking the wrong side of a ravine, which they expected soon to terminate, but which suddenly deepened into an impassable chasm. The officer in command signalled to the party an order to return. They mistook the signal for a command to charge; the brave fellows answered with a cheer, and charged. At the summit of the steep mountain was a triangular platform, defended by a breastwork, behind which were seventy of the foe. On they went, charging up one of those fearful paths, eleven against seventy. The contest could not long be doubtful with such odds. One after another they fell: six upon the spot, the remainder hurled backwards; but not until they had slain nearly twice their number.

"There is a custom, we are told, amongst the hillsmen, that when a great chieftain of their own falls in battle, his wrist is bound with a thread either of red or green, the red denoting the highest rank. According to custom, they stripped the dead, and threw their bodies over the precipice. When their comrades came, they found their corpses stark and gashed; but round both wrists of every British hero was twined the red thread!"

In "reverence" such as this I am happy to believe that the standard reached on the Stage is fully as high as in the literature of Fiction, and distinctly higher than what often passes without protest in Society.

Take, for instance, the treatment of *vice*. In Fiction, and in many a social circle, vice is condoned, and sentiments utterly vile and selfish are freely expressed, in language that would be hissed off the stage of a respectable theatre, unless put into the mouth of the stage "villain." In "The Silver King," as I saw it some years ago, when the gentlemanly scoundrel (splendidly acted by Mr. Willard) sent the coarser scoundrel, who served as his tool, on the hateful mission of turning out of doors the poor mother whose child was dying, it was good to hear the low fierce hiss that ran through the audience as the old wretch went off. Any one who witnessed that fine drama would, I think, believe with me that those who thus hiss— evil as their own lives may be in some cases— yet have their better moments, when the veil is lifted, when they see Sin in all its native hideousness, and shudder at the sight!

And, for an example of the sympathy shown by play-goers for what is pure and good, I may recall the experience of a few weeks back, when I went to see "The Golden Ladder" (produced by the same conscientious actor and manager— Mr. Wilson Barrett— who gave us "The Silver King"), and heard with delight the ripple of applause which greeted the soliloquy of the comical old greengrocer, Mr. George Barrett, about his child, to whom he gave the ambitious name "Victoria Alexandra."

"And I guv her them two names, because they're the best two names as is!" That ripple of applause seemed to me to say "Yes, the very sound of those names— names which recall a Queen whose spotless life has been for many long years a blessing to her people, and a Princess who will worthily follow in her steps— is sweet music to English ears!"

Years ago, I saw Mr. Emery play the hero of "All is not Gold that Glitters"— a factory-owner, with a rough manner but a tender heart; and I well remember how he "brought down the house," when speaking of the "hands" employed in his factory, with the words "And a' couldn't lie down and sleep in peace, if a' thowt there was a man, woman, or child among 'em as was going to bed cold and hungry!" What mattered it to us that all this was fiction? That the "hands," so tenderly cared for, were creatures of a dream? We were not "reverencing" that actor only, but every man, in every age, that has ever taken loving thought for those around him, that ever "hath given his bread to the hungry, and hath covered the naked with a garment."

My other example shall be a memory of the greatest actor our generation has seen— one whose every word and gesture seemed inspired, and made one feel "He has me in his power; he can make me laugh and weep as he will!"— I mean Frederick Robson. Who, that ever saw him in "The Porter's Knot", can forget the delicious pathos of the scene where the old father, who has sacrificed the earnings of a lifetime to save his son's reputation and send him abroad, is in an innocent conspiracy, with the girl to whom his son is betrothed, to keep the old mother happy by reading her a letter they pretend to have come from her boy. Unknown to him, the loving girl has resolved on giving her last earnings to the old couple, and has added a postscript "Dear Mother,— I am getting on so well that I send you this five-pound note," which the old man, reading the letter to his wife, comes upon so unexpectedly that he nearly betrays the whole plot. Then came the "aside"— with that humorous glance at the audience that none ever gave as he did— "Well! This here has growed since the morning!" And then, suddenly detecting the loving stratagem, and shaking his fist at the girl, "Oh, you little *rascal!*" As Borachio would say, "I tell this story vilely." Would that any words of mine *could* convey to the reader the infinite tenderness that breathed in those whispered "words of unmeant bitterness"!

And now, before narrowing the field of discussion and considering how "reverence" is due to subjects connected with religion, I wish to give to this word also a broader sense than the conventional one. I mean by it simply a belief in *some* good and unseen being, above and outside human life as we see it, to whom we feel ourselves responsible. And I hold that "reverence" is due, even to the most degraded type of "religion," as embodying in a concrete form a principle which the most absolute Atheist professes to revere in the abstract.

These subjects may be classed under two headings, according as they are connected with the principle of good or with that of evil. Under the first heading we may name the Deity and good spirits, the act of prayer, places of worship, and ministers; under the second, evil spirits and future punishment.

The "irreverence" with which such topics are sometimes handled, both on and off the Stage, may be partly explained by the fact (not unlikely to be overlooked) that no word has a meaning *inseparably* attached to it; a word means what the speaker intends by it, and what the hearer understands by it, and that is all.

I meet a friend, and say "Good morning!" Harmless words enough, one would think? Yet possibly, in some language he and I have never heard, these words may convey utterly horrid and loathsome ideas. But are *we* responsible for this? This thought may serve to lessen the horror of some of the language used by the lower classes, which, it is a comfort to remember, is often a mere collection of unmeaning *sounds*, so far as speaker and hearer are concerned.

And even where profane language seems really blameworthy, as being consciously and deliberately used, I do not think the worst instances occur on the Stage; you must turn for such to fashionable Society and popular Literature.

No type of anecdote seems so sure to amuse the social circle as that which turns some familiar Bible-phrase into a grotesque parody.

Sometimes the wretched jest is retailed, half-apologetically, as said by a child, "and, of course," it is added, "the *child* meant no harm!" Possibly: but does the *grown man* mean no harm, who thus degrades what he ought to treat with reverence, just to raise a laugh?

Again, can such jesting as that of the "Ingoldsby Legends," where evil spirits are treated as subjects for uproarious merriment, be tolerated by any one who realises what "evil" means, whether in disembodied spirits (whose existence he may possibly doubt) or in living men and women? Shall the curse of all the race, the misery of all the ages, serve us for a passing *jest?*

But the lowest depths of conscious and deliberate irreverence that my memory recalls have been, I am sorry to say, the utterances of *reverend* jesters. I have heard, from the lips of clergymen, anecdotes whose horrid blasphemy outdid anything that would be even *possible* on the Stage. Whether it be that long familiarity with sacred phrases deadens one's sense of their meaning I cannot tell: it is the only excuse I can think of: and such a theory is partly supported by the curious phenomenon (which the reader can easily test for himself) that if you repeat a word a great many times in succession, however suggestive it may have been when you began, you will end by divesting it of every shred of meaning, and almost wondering how you could ever have meant anything by it!

How far can the Stage use of oaths, or phrases introducing the name of the Deity, be justified? To me it is only when lightly and jestingly uttered that they seem profane. Used gravely, and for a worthy purpose, they are at any rate not to be condemned by any appeal to the *Bible:* one of the loveliest pieces of its prose-poetry, the well-known "Entreat me not to leave thee," &c., ends with an undeniable oath, 'the Lord do so to me, and more also, if aught but death part thee and me." And it is on Society, rather than on the Stage, that we should lay the blame of the light use of such language common in the last generation, when such phrases as "My God!" "Good Lord!" were constantly used as mere *badinage*, and when so refined a writer as Miss Austen could make a young lady say (in "Pride and Prejudice") "Lord, how ashamed I should be of not being married before three-and-twenty!" When quite common, such words possibly conveyed no meaning either to speaker or hearer: in these days they jar on the ear, for their strangeness forces us to realise their meaning. When Shakespeare wrote "Much Ado," Beatrice's "O God, that I were a man! I would eat his heart in the market-place," and Benedick's "O God, sir, here's a dish I love not; I cannot endure my lady Tongue," no doubt fell with equally innocent effect on the ear: but in our day, though the first may well be retained, as gravely said and on a worthy occasion, the second comes as a false note; and I think Mr. Irving, instead of toning it down to "O Lord!", would have done better by omitting it altogether.

The act of prayer is almost uniformly treated with reverence on the Stage. My experience furnishes only one instance to the contrary, where the heroine of a ballet, supposed to be in her chamber at night, and soon to be serenaded by her lover at the window, went through the horrid mockery of kneeling in semblance of prayer. But I see no objection to its introduction on the Stage, if reverently represented, as in the scene in "Hamlet," where Claudius is found praying: and I well remember the grand effect produced by Charles Kean (in "Henry V.," just before the battle of Agincourt), by kneeling, for a short passionate prayer, on the battle-field.

Places of worship, also, when made the subject of stage representation, are usually treated with perfect propriety: one must turn to the orgies of the Salvation Army, or the ribaldry of the street preacher, to realise how far religion can be vulgarised, and with what loathsome familiarity the holiest themes can by insulted. We have lately been privileged to see an instance of exquisite taste and reverent handling in the church-scene in "Much Ado" at the Lyceum. Some objected, at the time, to any such scene being put on the stage; yet probably none of its censors would condemn "sacred" pictures? And surely the distinction between a picture painted on canvas, and a picture formed by living figures on a stage, is more fanciful than real? To me the solemn beauty of that scene suggested the hope that some might see it— some to whom the ideas of God, or heaven, or prayer, were strange,— and might think "Is *this* what church is like? I'll go and see it for myself!" Yet *one* false note there certainly was to mar the beauty of the scene. The dialogue between Beatrice and Benedick, with all its delicate banter and refined comedy, spoken amid such surroundings, must have given pain to many to whom the previous scene had been a pure delight. I heartily wish Mr. Irving could see his way to transfer it to the *outside* of the church. Surely a manager, who could endure an interpolation so utterly alien to the spirit of the scene as "Kiss my hand again!", can have no *very* strong feeling about keeping the text of Shakespeare inviolate!

As for ministers of religion, I would not seek to shield them from ridicule *when they deserve it;* but is it not sometimes too indiscriminate? Mr. Gilbert— to whom we owe a deep debt of gratitude for the pure and healthy fun he has given us in such comedies as "Patience"— seems to have a craze for making bishops and clergymen contemptible. Yet are they behind other professions in such things as earnestness, and hard work, and devotion of life to the call of duty? That clever song "The pale young curate", with its charming music, it to me simply painful. I seem to see him as he goes home at night, pale and worn with the day's work, perhaps sick with the pestilent atmosphere of a noisome garret where, at the risk of his life, he has been comforting a dying man— and is your sense of humour, my reader, so keen that you can *laugh* at that man? Then at least be consistent. Laugh also at that pale young doctor, whom you have summoned in such hot haste to your own dying child: ay, and laugh also at the pale young soldier, as he sinks on the trampled battle-field, and reddens the dust with his life-blood for the honour of Old England!

Still, the other side of this picture is now and again given us on the Stage, and one could not desire a more gentle and lovable type of old age than the "Vicar of Wakefield," as played by Mr. Irving, or a more manly and chivalrous hero than the young clergyman in "The Golden Ladder," played by Mr. Wilson Barrett.

The comic treatment of such subjects as *evil spirits* must be regarded from a fresh stand-point. "What reverence," it might fairly be asked, "is due to the Devil, whether we believe that such a being exists or not?" My answer is, that *seriousness* at least is due in dealing with such subjects. The darkest deeds of lust or cruelty that have blasted human happiness have often seemed to the guilty wretch to be due to influences other than his own thoughts: but, even setting aside such evidence, the whole subject is too closely bound up with the deepest sorrows of life to be fit matter for jesting. Yet how often one hears in Society the ready laughter with which any sly allusion to the Devil is received— ay, even by clergymen themselves, who, if their whole life be not one continuous lie, do believe that such a being exists, and that his existence is one of the saddest facts of life.

In this respect I think the tone of the stage not lower than— I doubt if it be so low as— that of Society. Such a picture as Irving gives us of "Mephistopheles" must surely have a healthy influence. Who can see it and not realise, with a vividness few preachers could rival, the utter *hatefulness* of sin?

The same claim, for seriousness of treatment, may be made as to the subjects of Hell and future punishment. In the last generation the Stage, in its constant light use of words connected with "damnation," was simply following the lead of Society: and it is satisfactory to notice that the idle curses, no longer heard in respectable Society, are fast vanishing from the Stage. Let me mention one instance of false treatment of this subject on the Stage, and conclude with two of the better kind.

I have never seen Mr. Gilbert's clever play "Pinafore" performed by grown-up actors: as played by *children*, one passage in it was to me sad beyond words. It occurs when the captain utters the oath "Damn me!" and forthwith a bevy of sweet innocent-looking little girls sing, with bright happy looks, the chorus "He said 'Damn me!' He said 'Damn me!'" I cannot find words to convey to the reader the pain I felt in seeing those dear children taught to utter such words to amuse ears grown callous to their ghastly meaning. Put the two ideas side by side— Hell (no matter whether *you* believe in it or not: millions do), and those pure young lips thus sporting with its horrors— and then find what *fun* in it you can! How Mr. Gilbert could have stooped to write, or Sir Arthur Sullivan could have prostituted his noble art to set to music, such vile trash, it passes my skill to understand.

But I am no such purist as to object to *all* such allusions: when gravely made, and for a worthy purpose, they are, I think, entirely healthy in their effect. When the hero of "The Golden Ladder," claimed as prisoner by a French officer, is taken under the protection of a British captain (finely played by Mr. Bernage), and the Frenchman's "He is my prison-erre!" is met by the choleric captain's stentorian reply "Then, damn it, come on board my ship and take him!" the oath did not sound "irreverent " in any degree. Here was no empty *jesting:* all was grim earnest!

One more example, and I have done. No dramatic version of: "David Copperfield" would do justice to the story if it failed to give the scene after Steerforth has eloped with "little Em'ly", leaving her betrothed, Ham Peggotty, a broken-hearted man. Ham has brought the news to his father, and David is present.

"Mas'r Davy," implored Ham, "go out a bit, and let me tell him what I must. You doen't ought to hear it, sir."

"I want to know his name!" I heard said, once more.

"For some time past," Ham faltered, "there's been a servant about here at odd times. There's been a gen'lm'n, too . . . A strange chay and horses was outside town this morning . . . When the servant went to it, Em'ly was nigh him. The t'other was inside. He's the man."

"For the Lord's love," said Mr. Peggotty, falling back, and putting out his hand, as if to keep off what he dreaded, "doen't tell me his name's Steerforth!"

"Mas'r Davy," exclaimed Ham, in a broken voice, "it ain't no fault of yourn— and I am far from laying of it to you— but his name is Steerforth, and he's a damned villain!"

The critic who would exclaim, on witnessing such a scene, "Shocking irreverence! That oath ought to be cut out!", attaches such a meaning to the word "irreverence" with which I have no sympathy.

May I conclude with an allusion to the distinctly dramatic tone of much of the language of the Bible? In doing so I make no special appeal to Christians: any one, who possess any literary taste at all, will admit that, for poetry and simple pathos, it stands high in the literature of the world. Much of the vivid force of the parables depends on their dramatic character: one fancies, in reading the parable of the "Sower", that the recital was illustrated by the actual events of the moment: one pictures a neighbouring hill-side, with its sharp sky-line, along which slowly moves a figure, seen clear and black against the bright sky, and giving, by the regular swing of his arm, a sort of rhythmic cadence to the words of the speaker.

Whether the parable of "The Prodigal Son" has ever served as the basis of a drama I know not: the general idea has no doubt been so used again and again: but the story, as it stands, simply translated into modern life, would make a most effective play.

The First Act, with the splendour of the wealthy home, would be in picturesque contrast with the Second, where we would find the spendthrift in gaudy and ostentatious vulgarity, surrounded by unmanly men and unwomanly women, wasting his substance in the "far country." The Third might depict his downward career, ending in a deep despair— then the revulsion of feeling— then the pathetic words "I will arise, and go to my Father!" And when the Fourth Act took us back to the ancestral halls, and showed us the wretched outcast, pausing irresolute at the door, mocked by a troop of listless menials, who would fain drive the beggar back to starvation and death, and the old father rushing forth to clasp the wanderer to his breast— might not some eyes, even among the roughs of the Gallery, be "wet with most delicious tears", and some hearts be filled with new and noble thoughts, and a spirit of "reverence" be aroused, for "whatsoever things are just, whatsoever things are pure, whatsoever things are lovely", which would not lightly pass away?

---

### "Stage Children." *The Theatre* (2 Sept. 1889), 113-117.

An unbiased opinion on any subject from a competent judge of the point under discussion is at all times valuable. Mr. Lewis Carroll, the accomplished author of "Alice in Wonderland," and a valued contributor to this magazine, has addressed the following letter to the editor of the "Sunday Times," a letter written in such a dispassionate and judicial spirit as renders it most worthy of consideration by all those who wish to arrive at a just conclusion on the merits or demerits of the employment of children on stage:—

Sir,— I am neither a stage manager nor a dramatic author; I have no children of my own on the stage, or anywhere else; and I have no pecuniary interest in anything theatrical. But I have had abundant opportunities, for many years, for studying the natures of children, including many stage children, and have enjoyed the friendship of many dear children, both on and off the stage.

To these reasons for writing I may, perhaps, be allowed to add that I have given some attention to logic and mathematics, which help so largely in the *orderly* arrangement of of topics of controversy— and art much needed when so many controversialists are ladies. Long experience of that delightful sex has taught me that their system of arrangement is that of a circulating decimal, that with them analogy is identity, and reiteration proof, and that they always lay the *onus probandi* on their opponents. A beautiful instance of this occurred in a newspaper letter on this very controversy a few days ago (I forget the signature, but it was surely a lady's writing). She stated that the Americans are stricter in this matter than the British, and asked,

"Why should not we do as the Americans do?" forgetting that it might be asked, with exactly the same logical force, "Why should not the Americans do as we do?"

My contention is:—

I. That the employment, in theatres, of children under ten is *not* harmful.

II. That it *is* beneficial.

III. That, while this practice needs certain safeguards not yet provided by the law, it does *not* call for absolute prohibition.

(I.) The harm attributed to this practice may be classed under three headings— (1) physical; (2) intellectual; (3) moral.

(1) "Physical harm."— Take first the charge that it causes "excessive bodily fatigue." To this there was at first an additional item, "enforced by cruelty," which is now practically abandoned, it appearing, on investigation, that no evidence in support of it was forthcoming, while abundant evidence was produced of the kindness such children met with in theatres, and of their thorough enjoyment of their work. According to my experience, the work is well within healthy limits, and the children enjoy it with an intensity difficult to convey by mere words. They like it better than any game ever invented for them. Watch any children you know, in any rank of life, when thrown on their own resources for amusement, and, if they do not speedily extemporise a little drama, all I can say is that they are not normal children, and they had better see a doctor.

Take next such charges as "late hours, impure air, draughts, exposure to night air," &c. The good people who raise these cries seem to think that the homes of these little ones are perfect models of regular habits and good sanitary arrangements, and that such a sight as a child outside its house after 9 p.m. would thrill the neighbourhood with horror! Let them visit a few London alleys, and judge for themselves.

(2) "Intellectual harm."— This is asserted to exist in two forms, "excess of dramatic study," and "defect of other studies." A lady writer lately drew a sensational parallel between little Josef Hoffman, who was so nearly killed by being encouraged to give constant public exhibitions of his

precocious musical talent, and the ordinary stage child. It was not a fair parallel; in fact no really parallel case on the stage has yet been produced (the pathetic death of the Tiny Midshipmate in "Patience" was due to causes quite unconnected with stage work); and I have myself known intimately stage children who have played the heaviest child parts on record without receiving the slightest harm.

As to defect of other studies, if we contemplate the weary mass of useless knowledge which, in the present craze for teaching everybody everything, so many little minds are compelled, not to *digest*, for that is impossible, but merely to swallow, we may well hope that the stage child is all the better for escaping much of this. Frequent mental collapse among Board school children and pupil teachers is slowly teaching us the valuable psychological fact that a child's mind is *not* a sausage; but we have not quite learned our lesson yet!

(3) "Moral harm."— As this danger exists on every phase of human life, those who plead it in this controversy are bound to show that it is *greater* for children under ten than for older actors and actresses; otherwise they commit the fallacy of "proving too much."

Take first "immorality, whether of general tone or particular passage, in the play itself." Ignorance of the ways of the world, and of the meanings of most of the words they hear, is a protection enjoyed by young children, and by them only. The evil itself is undeniably great—though less, I believe, in this age than in any previous one— but it is almost wholly limited to the adult members of the company and of the audience.

Take next "the encouragement of vanity, love of dress," &c. Here, again, the danger is distinctly greater in the case of adults. Children are too deeply absorbed in attending to their stage "business," and in observing the discipline enforced in all well-conducted theatres, to have much opportunity for self-consciousness.

Take, lastly, the gravest and most real of all dangers that come under the category of "moral harm," viz., "the society of profligate men." For adult actresses this danger is, I believe, in well-conducted theatres, distinctly less than it would be in most of the lines of life open to them. Here again the good people, who see such peril in the life of an actress, seem to be living in a fool's paradise, and to fancy they are legislating for young ladies who, if they did not go on the stage, would be secluded in drawing-rooms where none but respectable guests are admitted. Do they suppose that attractive-looking young women, in the class from which the stage is chiefly recruited, would be safer as barmaids or shopwomen from the insidious attentions of the wealthy voluptuary than they are as actresses?

But if it be granted that young women of this class may choose a stage life with as fair a chance of living a reputable life as they would have in any other profession open to them, it is surely desirable to begin learning their business as soon as they are competent, unless it can be shown that they are in greater danger as children than as young women. I believe the danger is distinctly less. Their extreme youth is a powerful safeguard. To plot evil against a child, in all its innocence and sweet trustfulness and ignorance of the world, needs no common voluptuary; it needs one so selfish, so pitiless, and so abject a coward as to be beneath one calling himself a man.

II. My second contention is that stage life is beneficial to children, even the youngest; and this in three ways— (1) physically, (2) intellectually, and (3) morally.

(1) Physically. The deportment that must be acquired for even moderately good acting, and the art of dancing, which most stage children acquire, not only give grace of figure and of action, but are excellent for the health. In girls' schools, not so many years ago, spinal curvature was so common that an eminent surgeon, Dr. Mayo, put it on record that scarcely three per cent escaped it. I am glad to believe that they are more sensibly managed now, and that the days are passed away when it was "vulgar" for young ladies to run, and where the only bodily exercise allowed them was to walk two-and-two; but I feel sure that, even now, if one hundred children were taken at random from the highly educated classes, and another hundred from the stage, the latter would show a better average for straightness of spine, strength, activity, and the bright, happy look that tells of health. The stage child "feels its life in every limb"— a locality where the Board school child feels only its lessons.

(2) Intellectually. Comparing children with children, my belief is that stage life distinctly *brightens* the mind of a child. Of course the same result is produced at schools, whenever they can manage to *interest* the pupils in their work. But how often they fail to do this! How often are the poor little

victims made to do work "against the grain"! And all such work is not only badly done, but is intensely fatiguing and depressing to spirits and intellect alike.

3. Morally. I believe that stage life, in a well-conducted theatre, is valuable moral training for young children. They learn—

(*a*) Submission to discipline.

(*b*) Habits of order and punctuality.

(*c*) Unselfishness (this on the principle on which you always find children in large families less selfish than only children).

(*d*) Humility. This because, however clever they may think themselves, they soon find that others are cleverer.

III. My third contention is that, though it is desirable to provide, by law, certain safeguards for the employment of children in theatres, there is no need for its absolute prohibition.

The legislation that seems to me desirable would take some such form as this:—

That every child under sixteen (ten is too low a limit), employed in a theatre, should hold a licence, annually renewable.

That such a licence should only be granted on condition of the child having passed the examination for a certain "standard," adapted to the age of the child.

That a limit should be fixed for the number of weeks in the year that the child may be engaged, and for the number of hours in the day that he or she may be at the theatre. (This rule to be relaxed during rehearsals.)

That, during a theatrical engagement, the child shall attend a specified number of hours, during the afternoons, at some school; at other times in the year during the usual hours, if attending a Board school (High schools would probably adopt the same principle, and allow half-day attendance during engagements.)

That some guarantee be required that girls under sixteen are provided with sufficient escort to and from a theatre.

But I do not believe that the law can absolutely prohibit children under ten from acting in theatres without doing a cruel wrong to many a poor struggling family, to whom the child's stage salary is a godsend, and making poor children miserable by debarring them from a healthy and innocent occupation which they dearly love. . .

There is little doubt that opinions like the above— together with communications addressed to various journals by those so competent to judge as Mr. John Coleman and Mrs. Bancroft; from those who had had charge of Mr. D'Oyly Carte's Children Company, and others who *know* something about the matter— influenced the fate of the Cruelty to Children (Prevention) Bill.  Besides this, the subject has been ventilated, and such statements as those made by Mr. Winterbotham (which statements the hon. member most properly, generously, and publicly withdrew when he found he had been misinformed) and by others, who will persistently represent the stage is everything that is bad, have been refuted.  Had the bill been passed in its orignal [sic] form such plays as "A Winter's Tale," "A Midsummer Night's Dream," "Richard III.," "East Lynne," and a host of others, could not be acted in the future, and a great hardship would have been inflicted on the numerous children employed at the theatres, not to speak of the help which their earnings afforded their parents, who are not, as some would make out, for the most part drunkards and disreputable people.  The deputation that waited on the Earl of Dunraven included not only theatrical managers, but Mr. James Rodgers, Mr. John Lobb, and General Sim, of the London School Board, who bore witness to "the improvement in the appearance and manners of the youngsters after being connected with those places of amusement (theatres) for a little time." Thanks to the information afforded him on the matter, the Earl of Dunraven was the means of an amendment being passed in the House of Lords, which was accepted by the Commons, that children between seven and ten years of age could be employed on the stage, licensing powers for such employment top be granted by petty sessional courts.

C.H.

———————

# Notes

## Chapter 1

1. Stuart Dodgson Collingwood, The Life and Letters of Lewis Carroll (Rev. C.L. Dodgson) (London: T. Fisher Unwin, 1898), 20.
2. *Ibid.*
3. Quotations from Charles Dodgson's Diaries are cited in the text using the following abbrevation:

> D: *The Diaries of Lewis Carroll*, ed. Roger Lancelyn
> Green (New York: Oxford University Press, 1954).

4. Denis Crutch, "Lewis Carroll and the Marionette Theatre," *Jabberwocky The Journal of the Lewis Carroll Society*, vol. 2, no. 3 (Spring 1973): 7-9.
5. Lewis Carroll, "Children in Theatres," *St. James's Gazette*, 19 July 1887.
6. *Ibid.*
7. Lewis Carroll, "The Stage and the Spirit of Reverence," *Theatre*, n.s., vol 11 (1 June 1888): 292-93.
8. Charles Dodgson to Henry Savile Clarke, 17 September 1886, Alfred C. Berol Collection, New York University Library (hereafter cited as Berol MSS).

## Chapter 2

1. Quotations from and related to Charles Dodgson's published letters are cited in the text using the following abbreviations:

> L: *The Letters of Lewis Carroll*, ed. Morton N. Cohen
> (New York: Oxford University Press, 1979)
>
> LM: *Lewis Carroll and The House of Macmillan*, ed. Morton
> N. Cohen and Anita Gandolfo (Cambridge: Cambridge University Press, 1987)

2. Untitled advertisement, *Times*, 17 April 1876.
3. "The Royal Polytechnic," *Times*, 18 April 1876.
4. Untitled advertisement, *Times*, 29 May 1876.
5. Newman Flower, "Words by Carroll—Music by Sullivan," Radio Times 36 (26 Aug. 1932): 483.

6. Collingwood, 211-12.

7.  Kate Freiligrath-Kroeker, *Alice thro' the Looking-Glass and Other Fairy Plays for Children* (London:  W. Swan Sonnenschein and Co., n.d.), vi.

8. *Ibid.*, vii.

## Chapter 3

1.  Charles Dodgson to Henry Savile Clarke, 6 Dec. 1886, Berol MSS.

2.  Charles Dodgson to Henry Savile Clarke, 2 Sept. 1886, Berol MSS.

3. *Ibid.*

4.  Charles Dodgson to Henry Savile Clarke, 22 Oct. 1886, Berol MSS.

5.  Charles Dodgson to Henry Savile Clarke, 26 Oct. 1886, Berol MSS.

6. *Ibid.*

7.  Charles Dodgson to Henry Savile Clarke, 31 Oct. 1886, Berol MSS.

8.  Charles Dodgson to Henry Savile Clarke, 2 Nov. 1886, Berol MSS.

9.  Lewis Carroll and Wiliam Boyd, *The Songs from* "Alice's Adventures in Wonderland" (London:  Weekes & Co., [1870]), 9.

10.  Collingwood, 253.

11.  Charles Dodgson to Henry Savile Clarke, 2 Nov. 1886, Berol MSS.

12.  Manuscript of "'Tis the Voice of the Lobster," 31 Oct. 1886, Berol MSS.

13.  Charles Dodgson to Henry Savile Clarke, 7 Nov. 1886, Berol MSS.

14.  Charles Dodgson to Henry Savile Clarke, 28 Nov. 1886, Berol MSS.

15. *Ibid.*

16.  Charles Dodgson to Henry Savile Clarke, 29 Nov. 1886, Berol MSS.

17. *Ibid.*

18.  Charles Dodgson to Henry Savile Clarke, 30 Nov. 1886, Berol MSS.

19. *Ibid.*

20.  Charles Dodgson to Henry Savile Clarke, 13 Dec. 1886, Berol MSS.

21.  [M.E. Manners], "Wonderland," *Sylvia's Home Journal* (Christmas 1885).

22.  "Opening of the Prince's Theatre," *Times*, 19 Jan. 1884.

23. *Ibid.*

24. *The Dramatic Peerage 1892*, ed. Erskine Reid and Herbert Compton (London: Raithby, Lawrence & Co., Limited, [1892]), 188.

## Chapter 4

1.  "Prince of Wales's Theatre," *Times*, 24 Dec. 1886.

2. *Ibid.*

3. *Ibid.*

4.  Untitled advertisement, *Times*, 26 Feb. 1887.

5. "Prince of Wales's."
6. Untitled review, *Illustrated London News*, 8 Jan. 1887.
7. Untitled review, *Graphic*, 1 Jan. 1887.
8. E.R., "Alice in Wonderland," *Theatre*, n.s., vol. 9 (1 Jan. 1887): 49.
9. "A Christmas 'Carroll.'," *Punch* (8 Jan. 1887): 17.
10. "The Children's Choice," *Punch* (29 Jan. 1887): 60.

## Chapter 5

1. E.R., "Alice in Wonderland," *Theatre*, n.s., vol. 9 (1 Jan. 1887): 50.
2. Charles Dodgson to Henry Savile Clarke, 2 Feb. 1887, Berol MSS.
3. Charles Dodgson to Henry Savile Clarke, 31 Dec. 1886, Berol MSS.
4. Lionel A. Tollemache, "Reminiscences of 'Lewis Carroll'," *Literature* (5 Feb 1898): 145.
5. Henry Savile Clarke, *Alice in Wonderland—A Dream Play in Two Acts* (London: Court Circular, 1888), 40-41.
6. Sidney Herbert Williams et al., *The Lewis Carroll Handbook*, rev. ed. (Folkstone: William Dawson & Sons Ltd., 1979), 148.
7. Tollemache, 145.
8. Savile Clarke, 52-3.
9. Charles Dodgson to Henry Savile Clarke, 2 Feb. 1887, Berol MSS.
10. Charles Dodgson to Henry Savile Clarke, 6 Jan. 1887, Berol MSS.
11. Charles Dodgson to Henry Savile Clarke, 3 Feb. 1887, Berol MSS.
12. Untitled advertisement, *Times*, 16 Feb. 1887.
13. Untitled advertisement, *Times*, 26 Feb. 1887.
14. Untitled advertisement, *Times*, 1 March 1887.
15. Charles Dodgson to Henry Savile Clarke, 7 March 1887, Berol MSS.
16. Charles Dodgson to Henry Savile Clarke, 13 March 1887, Berol MSS.
17. Untitled advertisement, *Times*, 15 March 1887.
18. "A Theatrical Chat," *Punch*, 92 (19 March 1887): 137.
19. Lewis Carroll, "Alice on the Stage," Theatre, n.s., vo. 9 (1 April 1887): 179-83.
20. Charles Dodgson to Henry Savile Clarke, 27 March 1887, Berol MSS.
21. Collingwood, 254.

## Chapter 6

1. Charles Dodgson to Henry Savile Clarke, 7 March 1887, Berol MSS.
2. Charles Dodgson to Henry Savile Clarke, 14 Oct. 1887, Berol MSS.
3. Charles Dodgson to Henry Savile Clarke, 15 Oct. 1887, Berol MSS.
4. Charles Dodgson to Henry Savile Clarke, 26 June 1888, Berol MSS.

5. Charles Dodgson to Henry Savile Clarke, 4 July 1888, Berol MSS.

6. Charles Dodgson to Henry Savile Clarke, 6 July 1888, Berol MSS.

7. Charles Dodgson to Henry Savile Clarke, 16 July 1888, Berol MSS.

8. Irene Vanbrugh, *To Tell My Story* (London, Hutchinson, 1949), 18-19.

9. Charles Dodgson to Henry Savile Clarke, 5 Aug. 1888, Berol MSS.

10. Charles Dodgson to Henry Savile Clarke, 19 Aug. 1888, Berol MSS.

11. Langford Reed, *The Life of Lewis Carroll* (London: W. & G. Foyle, Ltd., 1932), 73.

12. Savile Clarke, 54-5.

13. Review, *Era*, 29 Dec. 1888.

14. Review, *Theatre*, n.s., vol. 13 (1 Feb. 1889): 116.

15. "Globe Theatre," *Times*, 27 Dec. 1888.

16. Charles Dodgson to Henry Savile Clarke, 3 Jan. 1889, Berol MSS.

17. Charles Dodgson to Henry Savile Clarke, 6 Jan. 1889, Berol MSS.

18. Charles Dodgson to Henry Savile Clarke, 11 Jan. 1889, Berol MSS.

19. Charles Dodgson to Henry Savile Clarke, 3 Jan. 1889, Berol MSS.

20. Charles Dodgson to Henry Savile Clarke, 8 Jan. 1889, Berol MSS.

21. Savile Clarke, rear cover.

22. Charles Dodgson to Henry Savile Clarke, 8 Jan. 1889, Berol MSS.

23. Charles Dodgson to Henry Savile Clarke, 20 Jan. 1889, Berol MSS.

24. Charles Dodgson to Henry Savile Clarke, 25 Jan. 1889, Berol MSS.

25. Charles Dodgson to Henry Savile Clarke, 11 Jan. 1889, Berol MSS.

26. Erroll Sherson, *London's Lost Theatres of the 19th Century* (London: John Lane The Bodley Head, 1925), 249.

27. Charles Dodgson to Henry Savile Clarke, 15 Jan. 1889, Berol MSS.

28. Charles Dodgson to Henry Savile Clarke, 25 Jan. 1889, Berol MSS.

29. Charles Dodgson to Henry Savile Clarke, 29 Jan. 1889, Berol MSS.

30. Untitled advertisement, *Times*, 5 Feb. 1889.

31. Graham Balfour, *The Educational Systems of Great Britain and Ireland*, 2nd ed. (Oxford: Clarendon Press, 1903), 24.

32. "London School Board," *Times*, 9 Nov. 1888.

33. "The London School Board," *Times*, 14 Dec. 1888.

34. Charles Dodgson to Henry Savile Clarke, 9 Feb. 1889, Berol MSS.

35. Charles Dodgson to Henry Savile Clarke, 12 Feb. 1889, Berol MSS.

## Chapter 7

1. "Entertainment at the Royal Free Hospital, Gray's Inn Road, W.C.," *Graphic* ( Jan. 1889).

2. Alan Mackinnon, T*he Oxford Amateurs* (London, Chapman & Hall, 1910), 200-201.

3. "Scenes from 'Alice in Wonderland'," *Sketch*, (26 June 1895): 453.

4. Verily Anderson, *The Last of the Eccentrics: A Life of Rosslyn Bruce* (?London, Hodder & Stoughton, 1972), 88-9.

5. *Sketch*, 453.

# Index

References to page numbers are given in italics; references to checklist items in roman.